With the Wind at His Back

The charmed and charitable life of Donald Baumgartner

KURT CHANDLER

Cedar Forge Press
Dexter, Michigan

With the Wind at his Back: The charmed and charitable life of Donald Baumgartner
by Kurt Chandler
© 2018 Kurt Chandler

ISBN: 978-1-943290-71-0
Library of Congress Control Number: 2018945700

All photographs, except where noted, are from the Baumgartner Family Archives.

Cover design by Lindsey Miller
Cover photograph by Donna Baumgartner
Copyedited by Carolyn Kott Washburne
Interior design and production by Kate Hawley by Design
Proofread by Paula Haubrich

Printed in the USA

Cedar Forge Press
7300 W. Joy Road
Dexter, MI 48104

He was born with a gift of laughter and sense that the world was mad.

–Rafael Sabatini, *Scaramouche*

Table of Contents

Introduction

first crossed paths with Donald Baumgartner at the Milwaukee Art Museum in early 2001. I was covering a news conference for *Milwaukee Magazine* as a reporter, and Baumgartner was leading the conference as the president of the museum's Board of Trustees. He had been a key player in the construction of the museum's much-acclaimed Santiago Calatrava-designed addition, which would open later in the year. I associated Donald Baumgartner's name with the art museum, and little else.

Years later, I heard him being interviewed on the radio. Much was being made at the time about his decision to turn over his manufacturing company, Paper Machinery Corporation, to his employees. Giving ownership of the family business to the people who built it into a multi-million-dollar success was good for the workers, he said, and good for the community.

"The company was not built by me alone, there are 250 people there. I'm one of them. My son, John, who's president of the company, is another one. But there are still another 248 people who contribute every day to the company. And they need to be recognized."

It was an admirable act. But what also struck me about the radio interview was Donald's natural ability to tell stories, *great* stories, told with humor and flair, filled with rich details and colorful characters. All the ingredients of a book.

Before long, I was sitting with Donald and his wife, Donna, at their home. With my voice recorder rolling, I asked Donald to repeat his stories. And through his vivid memories, he took me back to his early childhood in Chicago, brought me aboard his father's first powerboat, walked me through his mother's eighteen-stool diner in Milwaukee, guided me down the roads of Europe in an Italian sports car, and led me to the White House Rose Garden to meet Ronald Reagan. One story led to the next, and the basis for this biography began to take shape.

I shared these stories frequently with my wife and friends. "I've got another Donald story," I would announce, and recount the latest. My skill at verbal storytelling doesn't match Donald's, but I would manage to get across the gist of his tales—of crossing the Atlantic in a boat too small for the ocean; of landing a job as an extra in a Hollywood movie starring a young actress from Wisconsin; of stalking a family of gorillas in the Congo jungle with a long-lens camera.

The stories got reactions—a laugh, a shake of the head, or, most often, outright astonishment: "What? Are you kidding?" I took this as a good sign.

Barely two weeks after he transferred ownership of his company, Donald and Donna gave $8 million to the Milwaukee Art Museum. Combined with considerable donations to other major arts groups, the museum gift cemented the Baumgartners' place among the top tier of Milwaukee's philanthropists.

Donald is not a grandstander. It's not his style to showboat or seek publicity. "I never was social climber," he said to me, asking that I not make too much of his position in the pecking order of local benefactors.

In early 2018, Donald was honored as a "distinguished alumni" by his alma mater, Shorewood High School. "I have led the extraordinary life of an ordinary man," he said in a short speech. "I did not become the valedictorian of my class. I was not captain of the football team. I did not win science awards. But now I am able to make a difference in our community, and I am grateful to Shorewood High School for seeing that my humble beginnings led me to this fine award. . . . Thank you from my ordinary heart."

The ordinary man with an ordinary heart has made an extraordinary mark on his community and those who have crossed his path. Yet, partly because of his own reticence, Donald Baumgartner's life is an untold story. This book examines that life, the adventures and riches, successes and disappointments—a large life, the charmed life of a man true to himself and passionate about everything he does.

— Kurt Chandler

CHAPTER 1

Pulling Up Stakes

The employees of Paper Machinery Corporation in Milwaukee were on edge. The company's front-office executives had been acting out of the ordinary. They would disappear in the middle of the day for hours on end without explanation. On three or four occasions, legions of bankers and lawyers had filed into corporate headquarters, fifteen or twenty at a time, for long, hush-hush meetings in the boardroom.

Rumors swirled: The company was laying off workers. The company was being sold. The company was moving to China. Something was up. Something big was in the works.

Paper Machinery Corporation had been designing and building machines that make paper cups for more than sixty years. It was a family business, created by John Robert Baumgartner, an engineer, inventor, and entrepreneur. Since the 1950s, it had been run by his only son, Donald Baumgartner, now the chairman and CEO. In turn, Donald's only son, John Baumgartner, became president in 1999.

Outpacing competitors by producing state-of-the-art machinery, PMC was now a $100 million a year business, employing 250 people, the largest manufacturer of its kind in the world.

Things were about to change dramatically for the company.

Donald Baumgartner, far right, announces that his family business will become an employee-owned company. Right to left, Executives John Baumgartner, Luca Dellomodarme, Scott Koehler, and Mike Kazmierski look on.

May 2, 2016, was a brisk but sunny Monday. As first-shift employees began to arrive at work, they couldn't help but notice the huge, white tent in the executive parking lot. Sometime after lunch, an email from Donald Baumgartner showed up in the inbox of each employee. All were invited to a meeting under the tent for an important company announcement at 3 p.m.

At three o'clock, the plant emptied and the tent began to fill. Members of the Baumgartner family were seated in the front rows—Donald's wife, sister, children, grandchildren—most of them as much in the dark as the employees. With the tent overflowing, Donald took the stage. But instead of delivering the much-anticipated announcement, he launched into a long narrative and slide-show of the company's history.

"I'm going to hold you all in a lot of suspense while we go through a lot of slides," he said, "showing you how we got where we are today before I tell you where you're going to go tomorrow."

Nervous laughter reverberated through the crowd, the employees still unsure what was coming next. Donald laughed as well, artfully setting up his big reveal. After he ended the slideshow, he presented his son, John, who graciously thanked the workers for helping build the company into such a success. Then John turned to his father. "Dad, would you like to do the honors of introducing the *new owners* of Paper Machinery Corporation?"

Used with permission of the *Milwaukee Journal Sentinel*

Workers at Paper Machinery Corporation cheer the news.

The crowd stirred. "You heard right," Donald said, taking the microphone. "We have *new owners . . .*"—a drum roll rumbled as he pointed to the crowd— "And they're YOU!"

Silence, for one . . . two . . . three seconds. Then wild whoops and applause as the weight of the news sank in: Paper Machinery Corporation's entire workforce, all 250 people, now owned the company under a newly formed Employee Stock Ownership Plan.

"It's all yours," said Donald, his voice cracking, tears welling up in his eyes. "I mean, it's yours. It's 100 percent yours. We've turned all of the stock over to you."

The plan had been in the works since the fall. Donald Baumgartner, the principal owner of PMC, had met with friends, his personal lawyer, bankers, and investment counselors, looking for information and advice. Attorneys with Foley & Lardner, the largest law firm in Wisconsin, advised him not to pursue an Employee Stock Ownership Plan, an ESOP. He could make far more money for himself and his family by selling the company outright, they said.

"There's no question," Donald says, looking back. "I could have had instant gratification if I sold the company. I'd have the money right up front."

But he couldn't get the ESOP idea out of his head. He thought of his father, and how he had started two businesses in Milwaukee, turning each of them into successful companies, then selling them for a handsome profit.

"Even though the buyers said they were going to continue operations in Milwaukee," Donald recalls, "within a very short time, each of them picked the whole damned company up and moved. One company moved to Illinois and the other one moved all the way to California. People had roots here and they were not going to leave. So basically everybody lost their jobs."

Donald didn't want the scenario repeated at Paper Machinery Corporation. He had seen the consequences. Unlike his father, he would not sell out and pull up stakes.

"The people that have worked with me and with this company have been here a long time," he says. "We had a lot of thirty-year employees, twenty-five-year employees, three generations in more than one family. And these people made a contribution. They deserved the ESOP. They earned it, that's for sure."

His decision won widespread praise. In an age of mergers, buyouts, and soaring executive salaries, it was hailed as a magnanimous commitment to a local business and to the community itself. A photograph of elated PMC workers ran above the fold on *USA Today's* business page, and the next day appeared in newspapers and on websites worldwide. It was a feel-good story, a story of gratitude, of fairness for the average working guy.

Donald had traveled a long way with PMC. It was in his bones, it was part of his DNA, literally. His father's fingerprints were on the company's origins. When his father sailed into an early retirement, Donald took the tiller and steered the company into the future. With a nod to tradition, an eye for opportunity, and a certain measure of luck, he nurtured it, cultivated it, grew it into a worldwide market leader.

Like his father, Donald is an adventurer. He has traveled the world, set foot on all seven continents, sailed the Atlantic, driven racecars across Europe, dived the Great Barrier Reef, hunted Bengal tigers (with a camera), and listened to the rapturous voices of Italian opera singers in Verona's ancient Roman amphitheater. Donald Baumgartner could give lessons on How to Live Large.

Success provided a level of status to Baumgartner. He visited the White House to accept an award for international trade from Ronald Reagan. He was named Wisconsin Entrepreneur of the Year at a conference in Palm Springs, California. He sealed business deals with customers in Taiwan, Russia, Japan,

France, Australia, Korea, Israel, South Africa, and Latin America. He met with officials in East Germany just before the Berlin Wall came down, and traveled to Europe as a trade ambassador with the mayor of Milwaukee.

Donald had mixed feelings about stepping away from the controls. The company was his child, the workers his family. He had seen three generations arrive at PMC and grow into lifelong employees, shared in their stories, celebrated holidays with them, birthdays and Green Bay Packer victories. At his core, he was inexorably linked to Paper Machinery Corporation.

But he was ready to let go of company operations. He would move on without regret and begin another narrative. The next adventure was just around the bend.

Donald William Baumgartner opened his eyes to the world on November 21, 1930, in a hospital on Chicago's south side. His parents took him home to a four-story walkup at 8236 South Ellis Avenue near Jackson Park, an apartment building owned by his mother's parents, who lived two floors below.

Donald's parents had reached the Windy City from opposite directions, Mae Lucille Hayes from Georgia and John Robert Baumgartner from

John Robert Baumgartner and Mae Lucille Hayes on their wedding day in 1929.

Mae Lucille and John Robert on Lake Michigan's Miller Beach.

Minnesota. She was the second-generation child of Irish immigrants, he was the youngest son in a family of Minnesota farmers.

The two met at a Saturday afternoon dance at Chicago's famed Trianon Ballroom. Mae Lucille's red hair, green eyes, and freckles betrayed her Irish heritage. To win her over, John Robert, or Bob for short, posed as an Irishman as he approached her in the ballroom. "My name is Bob—Bob Casey. Would you like to dance?"

It's hard to say if the ruse worked or not. But Mae Lucille loved to dance, and she decided to take a chance with the tall, dark-haired young man who called himself "Bob Casey," though, with his sharp, angular features, he clearly didn't possess a drop of Irish blood.

Mae Lucille Hayes married John Robert Baumgartner in September of 1929. Just weeks later, the stock market crashed.

Donald's early beginnings were unconventional. When he was barely old enough to walk, his father and mother pitched a pair of tents along Lake

Michigan and lived on the beach with Donald for a summer. There, in the Indiana sand dunes community of Miller Beach, his father made a living by charging tourists twenty-five cents to ride in his speedboat, named the Mary Ann, and pulling the more daring ones behind on a surfboard tethered to his boat.

The Depression cut deep into the lives of working families. Living on Miller Beach was a temporary scheme and wouldn't go on much longer. One day Bob asked his wife to run an errand.

"Mae Lucille, I want you to go to the bank," he said. "I want you to not tell anyone where you're going or what you're doing and just go straight to the bank. When you get there, I want you to take all the money out of our account, every last cent. Get our money and then come straight back."

She did exactly what he asked: She went into the bank and made a withdrawal, every last cent. And as she walked out with the cash, the banker locked the door and pulled down the shade behind her. On the sidewalk a line of customers waited in vain to get in.

Mae Lucille hurried back to the beach encampment and they buried the money in the sand. By the end of the summer, the young couple was ready to pull up the tent stakes and try something else.

John Robert Baumgartner's family history traced a circuitous route. Born in the winter of 1907, he came from a long line of farmers on his father's side who emigrated from Switzerland to central Illinois. "Dad's family was not at all like my mother's," says Donald. "They were hard-working, humorless farmers. Think *American Gothic*." As a teenager, Bob was more interested in machines than livestock. He gave up the farming life and headed for the big city of Chicago when he was eighteen. He had ten dollars in his pocket.

According to church records, the Baumgartners' American roots originated in Rappersvyl, Switzerland, in the late 1700s with his great-great grandfather, Jacob Baumgartner. ("Baumgartner," a Swiss surname with German origins, translates to "tree gardener.") Jacob and his wife, Anna Maria, had four children. Their oldest son, John, sailed to the United States in 1848 and crossed the country to Chicago, Texas, and then California during the Gold Rush.

The second oldest son, Jacob Baumgartner Jr., bought two acres of land in Frankfort, Illinois, for $112.50 and a parcel of 323 acres for $2,000 to start his farm, setting aside one acre for the establishment of a Lutheran church, according to family records. Jacob Jr. married Philippine Maue, a native of Rheinfalz, Germany, and over the years farmed wheat, corn, oats, potatoes, and hay while operating a cheese factory with his brother and three other partners. Ten children were born to Jacob Jr. and Philippine between 1855 and 1874.

Industrious as well as prolific, Jacob was a respected citizen of Frankfort Township. He served as captain of the Horse Thief Detective Association and brought justice to bear after thieves stole three horses, including his own. In the late 1870s, he was asked by the estate of a friend in Switzerland to report on the behavior of a member of his friend's family, a "black sheep" living in Minnesota, who stood to receive a substantial inheritance. Jacob forthrightly reported back that this particular young man unfortunately was still a ne'er-do-well.

When the black sheep heard of Jacob's incriminating report, he tracked him down and shot him in the face. Jacob's sons apprehended the culprit, and were about to hang him from a tree for the crime, when Philippine, the boys' mother, intervened. The assailant was handed over to the authorities and banned from the State of Illinois for life, subject to hanging if he returned. Jacob, although disfigured, survived the gunshot wound.

August Frederick Baumgartner was the ninth of ten children, a strong and hardworking son of Jacob and Philippine. After the death of Philippine, Jacob sold the farm and moved to Chicago to open a butcher shop, Jacobus & Baumgartner, on Halsted Avenue. August, then seventeen, soon followed. But when his father died in 1893, August left the meat market and found work for a summer at the Chicago World's Fair. Looking for a change of scenery, he accepted a job from his older sister, Charlotte, and her husband on their farm in Sherburn, Minnesota. A couple of years later, he met and married Dora Lillian Benway from Iowa. With a wagon and a team of horses that he won in a raffle, along with a small inheritance from his father, he rented a farm on a lake. The story goes that August traded his violin for a haystack to feed his horses.

And so began the farm life of August and Dora Baumgartner. Five children were born to the couple, the fourth—John Robert, Donald's father—in Fairmont, Minnesota, a town bordered by five lakes not far from the Iowa state line. Over the years, the family pulled up roots several times, renting, buying, and managing farms in the Minnesota townships of Fairmont and Waseca, then the Red River Valley near Fargo, North Dakota, before moving back to Minnesota and the towns of Farmington and then Dassel, fifty miles west of Minneapolis, on Big Swan Lake.

Farm work was brutally hard. But young John Robert—known as a boy as Robert—found time for excitement and occasional mischief. He learned to drive when he was thirteen, piloting the family's second-hand Model T (purchased for $350) from the fields to the barn and back, fetching tools and spools of twine to lash together the grain bundles. And with his two older brothers, Leo and Roy, he never missed an opportunity to tease their younger sister, Charlotte.

Much of the work was done with draft horses. August raised horses. Hay was cut with a scythe-equipped mower pulled by Percherons and Belgians. But the gear-driven thresher, which separated grain seeds from the stalks and husks, was powered by a coal-fed steam engine. By World War I, tractors became more affordable, and August bought his first in North Dakota.

The Baumgartner farm in Dassel specialized in purebred Guernsey cows. Through a family connection, August was contracted to supply cream to the Radisson Hotel and the Donald's Tea Room in downtown Minneapolis. "Every morning, before daybreak, sixty-five cows were milked and the rich Guernsey cream separated," according to a family genealogy compiled years later by Carolyn Baumgartner Maruggi, Robert's daughter (from his second marriage). "The cream was put into ten-gallon cans, and it was Robert's job to take the cream, in the Model T, to the Dassel railroad station on his way to school. Here, the cream cans were put on the first train into Minneapolis."

Because of their experiences on the farm, the three Baumgartner boys became proficient handling machinery. Robert, though, had a special talent for inventing machines. He built a "pushmobile" that could be steered with his feet while he was sitting on a wooden frame. According to Baumgartner family records researched by his daughter, Carolyn, he built a propeller-equipped airplane with a twelve-foot wingspan. (Missing is any record of whether the airplane actually left the ground.) He built an elaborate "bag swing" that hung from a tree branch. Kids would climb a wooden tower, jump into the rag-padded seat, and swing through the air. In Farmington, when he was fifteen, he built a three-wheeled tractor from scratch and entered it in a contest at the Minnesota State Fair. As he drove past the judge's stand, the tractor suddenly stalled. Undeterred, he jumped out of the machine and cranked the engine back to life. The crowd cheered, and he won a blue ribbon.

He also was fascinated by radios, and built the first one in the Dassel area. Farmers were keenly interested in the weather reports, so Robert built and sold radios to the locals. In August 1923, when he was sixteen, he brought his "wireless" to school so classmates could listen to the inaugural speech of President Calvin Coolidge, the first inauguration broadcast on radio.

Robert had grown tired of life on the farm, as his daughter, Carolyn, notes in the genealogy. "Where his father loved horses, Robert loved machines. By 1925, at the age of eighteen, he was anxious to make his mark in the world."

He left Dassel and hired on with a couple of road building companies, but the labor was too similar to farm work for Robert's liking. With ambitions to find a union job as an electrician in Gary, Indiana, he jumped on a freight train going east, stopping in Chicago along the way to pay a visit to his favorite uncle who lined up a job interview or two in the city. After two or three false starts, Robert ended up with a company that made multi-layered paper bags for holding cement. He operated the machines that printed the bags, cut the paper to size, folded the paper, and glued the sides together. The experience would come in handy when his attention turned to paper cup machines.

Robert stayed with the company for two years while studying engineering at night. And in that time, the wheels in his inventor brain undoubtedly were spinning.

Donald's Irish grandparents, John and Angela Genevieve Hayes.

The Irish, and fun-loving, side of Donald's family—the forebears of his red-haired, green-eyed mother—drew a direct line to the Emerald Isle. His great-grandfather was born in Wexford, Ireland, a harbor town in southeast Ireland that was settled in the ninth century by Viking raiders. His great-grandmother came from Savannah, Georgia.

How they met is something of a mystery. But it is believed the two met and married after Donald's great-grandfather crossed the Atlantic and settled in Savannah, Georgia. There, in 1887, their son John Francis Hayes was born.

John Francis as an adult was a gifted storyteller with a lively sense of humor. He and his wife, Angela Genevieve, were devout Catholics. "They went to mass every morning," says Donald. "My grandfather and my grandmother were extremely proud of their Irish heritage. They were Irish snobs, to say the least. They totally believed that the Irish were superior people."

John Francis found employment with Flagler's Railroad, the first railroad to connect the Florida Keys to the mainland. A position with Illinois Central Railroad lured him and his family to Chicago somewhere around 1915. A few years later, he was hired as an accountant by the U.S. Interstate Commerce Commission, which over the years regulated railroads, bus lines, and the trucking industry.

John Francis held his government job all through the Depression. "As far as our family was concerned, he was very well off," Donald says. "During the war, he was transferred to Mare Island Naval Shipyard in San Francisco. They had a military base there, and he was given a rank of admiral as a civilian. He had a car and a driver and all the bells and whistles."

His prestigious position brought him a considerable salary, enough to support four daughters. Donald's mother, Mae Lucille, was the oldest. Born in Savannah in 1907, she was seven when her parents moved to Chicago's south side and enrolled her in a Catholic school.

Altogether different than the disciplined, dawn-to-dusk farm family that Donald's father had left behind, Donald's mother and her three sisters —Angela, Elizabeth, and Geraldine—were smart, extremely good looking, seductive, and excessively unmanageable. "Their Catholic father had a very hard time with them," says Donald.

While living just a couple of flights of stairs from his wife Mae's parents, Bob had steady employment for a year or two at Western Electric in Chicago. In 1931, however, at the height the Depression, he lost his job. For a short time, after leaving Miller Beach, the family moved to the Baumgartner dairy farm in Dassel, Minnesota. The exodus was temporary and they returned, happily, to Chicago.

A few years later, when he was around eleven, Donald spent a summer at the Dassel farm with his Aunt Charlotte and cousins, Jack and Kenny Storm. (Both cousins one day would go to work at Paper Machinery Corporation.) In the month of August, his father sent him a letter along with train tickets for the trip home. And, years later, Aunt Charlotte was crowned *Queen for a Day* on the nationally televised contest show of the same name. She was interviewed by host Jack Bailey and chosen as the winner of a farm tractor and a mink coat. (Donald later bought the coat from his aunt and gave it to his wife, Nancy.)

"I hope you have behaved yourself and had a good time up in Minnesota," Bob wrote to his son, "and also hope that you have not caused your Aunt Charlotte too much trouble and worry."

Unbeknownst to his father, Donald's summer had been eye opening.

The Baumgartners on the Minnesota family farm. Back row, left to right: Donald's father, Aunt Geraldine, mother, sister Jean, Aunt Charlotte, Grandmother Hayes, Aunt Gladys. Front row, left to right: Cousins Jack and Kenny Storm, Donald Baumgartner.

"I followed my cousins, the Storm brothers, around, and whatever chores they were doing, I joined in with them," he remembers. "But our biggest chore was hanging out in the hayloft and peeking through the holes at the hired hands with the milkmaids. That turned out to be very enlightening. I mean, the cows were doing it. The horses were doing it. The chickens were doing it. The milkmaids were doing it. The hired hands were doing it. And I returned from the farm at age eleven much more knowledgeable than when I went."

In 1933, after months of searching for work, Donald's father finally found a job in Milwaukee, ninety miles north of Chicago, as chief engineer of American Lace Paper Company. Operating in a newly built red brick plant on Port Washington Road in Glendale, the company fabricated paper soufflé cups, as well as lace paper placemats and other novelties. Bob designed machines that made some of these products.

The Baumgartners rented a house on the north side of Milwaukee, near Robert's job, then moved into another rental on Sylvan Avenue in Whitefish Bay, a leafy north shore suburb along Lake Michigan.

Bob and Mae Baumgartner, in what became known as their
"Bonnie and Clyde" photograph.

Meanwhile, Mae's rebellious youngest sister was causing headaches for her parents. Running out of patience, they decided to send fifteen-year-old Geraldine to a convent in Ann Arbor, Michigan, hoping her behavior would change. But life was not what she was accustomed to, and Geraldine did not get along with the nuns, understandably. Being an Irish lass, she had naturally rosy cheeks. The nuns, however, thought she was secretly wearing makeup. They would scrub her cheeks with hot water again and again to remove the red blush.

Geraldine wouldn't tolerate the nun's strict supervision. She soon ran away and hitched a ride to Milwaukee to live with her sister Mae and brother-in-law Robert. They welcomed her into their home.

In the summer of 1937, the couple's second child, Jean Mae Baumgartner, was born at St. Mary's hospital in Milwaukee. Jean was a round-faced girl with her mother's smile. In more than one family photo, her eyes are fixed adoringly on her big brother.

Seven years older, Donald overshadowed his baby sister. "Growing up in those very early years, he was another adult because he had the authority to boss me around," says Jean, now Jean McGrath. He picked out all the house furniture and his mother's dresses. "Our mother depended on him. She asked his opinion. And he was a big kid. He was always big for his age, tall, and husky. So he grew up, basically, as an only child, in my estimation."

Jean idolized her older brother. He was her protector. She recalls one memorable incident in which Donald gallantly rushed to her defense. It was Thanksgiving Day and the entire Baumgartner family was sitting down for a holiday dinner in Bob's home. But there didn't seem to be enough chairs around the table for everyone. Carolyn (Donald and Jean's half sister by his father's second wife) was seated in a table-chair—an oversized high-chair in which children could play and eat. There wasn't room for Jean.

"So they asked me to eat in the kitchen because this high-chair was taking up a couple of spaces at the table," says Jean.

Donald, outraged, jumped up and said, "If my sister eats in the kitchen, so do I!"

"And that was quite exciting that he was standing up for me," says Jean. "This was kind of a change in our relationship. I was really proud of him."

Perhaps as a way to compensate for growing up in the shadow of her brother, Jean

Sister Jean and a young Donald at the wheel of his first car, built by his father.

became a very social young woman. "I liked people," she says. "I had friends. I had activities. I had things I did, and just created my own life."

From first grade on, her father paid for her to attend exceptional, private schools: she went to Downer Seminary School and University School in Milwaukee from first through ninth grade, then Pine Crest boarding school in Fort Lauderdale, Florida, for grades ten through twelve. She enrolled at the University of Miami, joining the Kappa Kappa Gamma sorority and graduating in 1959 with a degree in speech therapy and education for the deaf. She completed a graduate level assistantship at Marquette University in Milwaukee.

"My sister is better bred than I am," says Donald. "She associated with a lot of pretty classy folks. Jean put on airs from the time she was very small. My mother felt she was being snubbed by her own daughter. My mother was earthy, to say the least, and Jean was just the opposite."

Like most older brothers, he took full advantage of his seniority by teasing and playing jokes on his sister. One year, when Jean was three or four, Donald got a tiger suit to wear for Halloween. "And he put it on and chased me around like he was a tiger," she Jean recalls. "He'd scare me half to death every time I saw that tiger suit. When we moved my mother left the tiger suit in the old house. That was great news to me because I was terrified of that tiger suit."

Before leaving the tiger behind, though, Donald managed to salvage a piece of fabric from the suit. Just the sight of the orange and black cloth sent his sister into hysterics.

Several years later, Jean got her moment of payback. Donald was about to turn sixteen, and as his birthday approached, his father bought a gift for him, a shiny silver canoe. His father locked it in the garage and hung newspaper in the windows so nobody could see in.

"Donald asked me if I knew what was in the garage, and I said it was his birthday gift. And he goes, 'Oh, it's in the garage?' I said, 'Well, it wouldn't fit in the house.' Naturally, he's thinking automobile, and naturally, I'm knowing he's thinking automobile. So every day I would give him a new hint, like, 'Oh, yeah. It's *transportation*. It's *silver*. There's *no top*. Only *two people* fit in it.' He's got it totally visualized: It's a silver sports car, a two-seater convertible.

"Of course," Jean continues, "His birthday comes and we open the garage door, and he sees that *canoe*. I had to run for my life. To this day, the word 'canoe' isn't a word he wants to hear."

The story doesn't end there: "The family had a little cottage," Jean continues, "and Donald left the canoe outside one day to be stolen, and of course it was stolen. Then a few days later we were eating dinner in a nearby restaurant, and I spotted the canoe out the window. I said, 'Oh, my gosh. It's the canoe!' And he's hollering, 'Leave it alone! Leave it alone!' He never really made friends with that canoe."

Donald remembers the prank all too well. "She got me good. I had no interest in canoeing up to that point—or after. I did buy a car. One of my dad's friends who had a used car lot sold me a black 1937 two-door Ford coupe with a sixty-horsepower engine for sixty dollars. But it had mechanical brakes, and no matter how hard you pushed on the damned brakes, it wouldn't slow the car down much. So it was real tricky. I learned a lot about driving at an early age. I mean, anybody can drive a car with brakes. I had a car but it would only go. It wouldn't stop. Could be a metaphor."

The Baumgartners moved to a house on Santa Monica Boulevard, another rental in Whitefish Bay. The challenges of supporting two children during the Depression years were daunting. But Bob and Mae Baumgartner were young—both turned thirty in the year their daughter was born—and they were ambitious. So determined was Mae that she took over a failing restaurant when she was still pregnant with Jean.

The restaurant had been built for Glenn Chapman. "He was my mother's sister Betty's husband," Donald explains. "He had worked for the White Castle people in Chicago and thought he knew the business. So my dad put up the money to build a White Castle on the corner of Capitol Drive and Port Washington Road. And business didn't go very well for Uncle Glenn. He couldn't pay back my father."

Glenn and Betty split up. "He had all kinds of horrible problems," says Donald. "A drunk, a gambler, a womanizer—you name it. All the evil things that a guy can do he was accused of. Of course whether any of that's true or not, I have no idea."

Donald's father regained ownership of the diner. "My mother moved into it and took it over, started running the damned thing herself."

Glenn's Grill, as it was named, was an eighteen-stool restaurant with a horseshoe-shaped counter. On the corner of the block with a large parking lot in the back, the white-tiled building with an "EAT" sign hanging above the door was hard to pass by. Serving a fare of hamburgers, Sloppy Joes, steaks, chops and "one-half milk-fed spring chicken with bread, butter, vegetables, potatoes and coffee, all for 40¢," it catered to neighborhood regulars—factory workers from a nearby manufacturing plant and teens from a high school two blocks away. The waitresses handed out green punch cards worth fifty cents credit to appreciative customers.

Mae Lucille managed the place as a twenty-four-hour diner, hiring a cook, three or four waitresses and a dishwasher. Occasionally she waited on customers and washed dishes herself. One of her hires was her sister, Geraldine, who had fled the convent and lived with the Baumgartners.

"My mother had heard about drive-ins in California," says Donald. "So she decided she would have curb service. She opened a window in the back of the restaurant, put up a big sign, CURB SERVICE – DRIVE THRU. Geraldine was going to be the curb-service girl. Well, the first car, a convertible, drove up and a handsome young guy behind the wheel started flirting with Geraldine. Before long my mother noticed a long line of cars at the drive thru, tooting their horns. Geraldine and the handsome young driver were nowhere in sight."

Donald took shifts after school washing dishes. "I progressed to become counter boy," he says. "And these burly, rough and tough guys would come in and order a cup of coffee. I'd put the coffee in front of them and if it was a quarter of an inch from the brim they'd yell. 'What the hell is this, boy? I want a full cup!' I learned a lot about human nature, not all of it good. But it was very popular place. Packed all the time."

Not yet ten years old, if Donald wasn't flipping burgers for his mother he was learning how to run machine tools from his father.

While holding down a salaried job at American Lace Paper Company, Bob, who was often called by his initials "JR," had set up a machine shop in a

Donald and his mother outside her restaurant, Glenn's Grill.

Mae Baumgartner, far left, at the counter of the eighteen-stool restaurant with her mother and sisters Geraldine, Betty, and Elizabeth.

two-car garage behind the family's rented bungalow. He called the company Reliable Tool & Machine Works. Run as a "job shop" and working nights and weekends, JR would make machine parts for local customers, following blueprint specs.

At his day job at American Lace Paper, he built a machine that made "soufflé cups," a flat-bottomed paper cup that was pleated on the side and is still commonly used as a pill dispenser. Drawing on his Chicago experience running a machine that made paper bags that held cement, he saw an opportunity to strike out on his own and soon left American Lace Paper.

"He worked there long enough to look at how they were making soufflé cups, and he thought he could do it better," Donald says. "Rather than stay there and make more machines for them, he went home to his shop and made a pleated soufflé-cup machine and sold it to their competitor, Milwaukee Lace Paper. People who grew up in the Depression had that mentality. Money was scarce as hell during the '30s. It was survival of the fittest."

With the money he was paid for the first machine, and a loan to fill orders for additional machines, he bought more machine tools to expand the business. Now with five employees, he moved into a 1,500-square-foot cement-block building—an old blacksmith shop—in Glendale on Port Washington Road, making soufflé-cup machines under contract for Milwaukee Lace Paper and machining parts as a jobber.

"He had lathes and milling machines and grinders and shapers, and a whole array of machine tools that you would need to make parts. I was learning how to run them all."

Mae kept the books at Reliable Tool. A graduate of the Moser Secretarial School in Chicago and the daughter of an accountant, she devised her own system for submitting bids to prospective customers: Taking the figure JR had calculated for building a machine or making a part, she would simply add 10 percent to every bid.

The economy began to roar back to life in the late 1930s with the run-up to World War II. As arms production surged throughout the country, the demand for manufacturing companies like Reliable Tool grew rapidly. One military contract called for the company to produce parts for the famous Lockheed Lodestar, the Army C-60 transport plane that was used to haul

Donald's father moved his first company, Reliable Tool & Machine Works, to a former blacksmith shop in the mid-1930s. Donald, at about age six, stands in the lot.

Inside Reliable Tool & Machine Works.

troops and supplies to New Guinea, where General Douglas MacArthur established an airhead to attack the Japanese.

Reliable Tool had moved to the Marine Terminal warehouse on the Milwaukee River in downtown Milwaukee's Third Ward. By 1943, the workforce had grown to 200. Ten years after setting up a tool shop in a backyard garage in the grip of the Great Depression, JR was shipping products halfway around the world.

"He put me to work at an early age," Donald says. "He made me industrious. He gave me a lot of responsibilities, and he counted on me. My dad and my mom both thought I knew what I was doing, even when I probably didn't."

After the war ended, JR received an offer to buy Reliable Tool from Bob McCullough, a wealthy Milwaukee entrepreneur. McCullough owned a motors company that produced racing-car engines and an aviation company that built helicopters.

JR accepted McCullough's offer and later, with the proceeds, started Mercury Engineering, a manufacturing company at 2100 North Farwell Avenue on Milwaukee's east side. McCullough moved the former Reliable Tool & Machine Works to California to manufacture chainsaws. Most of Reliable Tool's workers lost their jobs.

CHAPTER 2

The Captain and the Crew

A mong the many photographs of the Baumgartner family are child-hood portraits of Donald at a marina, or along a waterfront, or on a boat. In one photo, he's standing with his father on a dock at six or seven years old, wearing a round-brimmed, white sailor's cap and a black leather jacket like his dad's. And there he is, wearing the same cap and lying shirtless in the sun on the deck of a boat, his mother standing at a signal mast in the foreground. And there he is in the cockpit of a boat, dressed in an immac-ulately white sailor suit, a nautical insignia on his shirtfront, web D-ring belt around his waist, and penny whistle hanging from a lanyard around his neck.

Boats have been an integral part of Donald's life. As he was growing up, his father taught him everything about boats—how to dock a boat, pilot a boat, repair a boat, even how to build a boat.

Bob Baumgartner, known by many as "The Skipper," or JR, had an affin-ity for boats. Starting with the speedboat he anchored at Indiana's Miller Beach, to the sixty-six-foot motor yacht he sailed from Ft. Lauderdale to Key West at age ninety-three, he owned as many as fifty different boats by the time he reached the end of his life. He preferred powerboats to sail boats. He was a mechanic, after all. Working on machines was his second nature.

In 1937, Bob bought a thirty-seven-foot Chris-Craft and two mem-berships to the Milwaukee Yacht Club, one for himself and a junior

23

Clockwise from left: Donald with his mother on a dock; in a sailor suit on the deck of a boat in Milwaukee's marina; and with his father, "The Skipper."

membership for his son, who was seven at the time. Donald grew his sea legs on the Chris-Craft, christened the *Game Cock*.

"He was the captain, I was the crew," Donald says. "We spent a lot of my youth on the Great Lakes. His favorite port was Saugatuck, Michigan, straight across Lake Michigan from Milwaukee. We also spent time in the areas north of Door County. Mackinac Island was a favorite spot. I went to all of those places many times. We caught an awful lot of bad weather on the Great Lakes." If something broke down on the boat, Bob, the mechanical genius, was quick with his tool kit. "He was a hands-on guy, always moving, never sat down. He never sat on a beach in his life, ever."

With the start of World War II, Bob sold the *Game Cock* and bought a ninety-two-foot yacht called the *Verano*. Built by Consolidated Shipbuilding in New York, it was primarily designed for cruising on the Hudson River. "It wasn't a very good sea boat," says Donald. "It rocked like crazy. We had it for about a year or two, and he sold it. The guy that bought it sank it on the Michigan shore. I don't recall any of the details. There weren't any lives lost, but the boat sank."

Donald's nautical adventures shifted into high gear when he was in high school. "It started in 1946. I was fifteen, sixteen years old." World War II

Bob Baumgartner's Chris-Craft, the Game Cock, *docked on Mackinaw Island.*

had ended and the government began selling off surplus vessels. The Skipper bought an eighty-two-foot Coast Guard cutter. He planned to convert it into a yacht, and Donald volunteered to help.

The two traveled to Baltimore, where the cutter was anchored in the Navy shipyard on Curtis Bay. After finalizing the deal, Bob returned to Milwaukee, leaving Donald in Baltimore to hire a crew and prepare the vessel for the trip back to Milwaukee by water.

"I put an ad in the *Baltimore Sun*," recalls Donald. "I hired a deckhand, and I hired a cook. The cook was a German. He was down on his luck, an older guy named Ludwig von Hintenger, and he had cooked for the aristocracy in Germany. He told me he had been the cook for Count Felix von Luckner, who was a famous World War I naval hero and a boyhood hero of mine."

A German nobleman, powerfully strong, with a booming voice, Von Luckner was known as "the Sea Devil" for his exploits as captain of the *SMS Seeadler*, a converted, three-masted merchant ship, in the war. Commandeering the *Seeadler* in 1916 and 1917, von Luckner disrupted the Allied supply chain, sinking fourteen ships in his Atlantic and Pacific raids while being responsible for the death of only a single Allied seaman. His memoir about his wartime adventures became a bestseller in Germany, and a subsequent book about his life by Lowell Thomas spread his fame internationally. Donald had read all about von Luckner's *Seeadler* adventures and was fascinated by his story.

During World War II, Adolf Hitler attempted to exploit von Luckner's popularity in Nazi propaganda campaigns. But von Luckner did not back Hitler's regime. In 1943, he rescued a young Jewish woman living in Germany by providing her with a bogus passport that allowed her to escape to the United States. After the Nazis condemned him to death, he never returned to his homeland, and instead lived out his years in Malmo, Sweden.

"When Ludwig told me he had cooked for Count von Luckner, that sealed the deal. I hired him straightaway. Ludwig had a very thick German accent. He had somehow managed to get out of Germany and make it to these shores. He cut an impressive figure, and he became the family cook forever. Not just on the boat, but he wound up cooking for my dad at his apartment at the Astor Hotel in Milwaukee.

Donald at the wheel of a decommissioned Coast Guard cutter en route from Baltimore to Milwaukee, where he helped his father convert the boat into a pleasure yacht.

"The other guy I hired was named Charley Rogers. He was a good-looking guy, lost all of his money gambling, womanizing. He provided an eye-opening education for me. I learned all sorts of wonderfully inappropriate things that an impressionable fifteen-year-old would from a guy like Charley."

The decommissioned Coast Guard cutter set sail out of Chesapeake Bay, bound for Milwaukee, crewed by a rounder named Charley as the deckhand, a down-and-out German immigrant as the cook, and an adventurous high school student. "That's all we needed," Donald says.

They headed north along the Eastern Seaboard to New York Harbor, then up the Hudson River to Albany, where they turned west and traveled through the Erie Canal for 360 miles before exiting into Lake Erie near Buffalo. From there, the boat motored past Cleveland, Toledo, and Detroit, passed into Lake Huron going north, brushed past Mackinaw Island and into Lake Michigan, then cruised south to Milwaukee.

"I made the whole trip," says Donald. "My dad laid a lot of responsibility on me, but I knew what I was doing. I was a big kid, six feet and 200 pounds. I always looked older than I was. I had no trouble going into a bar at sixteen and ordering a beer."

The voyage took approximately two months. "We tied the boat up in back of the Metropolitan Block in downtown Milwaukee, which was on the river at the State Street Bridge. There's no building there anymore, but we had a shop in the basement of the Metropolitan Block where we worked on the boat. I helped nights and weekends, and just volunteered my time with my dad. I wound up painting the thing, scraping and cleaning bilges, tuning engines, tearing everything apart. I learned a lot of trades, plumbing and electrical and who knows what else. It was a lot of work. It was a big boat, eighty-three feet."

Named the *Trenora*, Bob used the reconditioned boat to launch a new business with his son, Milwaukee Shipbuilding. The idea was to buy and convert surplus warships that were mothballed and sell them as pleasure boats.

The idea went nowhere, and Milwaukee Shipbuilding went dormant until the Korean War.

Bob and Donald—father and son, skipper and crew—often cruised the waters of the Great Lakes on the *Trenora*, but rather than keep the yacht in Milwaukee, the Skipper took it to Florida, sailing down the Mississippi

The reconditioned Trenora, *at anchor.*

River, around the Gulf of Mexico's arc, through the Florida Keys, and north to Fort Lauderdale, where it remained until Bob finally sold it in the 1960s.

"The boat didn't pan out as a business," says Donald, looking back. "But it worked out, as my father got himself one nice yacht."

In the image of his restless father, Donald was a venturesome, curious boy, always looking for new experiences. His first several years of school, though, seemed to go against his grain.

His mother came from an Irish Catholic family and had been educated by Roman Catholic nuns. So it made sense that she and Donald's father would send him to the parochial St. Monica School two blocks from their home in Whitefish Bay for his elementary education.

Named after the mother of Saint Augustine, the parish of St. Monica was established in 1923. Its first mass was held in the Whitefish Bay Village Hall on Christmas Day. The following spring, parish leaders purchased fifteen acres along Silver Spring Drive and converted an old barn into a makeshift chapel. St. Monica School opened in the repurposed barn in 1928, and the worship space was moved into the basement. Construction of a new church and school was slowed by the Depression and World War II until years later.

The academic successes of the school were encumbered by a limited budget, a small space, and high enrollment, which was a concern to Donald's mother, who valued the importance of education. She worried that the large class size of fifty-two students for each teacher was hindering her son's learning.

"In fourth grade, I still wasn't reading very well," Donald says. "So my mother came to school one day to find out what was going on. She asked the teacher, Sister Daisy, if she could point out her son in the classroom. And Sister Daisy didn't know who I was. 'Donald who?' was her response."

Mae Baumgartner pulled her son out of St. Monica School at the end of the school year and, with Donald's father, enrolled him that fall in Milwaukee Country Day School, a private, all-boys school in Whitefish Bay, with fifteen students in each class.

Based in three, Tudor-styled buildings, with ivy climbing its brick walls, the school held an air of exclusivity.

"My father agreed to pay the tuition at Country Day, which was quite a lot of money at the time. It was an expensive school with a very small enrollment. There were just fifteen of us in fifth grade, and we had five teachers for five different subjects."

He was relieved to leave St. Monica behind. Catholicism had run its course for Donald by the time he was ten. Although he had been raised a Catholic up until then and had sung in the church choir, one particular event conclusively soured him on the faith.

"The archbishop of Chicago had come to our church," he says. "He was sitting in a sedan chair with wooden arms that extended from the back. They put me in a black gown with a white top over it like altar boys wear. There were nine of us carrying him on our shoulders—the archbishop's in his chair with an incense burner, waving it back and forth, blessing the congregation. I felt like a galley slave. It was right out of a movie, and it was all I could stand.

"That, and I had a problem with confession. I wasn't really sinning, so I had to make up sins. I felt that this was strange, confessing: 'Forgive me father for I have sinned. . . .' Then I'd have to lie to the priest, which was a sin. So I quit. I walked out and never went back. It wasn't for me. I didn't believe any part of it. I just couldn't handle it."

Milwaukee Country Day School seemed like a good fit for Donald. The smaller class size and individualized teaching approach suited him. And the rousing school motto, "Don't wait to become a great man—be a great boy," was a ready-made credo for any over-animated ten-year-old boy.

"I was at Country Day from fifth grade through the tenth grade—six years," Donald says. "I built model airplanes in fifth and sixth grade with my friend Phil Krueger, who lived in a big, red, stone house with a turret on Wahl Avenue, overlooking the lake. His father was president of the Worden-Allen Company, a steel company in Milwaukee. Phil and I would ride our bikes down the stairs from the North Point Water Tower down to the lake. There was a set of stairs straight down St. Mary's Hill to Lincoln Memorial Drive. I look at those stairs now and I think, 'I can't believe we did that.' Bumpity, bumpity, bumpity bump."

At the end of the fifth grade, Country Day sent an itemized invoice to Donald's father for the cost of school supplies for the year: $1.08 for art supplies, 50 cents for writing supplies, 45 cents for an arithmetic book, 30 cents for a dictionary workbook, and $2.00 for the book *Fathers and Sons* (the classic by Russian novelist Ivan Turgenev). Judging by the last item on the list, Donald apparently ran into a little trouble that year. At the bottom of the invoice is a charge of 50 cents for a broken window.

Donald was promoted from the school's junior division to its senior division in 1944. Two years later, near the end of his sophomore year, he was brought before the faculty to face accusations far more serious than a broken window. Gathered in a tribunal-like panel were some of his favorite teachers, who told him he had been seen making out with a student from Downer Seminary, a private girls' school located on what is now the University of Wisconsin-Milwaukee campus. The girl, Mary, was Donald's first girlfriend.

Donald emphatically denied the allegation. "I was shocked. I had no idea what they were talking about," he says, looking back. "Mary was a girl who I had held hands with, at the most, if I had even done that. Their accusations were preposterous."

The school insisted that he withdraw or be expelled.

"I was blindsided and totally devastated," he says. "These were some of the best teachers I ever had or ever would have: Gledden Santer, the headmaster and Latin teacher; Chuck Boesel, mathematics teacher; Ken Laird, English and football coach; and Bill Church, a science instructor. I had absolutely no idea where they were coming from. It took years to get the answer."

The answer arrived in the form of his one-time best friend, Dick Walton, who showed up at his front door unexpectedly thirty years later. Without prompting, Walton, a classmate at Country Day School, began to unburden himself about his alcoholism, his failed marriages, and other problems. "Then he told me this incredible story and started apologizing for what had happened at Country Day. He confessed that he had set me up. He had spread rumors that I was having a torrid affair with Mary because he was jealous."

Walton told Donald he had joined Alcoholics Anonymous, and Donald speculates that his sudden confession might have been motivated by AA's twelve-step program, which requires members to "make direct amends" to people that they have wronged.

"I knew Dickie Walton had a dark side when we were in fifth grade and he announced to me that he had an extremely hard head and could take any blow. Waiting to hear the approaching footsteps of the teacher, he said, 'Go ahead hit me with this encyclopedia as hard as you can.' Just as the book came down on top of his head, the teacher walked in the door. Maybe it was an early indication of where things were going with Dickie."

Apparently his confession was not enough to quell his demons. Haunted by guilt and his failures, and wracked by alcoholism, he took his own life soon after confessing to Donald.

"I had no concept that he was the root of all of my problems with Country Day," says Donald, bowled over by the turn of events. "But instead of ruining my life, it opened up a whole new world to me because I went to Shorewood High School, a much bigger school. It was coeducational, I got to meet girls, and I got to play football, which is something I really enjoyed doing on a much bigger platform, in a much bigger program."

Years later, after Donald had established himself as a successful businessman and philanthropist, Country Day School "had second thoughts about what the hell they had done," Donald says. "Even though I did not graduate from Country Day, they listed my name as a member of the class of '49. It was too late."

In 1963, Milwaukee Country Day merged Downer Seminary and the Milwaukee University School to become University School of Milwaukee. "I wound up sending my daughter and grandchildren there and have been a regular donor to the school. Years after they forced me to leave, the school asked me to host the Class of 1949's 50th Reunion, which would be celebrated at my house."

At Shorewood High School, a public school built in 1925 that grew into a college-sized campus, Donald played football, ran track, and threw the shot put in his junior and senior years. He had played some football at Country Day, but the small student population made it hard to field a competitive team. Shorewood's football games were very well attended. "Friday Night Lights" was a family affair. Donald's mother, Elmer (her second husband), and his grandfather, Grandpa Hayes, came out to watch him play.

Donald was the first-born grandchild and first-born grandson of the Baumgartner and Hayes families. Having raised four daughters, his

Donald hanging out with his Uncle David, the husband of his Aunt Geraldine.

Donald trimming a sail with his Grandpa Hayes.

grandfather—John Francis Hayes, known as Dad Hayes—was delighted to spend time with Donald.

The feeling was mutual. "My grandfather had a good sense of humor and a big, hearty laugh," says Donald. "And what a storyteller—in the best Irish bullshit tradition. He had a big influence on my life. He's the one that got me into the Catholic school, even though it was a terrible school. He came up from Chicago and watched me play football when I was in high school. And he took me to a Notre Dame-Northwestern game. As an Irish Catholic, I mean, he was a rabid Notre Dame fan."

By contrast, his father knew nothing about football, Donald says. "He couldn't have cared less." Naturally, the teenaged Donald gravitated to the large personality of his grandfather.

"Dad Hayes was very gregarious," recalls Donald's younger sister, Jean McGrath. "He had a lot of friends, a lot of interests, was active in the church, active in the Knights of Columbus. He was a big southern Democrat, very friendly, loved people. He was a wonderful storyteller, and Donald gets that from him."

Donald played football at Shorewood High School in his junior and senior years.

For his junior and senior years at Shorewood High, Donald starred on the football team. At six feet and 215 pounds, he played center and pulling guard on offense; he played defensive end and linebacker on defense. He was named to the all-conference team by both *The Milwaukee Journal* and the *Milwaukee Sentinel* for two years straight.

"We did very well," he says. "Our major mission was to beat Whitefish Bay. And we did."

Donald fell in with a group of like-minded friends in Shorewood who were good at hatching schemes and pulling pranks. Bill Schwab, a running back on the football team, introduced Donald to the art of wedding crashing, and quickly became Donald's best friend.

"On Saturdays, we would go around town looking for wedding receptions at union halls," Donald says. "The halls would hold union meetings at night and weddings on the weekends. Bill and I would go from hall to hall, pretending we were friends of the bride or friends of the groom. We would have all the beer we wanted and all the food we wanted, and danced with all the pretty girls."

Don Tomasini also played football, the team's fullback. "He was a pole vaulter and worked for his dad, who was a sewer contractor. Don was by far the strongest kid I knew," Donald recalls.

Donald met Gil Brandt through Bill Schwab. "Gil showed up after one of the football games at a student center where there was a little dance going on. He came up to Bill and me. 'I was watching you play football. You guys are pretty good,' Gil said. 'You guys want to meet some *goyls?* I've got some *goyls* for you.' So that's how I met Gil.

"Gil went to North Division High School on West Center Street. He lived across the street and played football for North Division. He was just

Left to right: Donald with his high school traveling companions, Bill Schwab and Gil Brandt.

about the only white kid in the school and had the unique ability to speak the hip lingo of the black kids. He went on to work for the Dallas Cowboys under Coach Tom Landry, when the Cowboys were first formed and came from out of nowhere to become a world-class team. Gil was given credit for building that team. He was their player personnel manager, in the news constantly. He was always on television. He became the expert on football."

In one of their more ambitious schemes, Donald and his three friends decided to drive to Alaska via the recently opened Alaska-Canadian Highway. Built as a military route during World War II to connect the lower forty-eight states to Alaska across Canada, the Alcan became accessible to the public in 1948, in the summer between Donald's junior and senior year of high school.

Donald, Bill, Gil, and Don bought a used Jeep and hit the road, fueled by the sheer exuberance of youth. "We painted a sign on the side, 'Alaska or Bust.' They had just finished the Alcan Highway, and we were going on this adventure. We piled into this little jeep, just the four of us."

They made it to the Canadian Rockies before the Jeep gave out.

"We got as far as Lake Louise, near Banff in Alberta. Mechanically the Jeep just would not go another inch," says Donald.

Gil decided to forsake the Alaskan dream and bought a train ticket home. The other three boys knocked around Banff for a while, not ready to give up on their adventure.

"We're stranded there and, *bam*, out of nowhere, we see there's a movie being made," says Donald. The cast was straight out of Hollywood—Randolph Scott, J. Carrol Naish, and a young actress named Nancy Olson, originally from Wauwatosa, Wisconsin.

"We heard she was from Wisconsin and went over to the set and introduced ourselves. We told her we were from Shorewood, and she got us a job on the set as movie extras. We were running out of money, running out of food, running out of everything. So Nancy took care of us, and we spent three days as extras on the job."

The movie, *Canadian Pacific*, was Olson's first big role. The following year she starred in *Sunset Boulevard* and was nominated for an Academy Award for best supporting actress.

In their dramatic roles in *Canadian Pacific*, the three boys were given just a single line of dialogue: "We want our pay *now!*" Their dialogue didn't survive the final cut. But moviegoers across the country would see them on the silver screen, larger than life—running across a railroad track.

After their work as extras, the stranded trio abandoned their plan to make it to Alaska and looked homeward. Don Tomasini's parents wired him train money, while Bill and Donald started to hitchhike.

"That didn't work real well," says Donald. "So, taking a cue from my father, who had ridden the rails from his family's farm to Chicago, we started riding open boxcars. That didn't work out so well either. We managed to get from Canada down somewhere into North Dakota, and I think we walked across the entire state of South Dakota. We were so filthy from the boxcars that nobody would pick us up hitchhiking. I don't know how far we got before we finally called it a day and called home for bus money. Maybe we made it to Iowa."

The abbreviated journey made the newspapers. An article and photo of the three boys with their movie star friend Nancy ran in *The Milwaukee Journal's* Green Sheet, with Donald, Bill, and Don dressed in cowboy hats and kerchiefs around their necks, costumes from their Hollywood debut.

Sometime in the late 1930s, as Donald's father began to expand Reliable Tool & Machine Works and his mother took over Glenn's Grill, his parents' marriage started to unravel. JR had become involved with a woman he met named Thelma Kohl, and before long, he and Mae separated. "Your father left us," Mae said to Donald. "You're the man of the house now."

When they met, Thelma worked at Milwaukee County Hospital, but her roots were from a farm near Marshfield, Wisconsin. She and JR were cut from the same familial cloth. "Oh hell, Thelma, we're just a couple of farmers," he would say when invited to a formal social event or dinner at a fancy restaurant. Throughout his life, he made no pretense of being cultured or sophisticated.

JR and Thelma moved into an apartment at the Astor-on the-Lake Hotel near Lake Michigan. They stayed there through the war years, then rented a house on Grant Boulevard on the city's west side.

THE MILWAUKEE JOURNAL
Green Sheet

Milwaukee, Wis.　　　Monday, September 13, 1948　　　*Copyright, 1948, by The Journal Company*

Movie Vacation

Three Shorewood high school football players have returned from a vacation trip in which they had their share of adventure, including an appearance in a movie. The boys are Bill Schwab, Don Baumgartner and Don Tomasini. They went into Canada in Schwab's jeep, but it broke down three times and they had to sell it. Near Banff, they went to see Nancy

When three Shorewood high school football players were stranded in Banff, Canada, after their jalopy broke down, they found that they were in luck. Nancy Olson of Milwaukee was in Banff on location, playing in the movie "Canadian Pacific." She learned of the misfortune of her friends from Shorewood and promptly got busy. Her first maneuver was to get them jobs as extras in the movie so they could get enough money to have their jalopy fixed and extra cash for cakes on their return voyage. This picture with Nancy was taken after the boys were in their costumes. They are (left to right) Bill Schwab, 525 Clovernook lane; Don Baumgartner, 2321 E. Menlo blvd., and Don Tomasini, 9012 W. Hampton av. They are back in school now.

Olson of Milwaukee, who has the feminine lead in "Canadian Pacific," which was being made there. Nancy helped them get three days' work as extras in the picture. Finally, they hitchhiked home.

Hometown movie stars.

Thelma, known for her exceptional cooking and infectious laugh, married JR in 1947. A year later their daughter Carolyn was born, followed by Roberta in 1950. "Thelma was a caring mother and stepmother to JR's children," Donald recalls. In years to come, his two half-sisters and his first two children would spend much of their childhoods together.

"My mother would have big family parties," says her daughter, Roberta Axelrod. "She wouldn't be afraid to cook two Thanksgiving turkeys for everybody. She was beautiful and always cheerful and liked to dance. She was a person who was really easy to get along with, and devoted to her family. That's who she was. We were lucky to have her as a mom."

Mae, meanwhile, purchased a two-story stucco house for $7,000 on tree-draped Menlo Boulevard in Shorewood, halfway between Shorewood High School and the Lake Michigan shoreline. She took up golf after her separation from JR, and soon met Elmer Percy Greenwald, a golf pro who gave lessons and ran a driving range called Stop & Sock at Santa Monica Boulevard and Hampton Road in Whitefish Bay.

By then, the United States had entered World War II, after declaring war against Japan and then Germany days after the December 7, 1941, attack on Pearl Harbor by Japanese fighter planes. Elmer was drafted into the Army and began basic training in the Signal Corps the following summer at Fort Sheridan Army Base north of Chicago. He married Mae on October 3, 1942—two days after Mae and JR's divorce was finalized—and shipped out within weeks, assigned as a radio operator in a Sherman tank division led by the legendary General George Patton.

"I went down to Fort Sheridan for his graduation, and I was in the picture with all these soldiers as sort of the mascot of the class," remembers Donald. "They would all become tank radio operators in our gasoline-driven Sherman M4s, which were no match for the German Panzers. God, the Axis forces just knocked off tank after tank. Elmer was one of the few that survived from that group."

Elmer's tank division landed in Casablanca as part of the North African Campaign in November 1942. He took part in the Allies' invasion of Sicily in July 1943, fighting against Mussolini's Italian Royal Army. "He then fought his way with Patton's 7th Army across Germany," Donald says. "He was one of the first to go and one of the last to come back. He fought

Left: Donald's mother, Mae, married Elmer Greenwald during World War II, weeks before he shipped out.

Right: Elmer, right, fought in the North Africa Campaign and across Europe.

Jean and Donald with their mother and Elmer before he left for the war, 1942.

the whole war. And during the war, we corresponded. They had a thing called Victory Mail, V-Mail, really thin paper. And he would send me these V-Mails. The two of us corresponded. He would talk about the equipment and the machinery. He knew I was interested in machinery and equipment. He talked about the planes, he talked about his buddies and what they were doing. He always made it sound fun."

Elmer sent the following V-Mail on March 17, 1943, from somewhere in North Africa:

> Hi Don,
>
> Well, this being St. Patrick's Day I thought I might dedicate this letter to you. How are you getting along with your schoolwork? I suppose by the time this reaches you, you will be out for baseball. Don't forget that outside pitch to right field. We have been playing quite a bit of ball here. Our ball field is surrounded with cork trees. . . . Your mother tells me you two have been seeing quite a few shows. Well so have I. We have an outdoor theatre here and they run off some very good shows. Tonight we are having "Yanks in Burma." You would sure be in your glory with all these different types of planes flying around. I believe now I could outsmart you on the different names and types. How do you like the new P-38? Have you seen the P-47? Boy is that thing fast. We had two of them fly over our camp, and they came so fast one couldn't even get a good look. . . . Well Don, study hard, and take care of your mother for me.
>
> The African Bullet Dodger,
> Elmer

Donald held Elmer in high regard, as a veteran of war and for his athletic ability as a golfer and minor league baseball player. "Being a kid with a lot of aspirations of playing serious football, and he being an athlete was inspiring to me. He would come to the practices. He would come to all of the games. He knew the sport intimately. My father didn't know a damn thing about football, but Elmer sure did, and all of my buddies at school knew him and liked to hang around with him. A gifted athlete, ambidextrous, a switch hitter—he could do it all. Golf, baseball, he had once played for the New York Giants. He never bowled under 200, and you didn't want to play pool with Elmer.

"He was at one time Milwaukee billiards champion. He could call a shot on the break and clean the table while you stood there like an idiot chalking your cue. We had a pool table and two slot machines and a bar that we'd set up in the recreation room in the basement. Because it was a small basement, you didn't have a lot of room around the pool table. So, we had these little short cues you could use when you had a shot from the side. And even with these little three-foot cues, Elmer would consistently make shots. He was one of these truly gifted guys with hand-eye coordination. He was a natural."

The letters Elmer wrote to him did not paint a "war is hell" portrait. To the contrary, Elmer never seemed to be in harm's way. "The way he wrote his letters did not indicate that he did anything except manage to somehow survive. He was in a gasoline-powered M4 Sherman tank, for God's sakes. It was a death warrant, but he was always in the right place at the right time, and I was very proud of the fact that he survived the war, and I was proud that he served in it of course. But I never saw him as a war hero, like some Hollywood star. I never thought of him as a John Wayne figure. Never. He was just too nice a guy and too gregarious to be John Wayne."

As with most men of his generation, World War II had an enormous influence on Donald. He followed every major battle, watched every move made by the Allies and the Axis powers—Germany, Italy, Japan—and knew intimately every piece of equipment both sides employed. "The generals became heroes and role models," he says. "These larger than life figures— George S. Patton, who Elmer served under in the Third Army; and Erwin Rommel 'the Desert Fox,' who Elmer fought against in North Africa; and Douglas MacArthur, who spoke with such authority and conviction—all had me mesmerized."

While Elmer was overseas, Donald proved to be a hero of sorts, at least in the eyes of his sister, Jean. Their mother had taken in a boarder, a particularly disagreeable man named Wally.

"I totally disliked him," Jean recalls. "So did Donald. I mean, he was just an unpleasant, nasty guy. But he was there. And mother kept saying that he was leaving, he was leaving, he was leaving. But he never seemed to leave. So finally Donald decided that the time had come for him to go. Donald, in a most dramatic fashion, as only Donald can, grabbed all of his clothes and threw them out on the lawn. And I'm cheering, 'Yaayyy!' I was so proud of him. Bear in mind, I was only six or seven years old, and it was just the most glorious moment of my life, getting rid of that guy. Donald was my hero, and of course he's done so many things since then to reinforce being my hero."

Donald, right, boxes with older cousin, Kenny Storm.

As Donald remembers it, his mother might have been somewhat more complicit in Wally's living arrangement. "He wasn't a boarder, he was my mother's wartime lover," he says. "He was a crude loudmouth with a giant potbelly, a cigar-smoking creep who I couldn't stand. The guy's six-foot-two and weighed 230 or 240 pounds, and I was thirteen or fourteen, at the most. But I was a big kid and fearless. I hated this guy. So I kicked him out.

"Worse than that, my mother, who always had my father's ear, managed to get Wally a job in a war plant so he didn't have to get drafted. Now, mind you, Elmer doesn't take a job in a war plant. He goes off and fights the war, and this lout is working for my father in a defense plant."

While his mother may not have been the most faithful war bride, she welcomed Elmer home from war, and he promptly moved in with Mae and her two children.

Donald and Elmer became close. He was a storyteller, like Donald's grandfather. And, like his grandfather, Elmer's humor undoubtedly shaped Donald's.

"Elmer was a character," says Donald. "He had a great laugh, and he liked to kibbitz. He could bullshit with anybody, I mean, even little kids. I'm sure a lot of the pithy humor I have came from my association with Elmer because we joked all the time. He spent a lot of his youth playing minor league baseball, in Clarksdale, Mississippi, and Texarkana, Texas. And he hung out at the local burlesque show. The burlesque was more standup comedians than strippers. Elmer had good recall, and he remembered all these stupid jokes. He had more one-liners than Henny Youngman: *You can't put a feather in a chicken's ass and call it a Peacock. . . . Learn a trade so you know what kind of work you are out of. . . . A girl with short legs should sue the city for building the sidewalk so close to her ass. . . .*"

Elmer attended North Division in Milwaukee, a high school in a then-predominantly Jewish neighborhood. He insisted that the school fight song went like this:

> Gefilte fish gefilte fish
> We are the boys from North Divish
> Izzy Ikey Morrie Sam
> We are the boys that eat no ham

Home from war, Elmer returned to his job teaching golf and operating a driving range. Mae meanwhile continued to run Glenn's Grill, with the occasional help of her kids.

Owning a 24-hour restaurant was demanding work. "Keeping meat on the menu was a challenge," Donald says, "especially during the war years. My mother had made a connection in Bonduel, Wisconsin, way up north past Green Bay. The dairy cows, when they died a natural death at this farm, were not necessarily subjected to meat rationing or grading by the U.S.D.A. There were no blue stamps on them. They were black market.

"We'd drive up there, put a canvas over the dead cow, put it in the back of mother's station wagon, and drive it back to Milwaukee. My job was to take that cow and turn it into hamburger. So in our basement at the house, I skinned the whole damned carcass."

Donald would butcher it. His sister, Jean, would apply a very creative rendering of the blue U.S.D.A. stamp to the butchered beef.

"We had a big hamburger grinder in the basement," Donald says. "Whatever would come out of the grinder wound up as hamburger on the menu."

Meticulously organized even at a young age, Jean had pitched in before. She recorded the daily receipts at the restaurant, starting in first grade—the savant bookkeeper, sorting the bills by amount and by color.

Her mother was audited one year by the Internal Revenue Service. An auditor came to the restaurant to examine the books and meet the bookkeeper. "It was wintertime," Jean remembers, "and it was quite chilly in the basement where my mother's little office was, not the kind of place you'd want to hang out. She introduced me to the IRS man as the bookkeeper, and she offered him a glass of ice water. So I showed him my system. He's down in this cold basement with this kid and all these bills piled around him. After ten minutes or so, he said, 'You know, it looks good to me,' and he left. That was my first audit. To this day, I enjoy balancing my checkbook to the penny. I had a very early start."

Seven years younger than her brother, Jean didn't exactly fit in with Donald and his friends. They generally ignored her. Unless they needed money. Then she called the shots.

"Donald and his friends were broke all the time," she explains. "When the weekend would come, they'd want to go someplace or they had a hot date or something. So it occurred to me that I could loan them money and charge them a very high interest rate.

"I saved my allowance money and Donald spent his, so I became my own loan officer. I had my own little bank account, I had my own little bank. They'd pay me back with interest, and then, sure enough, a week later, they'd be borrowing again.

"I'd keep detailed records like my bookkeeping at Glenn's Grill—which ones paid, which ones I would lend to, which ones I wouldn't. Yeah, I got to know his friends quite well. I had a wonderful thing going."

It was not so wonderful for Donald and his cronies. "She should have been charged for usury," he says, shaking his head. "Jean was very, very frugal, and she always had money. If you wanted to borrow one buck, it was two bucks."

Mae and Elmer began to spend winters in Florida, leaving Donald in charge of Glenn's Grill. To bring in a few more dollars to the business, he came up with a couple of enterprising ideas. "We put an advertising sign on the roof for Miller Brewing that was as big as the restaurant. And then, instead of having free parking for restaurant customers, we rented out the parking lot behind the Grill as a used car lot. So we had revenue coming from the used cars and revenue coming from the Miller sign on the roof. There was a lot of traffic at that corner."

Donald was also responsible for taking care of his mother's house while she and Elmer were gone. "Let's just say I had some great parties in high school," he says. "It was an open house. We had a bar in the basement and slot machines, and I had the key to the slot machines. I offered cannibal sandwiches from the Grill and beer on tap, kegs of beer, and I would pay for it all with the money I got out of the slot machines from all the kids that came by. We ate a lot of raw beef with raw onions."

From the outside looking in, Donald's family might have appeared topsyturvy, constantly in flux, an ever-shifting representation of what defined a family: the change of partners, his father and Thelma, his mother and Elmer, his sister, Jean, and half sisters Carolyn and Roberta, aunts and uncles and cousins from both sides of his family, with homes in Milwaukee, homes in Florida, dual Christmas parties, dueling agendas, lots of kids, and lots of movement.

But in time, it became manageable, and remarkably cohesive. "It's always been one big, blended family," says Donald's half sister, Carolyn Baumgartner Maruggi, the family genealogist. "The exes, the ins, the outs—everybody was always together. It was kind of a normal thing growing up."

Donald describes his family in a similar way. "A lot of people have problems with one or two parents. I had four parents that were great. My mother and Elmer were a terrific team, and as were my father and Thelma. Thelma was a good mother and just a very warm and loving person. So I had four really good parents, and they got along well. We started celebrating holidays together, with all four parents after I married Donna."

"There was never any jealousy," he adds. My mom and dad still flirted. They always liked each other. And Elmer and my dad, they couldn't have been two more different people, but they got along well."

Donald and Nancy, high school sweethearts and husband and wife at age 19.

In his senior year of high school, Donald started dating a cheerleader named Nancy Prestin. Blonde hair, barely five feet tall, Nancy was a Milwaukee native, seven months older than Donald. Donald expected the romance would be short-lived. Having been accepted into the University of Wisconsin, Donald moved to Madison in the fall of 1949 for his first semester in college, leaving Nancy behind. But a week or two later, he drove back to Shorewood.

"Nancy's older brother, Eugene, had decided to elope with his girlfriend, Pat," Donald says, "and they wanted Nancy and me to be witnesses. I was going to go along and be his best man. The wedding was going to be in Waukegan, Illinois, and then we were all going to drive into Chicago and stay at the Palmer House hotel. This was back in a time when social mores were very different, and if you were very young like we were, you had to prove you were married to get a room at the Palmer House.

"Well, Eugene had found this sort of 'marriage shop' in Waukegan. You just give this guy a few bucks, they handed you a marriage certificate, and you were married. I thought, *This is just justice-of-the-peace bullshit. This isn't a legal marriage.* It was a joke, actually. So I decided, *Well, Nancy and I will get married too. We'll get a certificate and use that to get a room at the*

Palmer House. We had a choice of two or three different songs that they would play on a 78 rpm record player. We had them play *Clair de Lune.*

"I can't believe the stupidity of it, but that was my thinking at the moment. I didn't believe it was a true marriage. No questions were asked, and no license was required. I did it as a lark. So we drove to the Palmer House. They wanted to know if we were married. I showed them the marriage certificate, and we were admitted. This was September 10, 1949. I drove back to Milwaukee, dropped off Nancy, and went back to college. And I never believed for a minute that I was married or gave it another thought."

When he went home for the holidays, Nancy questioned him about their marriage. She believed the wedding was legitimate and wanted to know his plans. To Donald, it was a mistake, a sham. He never imagined it would stand legally. But when Nancy persisted, he went to his father for help, thinking he could get the marriage certificate canceled or annulled.

"I had gone to him with the thought of maybe finding a lawyer and getting out of this mess. I told them the story, and his response was, 'Well, what the hell is this going to cost me?' That pissed me off, and I said, 'It's not gonna cost you a goddamn thing!' And it didn't. I took Nancy to Madison with me. We found student housing. And all of a sudden I became married."

CHAPTER 3

A Wife, Two Kids, and Three Great Danes

n the latter half of the 1800s, a rising number of immigrants from Germany and East Europe began to settle in Milwaukee. Many were highly skilled machinists, mechanics, and toolmakers. As industrialization surged across the nation, some of the best and the brightest of these immigrants—with last names like Falk, Allis, Harnischfeger, Nordberg—became Milwaukee's new industrialists, building foundries, forges, iron mills, and job shops across the city.

By the turn of the twentieth century, Milwaukee was recognized as a major manufacturing town, earning the label "Machine Shop of the World" and turning out all types of machinery, from electric motors and cranes to steam engines and mining drills to farm machines and motorcycles.

JR Baumgartner's Reliable Tool & Machine Works burgeoned in the late 1930s and throughout World War II, as the company geared its production to the war effort. After the war, JR sold the business for a considerable profit and started all over again in 1945 with the start up of Mercury Engineering on Milwaukee's east side. Donald had been studying mythology in school, and his father was inspired to name the company after the fleet-footed Roman god Mercury.

Mercury Engineering had two divisions: Its machine tool division had a line of production grinders and specialty machine tools. Its paper converting division built JR's soufflé cup machines that he had designed years ago in his job shop. They mainly turned out "inline printer blankers" that were used in

Mercury Engineering occupied two buildings on Farwell Avenue in Milwaukee.

the folding carton industry. These machines, manufactured by Mercury, would make the first paper six-pack soda carriers for Coca-Cola and Pepsi-Cola.

More opportunities were on the horizon. With a military conflict in Korea drawing the United States into war in 1950, JR saw a potential to once again build machinery for the military.

Donald was in college at the time, living with his new wife Nancy in an off-campus housing unit called Badger Village, thirty minutes from the University of Wisconsin. Set up for married students and veterans, the complex was the former site of the World War II Badger Ordnance plant. The dormitories once used by factory workers were bought by the university and converted to student apartments for veterans and families.

"Badger Village was a hustling, bustling place," he recalls. "This is in the early '50s. There were mostly World War II veterans who were in college on the GI Bill living there at that time. Nancy and I were by far the youngest couple there. We were still in our teens."

The living arrangements were basic at best: a combined living room-kitchen and a bedroom. "They didn't have individual bathrooms," he says. "There were community bathrooms, with a community shower. It wasn't exactly luxurious."

As a freshman at the University of Wisconsin in Madison, Donald and his wife, Nancy, lived at Badger Village near Madison.

Donald served two years in the Reserve Officer Training Corps, ROTC, the on-campus military training program. "That was mandatory in Madison at the time," Donald says. "It was kind of embarrassing putting on my ROTC uniform in front of all these seasoned veterans from World War II, my neighbors and my friends."

He also tried out for UW's football team. "I was trying out for lineman and deep snapper. I started right after Harry Stuhldreher left as head coach. He played quarterback at Notre Dame as part of the legendary Four Horsemen backfield. But Wisconsin had had a terrible losing record under Stuhldreher. It was one of the worst teams in the Big Ten. So they hired Ivy Williamson as coach, and it was his idea to increase the speed of the team. He thought the team was too fat and too slow. So we had speed drills every day, and the guy that came in last turned in his uniform. I managed to stay with the team.

"In my second year, we had a young guy from Kenosha by the name of Ameche, Alan Ameche," he adds. "He was one of the great running backs in the history of the program and would play in the NFL for six seasons with the Baltimore Colts. He left records at UW that still remain today and went on to win the Heisman Trophy. The team went to the Rose Bowl two years later. Wisconsin hadn't been in a Rose Bowl in a long, long time, so it was a big deal. I didn't go. I had already left school."

In the spring of his freshman year, Nancy found out she was pregnant. The couple's first child, Sally, was born November 14, 1950, while Donald was taking a chemistry exam. Seven days later, he turned twenty.

College life got more complicated with a family. Following his sophomore year, Donald changed course. "I was married with a child," he says. "The Korean War was raging and I got very involved helping my father during my summer break. So I made an executive decision to not go back to school." At the end of summer recess, he moved his family back to Milwaukee.

Donald, Nancy, and daughter Sally moved from the Badger Village dorms to a huge cluster of modern, red-bricked apartment buildings in Whitefish Bay known as Schroedl's Cradles on Wilson Drive. Their apartment was a comfortable size for a compact family of three: Living room, dining room, kitchen, two bedrooms, and a bathroom.

Born a month before Christmas in 1950, Sally was the first child of Nancy and Donald.

With Donald back in the shop, JR reactivated Milwaukee Shipbuilding in the fall of 1951. "Milwaukee Shipbuilding had been incorporated in 1947, and I was given one-third of the company," Donald says. "There was another member, a nonfamily member, who was part of the company, and that was my father's partner from his new business Mercury Engineering. His name was Ralph Martin—'R.O.,' we called him. He had one-third. My dad had a third. I had a third."

JR had shut down the company a few years before the Korean War, abandoning the business plan after failing to find a buyer for the Coast Guard cutter that he and Donald had converted into a yacht. Now, with the war going full throttle, there were new possibilities for growth.

Under its first defense contract, Milwaukee Shipbuilding was hired to make a machine that would correct a defective design in a line of tanks. The ring-shaped openings that supported the tanks' revolving gun turrets were out of round.

"When the tanks were assembled, they welded together the sections of the hull and the turrets would not turn," Donald says. "All of these new tanks were sitting in the field at an Army base in Detroit where ordnance was tested. So my father designed and I built a machine, a portable planetary grinder that could be used in the field. You could snake the planetary grinder into the hull of the tank and grind out the turret opening so that it was round and the turret would turn freely.

"Dad designed the machine in one night over dinner," he recalls, "and I got the job of building it from his sketches. We built dozens of these machines. The grinders could be dropped into the tanks, then grind out the race, the circular groove, so that the turrets would turn freely 360 degrees."

During the course of the war, Milwaukee Shipbuilding also developed a robotic flame cutter that could cut through thick steel to form precise patterns and shapes. Again, it was used in the Army's tank-building program.

While some of his friends had been drafted into the Korean War, Donald qualified for a military exemption because he was married with children and because he was an employee of a defense plant that made products essential to the war effort.

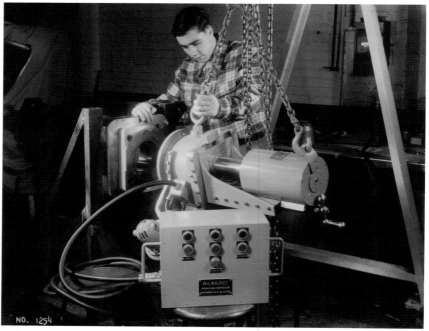

At his father's company, Donald built portable grinders that were used to repair the revolving turrets in U.S. Army tanks during the Korean War.

The more contracts Milwaukee Shipbuilding landed, the more responsibility Donald assumed. "I wasn't just running machinery, I was assembling machines and buying parts for the machines. At a very early age, I had learned how to read a blueprint, and I knew what I was buying. The Korean War was raging, and we were busy as hell doing our bit. But we couldn't make all the parts that we needed. So I started subcontracting stuff out. I was in charge of managing the projects, expediting and subcontracting, bringing parts together from companies all over the city, then all over the state. Pretty soon I was buying parts from all over the country."

The Korean War came to an end in July 1953. An armistice was signed, and a Demilitarized Zone was created to separate North Korea from South Korea. Donald's father was running two companies at the same time, Milwaukee Shipbuilding and Mercury Engineering. "We had the portable planetary grinder, we had the flame-cutting machine, and we were taking in any kind of military work we could," says Donald. "But, you know, the Korean War ended, and all that work ended."

With contracts to war plants drying up, they were looking for new products to manufacture. "In those early years, we tried just about everything to get going. Our chief engineer designed an egg-carton set-up machine. By this time, we were getting desperate to stay alive, taking such risky assignments as a machine to tape shut dynamite boxes for DuPont."

His father turned his full attention to running Mercury Engineering, designing and building folding carton machinery and making machine tools. Donald, meanwhile, continued to manage Milwaukee Shipbuilding in an office and industrial warehouse at Third and State Streets in Milwaukee, where he and his father had rebuilt the Coast Guard ship. "I had a machine shop. I had some machinery. I had some mechanics. I had some engineers. I had this operation—all I needed was a product."

In the midst of the war boom, on August 25, 1952, Donald and Nancy's apartment got a little smaller with the birth of their son, John, named for his grandfather, John Robert Baumgartner. A couple of years later, the Baumgartners moved a mile or so into Glendale. Sally was in first grade, and John was a toddler.

Around this time, Nancy became interested in raising dogs, specifically, Great Danes. She first brought a terrier home from the pet shop, but Donald was not impressed. The dog was too small and barked too much. She exchanged it for a Great Dane. They called him Jody.

"The dog was just totally unmanageable. It was just wild and crazy," Donald says. "So we took him to an obedience training class, and during the training class, we met people that were showing dogs. They told us we had a dog that was very good-looking and said we should take him to the dog show. We did, and he won a ribbon. Well, we became enthused with this, and we started taking him to other dog shows."

They entered Jody in a few out-of-state competitions, and he soon accumulated enough points to become a "dual champion," winning titles of Champion in Obedience and Champion in Conformation. "Champion Dana's Jody of San Sou, CDX" (Champion Dog Excellent) was his full title. Jody was a "Will Judy Award" recipient for excellence in obedience as well.

Top: Sally and her younger brother, John, sit behind the wheel of their father's car.

Bottom: As a trainer of Great Danes, Donald entered his dogs in many competitions. His dogs won awards at the prestigious Westminster Kennel Club in New York City.

Before long, Nancy and Donald were traveling to dog shows across the country—with two kids and three Great Danes in the back of their station wagon. "Mom and Dad would sit in the front with a gate behind the seat," recalls Sally, a retired nurse in Glendale. "And John and I would be in the back of the car. Sometimes we had all three Great Danes with us, and they would be slobbering on us, drooling on us, passing gas—all the things that big dogs do. Not a lot of fun going to all those shows, but we loved the dogs. At the shows, we would wander around and just look at all the dogs."

Donald and Nancy began acquiring more Great Danes and breeding them for sale, while entering others in dog shows. "We were breeding, so a lot of them were just puppies," Donald says. "We sold dogs to a lot of people around the country, show-quality Great Danes. They're beautiful dogs. I got very involved." Donald and Nancy became members of the Great Dane Club of Wisconsin, and, eventually, Donald was named president. He was also licensed by the American Kennel Club to judge dog competitions, and once won the brace at the Westminster Kennel Club in New York's Madison Square Garden, the biggest dog show in the country.

Moving their family once again, this time to a big, corner house on Bartlett Avenue in Whitefish Bay, Donald and Nancy filled the basement with contest ribbons, trophies—and dogs. "It was exciting for them," says Sally. "We mostly had three Great Danes, Gypsy, Jody, and Tar Baby. They were brindles. Then we had Sunny, who was a fawn, looked kind of like a deer coloration. And we had a couple litters of puppies. My mother started what she called Nan Dane Kennels out of the home. We had dogs all over the place, so we were known as the house with the big dogs. It was a major part of my life from when I was in first grade until almost a senior in high school."

Donald's half-sister Roberta Axelrod, the daughter of JR and his second wife Thelma, was the same age as Sally. She remembers helping Donald train the Danes. "We would all ride in a big, old station wagon with the back down and a dog running behind us on a leash," says Roberta, a retired medical technologist who now lives in North Carolina. "We'd hold the leash and the dog would run, and this is how he would muscle them up. Donald was such a showman himself, running with his dog in the arena. He would just put on a good show for everybody. So he was very successful that way.

"I was around seven," she remembers, "and Sally and I are just four months apart, so we were almost like sisters. I spent a lot of time with her, overnights and stuff, and Donald seemed to be a really fun dad. He would actually play with you, take you out to drive-in movies. Whereas my dad never did any of that, he was always too busy. You know, pat you on the head and say, 'Go play now. Get outta here, I'm busy.' Well, everyone loved Donald."

Having a house full of dogs when they were growing up made a lasting impression on Sally and her brother. John became an avid horseman, riding since before his teenage years, eventually training horses and competing as a jumper. He was at the top in his age category. Sally became an animal lover, always caring for pets—dogs, cats, turtles, and birds, including a parakeet she had as a girl that was named Tweety, an ill-tempered clump of feathers.

"I had this pet bird that was never finger-tamed and very vicious," Sally says. "If I put a pencil in its cage, it would bite the pencil. I was scared of this bird. One day it got out of its cage and flew through the house and somehow landed in the toilet. I thought it was dead because it was floating downward and its wings were spread out. I got hysterical. My dad calmly came in and took Tweety between his hands and shook the water out of the bird's lungs. Then he did mouth-to-mouth resuscitation on this parakeet. The next thing I knew it started to move, and all of a sudden it bit my dad on the finger.

"I was afraid to even take it out of the toilet. I was freaking out, and it's swirling around, and my dad just came right in like you would have thought he knew how to do mouth-to-mouth on a bird."

While he found the time now and then to travel to dog shows and maybe bring his kids' pets back from the dead, Donald's commitment to expanding his fledgling business grew deeper and deeper. Propelling him, perhaps, was a rivalry with JR and a need to separate his father's strengths and ambitions from his own, the goal of every father's son.

He admired and emulated his father as a boy, learning about boating from him, learning how to use all types of tools. "I was once referred to as his shadow," says Donald. There was no teenage rebellion from any of his kids against the Skipper, an imposing and commanding figure. Nor was there a spoken agreement on his father's part that Donald would take over the family business. For Donald, doing something else never crossed his mind.

"There was no way I was going to open a damned restaurant. That was out of the question," he says. "No, I knew I wanted to stay with machinery manufacturing. From the time I was a kid, it was in my blood. I was exposed to it every day, and knew I wanted to stick with it. I was good at it, I enjoyed it. I never thought of anything else."

Donald with his two children, John and Sally, in the wheelhouse of the Trenora.

His father was a very important part of Donald's life. But Donald was not his father's double, and he never wanted to be.

"Dad was a man for all seasons," he says. "He could run every machine in the shop better than his best mechanics. He was an expert draftsman and a creative designer. In short, he could do it all and expected me to do the same. But that wasn't my forte. What I did, and did very well, was get things done."

CHAPTER 4

Paper Chase

When tracing the origins of the paper cup, one finds an obscure version that credits a certain "John Lackner of New York City" for making one-piece water cups by hand in 1874. His daughter, Harriet Hill, apparently went on to design a rudimentary machine in 1908 that made pleated paper cups. These would evolve into what became known as "tulip sprinklers," the instantly recognizable baking liners that have formed the shape of countless cupcakes and muffins for decades.

A more accepted version of the beginning of the paper cup dates back to the turn of the twentieth century and the expansion of the railway system. At the time, public drinking water was dispensed to thirsty train passengers from a jug or barrel using a common glass or ladle, called a "tin sipper." The sipper was convenient, but hardly sanitary.

In 1907, a Boston lawyer named Lawrence Luellen came up with a better idea—a water cooler with an accompanying paper cup dispenser. Fashioning a tall, porcelain ice cooler with a five-gallon glass water bottle on top, he attached to the face of the cooler a wide, brass vertical cylinder that could hold dozens of nested, envelope-shaped paper cups. A train passenger would be able to pluck an individual cup from the dispenser and enjoy a drink of cool, clean water without risking the scourge of someone else's germs.

In early 1908, having enlisted a group of investors, Luellen founded the American Water Supply Company of New England. After experimenting with two or three cup designs, he hired Taylor Machine Works at Hyde Park, Massachusetts, to make a machine that produced a two-piece cup made out of a blank of paper and a separate bottom piece, according to archive files at Lafayette College in Eaton, Pennsylvania.

Luellen's inventions caught the attention of his young brother-in-law, Hugh Moore, a Harvard student at the time. Seeing the business possibilities, Moore quit Harvard and teamed up with Luellen to market the paper cup dispenser and wage a national campaign to banish communal tin sippers.

That same year a biology professor at Lafayette College published a damning investigation titled "Death in School Drinking Cups," which reported in graphic detail the public health dangers of shared-use glasses. Analyzing a drinking glass used for nine consecutive days in a Pennsylvania school, the biologist found "not less than 100,000 bacteria present on every square inch of the glass."

The study caused a stir. Less than a year later, health officials in Kansas promoted the passage of a law that banned tin sippers on trains. Other states soon followed, launching efforts to abolish common drinking glasses on trains and in schools, amusement parks, stores, hotels, and other public venues. One newspaper ad in the *Pioneer Press* of St. Paul, Minnesota, included an illustration of a glass in the shape of a human skull chained to a water dispenser. "One public drinking glass can spread more disease in an hour than a Board of Health can eradicate in a year," read the ad.

Riding the wave of change in public health policies, Moore and Luellen started the Individual Drinking Cup Company in New York City, condemning the dangers of public drinking utensils and extolling the safety of disposable paper cups. The company patented and sold its cup as the trademarked Health Kup, expanding its market to drugstores and soda fountains.

In 1918, a deadly flu epidemic gripped the nation, spurring a boom in the number of paper cup makers. To set themselves apart from competitors, Moore and Luellen changed the name of their cup to something less mundane. The Health Kup became the Dixie Cup, named after a popular line of toy dolls in New York City. A star was born; the Dixie Cup remains synonymous with paper cups 100 years later.

Paper cups became ubiquitous, entrenched in American culture. Palm-sized, pleated cups were made as convenient containers for eating Italian ice. Lids were added to Dixie Cups to hold individual servings of ice cream. Waxed soda cups became a new market as the first drive-in movies opened in the mid-1930s.

The mass production of paper cups owed a large debt to the introduction of the vending machine. Remarkably, the first documented vending machine goes back to the first century, when Hero of Alexandria, a mathematician and engineer, designed a cylindrical container that dispensed splashes of holy water in the temples of Egypt with the drop of a coin. In the early 1600s, the taverns of England sold tobacco from coin-operated machines. The first beverage vendor came upon the scene in Paris in 1890, offering wine, beer, and liquor. And in America, patents for automated vendors in 1888 led to the installment on New York train platforms of machines that would dispense a stick of chewing gum for a penny.

Following World War II, as the massive armaments buildup came to an end, manufacturers ramped up the production of domestic goods, including packaged foods and beverages that could be sold ready-to-consume from a vending machine. With the widespread popularity of carbonated beverages such as Coca-Cola and Pepsi-Cola, automatic cold drink machines could be found virtually everywhere. By 1946, coffee vendors had been invented.

Bob Baumgartner had a leg up on constructing paper cup machines. He had started building soufflé-cup-forming machines in the mid-1930s at his first company, Reliable Tool & Machine Works. A small cup formed from a single blank of paper and box pleated on the sides crowned with a rolled rim, the paper soufflé cup was used by dentists, doctors, and nurses to dispense pills. Bob began building them again at Mercury Engineering and, when the Korean War ended, switched the line over to newly activated Milwaukee Shipbuilding.

"The markets were looking for machinery, and we were looking for markets," says Bob's son, Donald Baumgartner. "We had made war machines, and then, after the war, we shopped for a product. We had a small setup with engineers, assemblymen, and machinists, and we tried a number of things. And then we got into making my dad's soufflé cup machines. That was our first cup forming machine."

In 1955, his father's longtime business partner, Ralph "R.O." Martin, hired an engineer who was with the Solo Cup Company in Chicago. "His name was Russell Anderson," says Donald. "He came to work for Milwaukee Shipbuilding but worked out of his home in Chicago. He told us he could design a machine that made conical paper cups, the cone cups that they used for ice cream, drinking water fountains, and shaved ice. Cone cups were quite popular back then.

"Solo Cup was a major manufacturer of cone cups and had designed their own cone-cup-forming machine. I got suspicious because of the way the drawings were flowing in that Russell was tracing from a set of drawings he had taken from Solo. So as his drawings came in, I had our engineer, Ray Bodendoerfer, redesign everything. We redesigned every part of the machine, adding a new drive and in every way improving what Russell was sending in. And at the end, I guess we got a little sloppy. Out of maybe a thousand drawings, we missed a few blueprints of one part of the machine in our redesign."

When Milwaukee Shipbuilding introduced its cone cup machine to the market, it sold right away, Donald says. "One of the machines went to Solo Cup. They took at look at it and said, 'Parts of your machine look a lot like our machines. You've got Russell Anderson working for you, don't you.' And they sued us."

When the case went to court, Milwaukee Shipbuilding claimed it had completely redesigned the machine. Attorneys for the company presented evidence that the firm had not violated Solo Cup's patent on the machine. But the judge found that Anderson, in his design of the cup machine, had come into possession of Solo's drawings illegally.

"The judge found us guilty and ordered us to cease and desist. No more cone cup machines," says Donald. "We also were ordered to pay reparations to Solo."

The court held that R.O. Martin, who had hired Anderson, was "an actual participant in the tort and, therefore, liable." The court also held Bob Baumgartner liable, as president of the company.

In the meantime, Anderson had been designing a two-piece, 7-ounce cup machine for Milwaukee Shipbuilding. "I thought, *It's also traced, no doubt.* So I threw all the drawings into the garbage, and Russell Anderson and the company parted ways."

Donald then confronted R.O. Martin. "He knew damned well Anderson had Solo's drawings. I didn't care for all that crap. My idea of running a business was not taking somebody else's drawings. So we bought Ralph out."

Operating in a 2,000-foot rented manufacturing plant, Milwaukee Shipbuilding soon moved to a larger plant in an industrial tract at 37th Street and Lancaster Avenue on Milwaukee's north side. On March 13, 1956, Donald entered into a purchase agreement with his father to buy his stock in Milwaukee Shipbuilding. Two days later, the company's name was changed to Paper Machinery Corporation, or PMC for short.

The assembly floor at Paper Machinery Corporation's Lancaster Avenue plant.

The next year, JR Baumgartner sold Mercury Engineering. He spun off the company's machine tool division to Mattison Works in Rockford, Illinois. Meanwhile, Mercury's paper converting division, which produced the machines that formed the first six-pack cartons for Coke and Pepsi, was acquired by Chicago-based Miehle-Goss-Dexter, the nation's largest supplier of printing presses.

Bob accepted shares of stock in the purchase agreement. Although he was advised to sell the stock, he held on to it instead. When the industrial giant Rockwell International purchased Miehle-Goss-Dexter in 1973, the value of the stock soared, making JR a wealthy man.

Donald was again disappointed that his father had sold the business to out-of-town firms. The sale, again, had displaced hundreds of devoted Milwaukee workers. The move stuck in Donald's craw for the duration of his business life.

By 1958, Donald had moved up the ladder at PMC. He was made executive vice president when he was twenty-eight years old. Even though his father remained president, he did not keep an office at the plant.

In the early years, JR had an itch to build a two-piece cup machine. His first attempt failed. In a second attempt in 1949, a two-piece cup machine was offered to Solo Cup, one of the biggest cup makers in the land. Solo rejected the offer—strike two. Milwaukee Shipbuilding picked up JR's design. With engineers that were supervised by Donald, the company—by then called Paper Machinery—finally created its first successful two-piece cup machine and went to market with it. It sold one of its first machines to the cup manufacturer Sutherland Paper in Kalamazoo, Michigan.

PMC's two-piece cup-forming machine, operated by Donald's cousin, Jack Storm.

The generational shift was complete. Donald Baumgartner was now at the tiller, controlling the mechanical inventions and the business that his father had forged when he was precisely the age of his son.

A gung-ho American economy in the 1950s fueled a steady rise of employment. Industries thrived, manufacturing plants expanded, and new products flooded the markets. Water coolers and vending machines became convenient fixtures in workplace break rooms and on production floors. Drop a dime in a vending machine, get a cup of hot coffee in a 7-ounce disposable cup.

But breaking into the cup-machine market was nearly insurmountable for a newcomer. At the time, the paper cup market was dominated by five major cup-making companies that each had its own in-house machine-building program. All of the "major" cup makers—Dixie, Lily-Tulip, Solo, Sweetheart (or Maryland Cup), and Bondware (Continental Can)—built the machines from their own designs.

"These five companies were producing vending cups for coffee," Donald recalls. "They got real cozy together, and we were having a hell of a time selling the cup machines. The companies that were making their own machines sure as hell didn't want to buy ours. They didn't want us selling machines. They saw us as a threat."

A friend of Donald's named Oswald Jaeger came up with an idea. "Ozzie Jaeger was the heir to the Jaeger Baking Company in Milwaukee, and he thought he could sell paper cups along with Jaeger's bread on the bread routes. So Ozzie and I bought one of PMC's own machines, as partners, and moved the machine off the floor at the Lancaster plant. Ozzie rented space in a mortuary on 12th Street. We set the machine up in the mortuary's casket display room and we started producing cups.

"We named the company Holiday Cup, and we had the cups in red-white-and-blue striped polyethylene sleeves. We soon found ourselves up past our ass in cups, producing cups an awful lot faster than Ozzie was selling them. Getting rid of all these cups was problematic. Ozzie and I thought we needed a partner, someone who had some marketing ideas and skills."

Donald decided to ask his uncle, David Flaxman, if he wanted to go in as a silent partner. "David was the husband of my mother's sister, my Aunt

Gerry. [He also was the father of Donna Flaxman, whom Donald would marry many years later.] David was president of Universal Foods in Chicago, which had just merged with Red Star Yeast in Milwaukee. With the merger, we thought the timing might be right, as he would be looking for something else to do. So we invited him to dinner.

"My wife, Nancy, prepared this game dinner of ducks that Ozzie and I had shot, along with a wonderful wild rice casserole called Russian Fluff. We put out our best wine. We put our best foot forward. During dessert, David reaches in his pocket for his checkbook. 'What's this going to cost?' he asks. And, speaking without thinking, Ozzie says, 'Well, if we split the lemon three ways . . .' And after hearing the word 'lemon,' David slowly slipped his checkbook back in his pocket and excused himself. That was the end of David for a partner. With Ozzie referring to the company as a lemon, his enthusiasm for partnering with us cooled very quickly."

The meeting was a letdown for the flailing startup. But not long after, the owner of a local vending machine company got wind that Donald and Ozzie were manufacturing paper cups. Herb Geiger, president of Geiger Automatic Sales Company, ran into Ozzie at the Milwaukee Yacht Club, where they both had yachts. He asked Ozzie to see Holiday Cup's machine.

"Herb had vending machines in industrial plants throughout the city," says Donald. "He was buying vending cups and thought he was paying too much. The market was pretty much fixed on the price. He knew it and he didn't like it. So we gave him a look at our machine, and he said to us, 'I'll make my own cups. I don't want to be your partner. I want the whole damn thing.' So Ozzie and I sold the company to him, and he started production right there in the mortuary."

Geiger soon moved the machine to Menomonee Falls, where he built a factory and started buying more cup-forming machines on a regular basis. "He was our first serious customer. Up to this point, PMC would sell a machine here, sell a machine there. We were a small company, twenty, thirty employees maybe. This was our real start. It put us on the map."

There were plenty of other independent vendors who were grudgingly buying cups at a premium price. When they saw what Geiger was doing with Holiday Cup, they wanted the same.

"That was the beginning," Donald says. "From there, we sold another machine in Cleveland. Then we sold one out on the East Coast. Our next big customer was Imperial Cup, which was started by a guy named Dick Allen in 1958 in Kenton, Ohio. We supplied the machines that produced 7-ounce cups for the vending machines in all the big auto plants."

Allen sold the business to Federal Paper Board for $100 million in 1989. A few years later, Federal sold the company to International Paper, a world-leading manufacturer of paper cups.

"Everything was in 7-ounce coffee vending, and the company grew around that. We were supplying vendors with their own machines so they could make their own cups. That was the kick-start for Paper Machinery Corporation. And here we are now, back to where we started. It's all about coffee again."

More and more, Donald was in the driver's seat, working on deals, supervising production at PMC, while his father spent time out of state. JR had purchased property along the Intracoastal Waterway in Florida, with a dock big enough to accommodate his ninety-two-foot yacht. He formally retired to Fort Lauderdale in 1960 with his wife, Thelma, and their two daughters, Carolyn and Roberta, He was just fifty-three.

On the Baumgartner home front, Donald and Nancy welcomed a third child into their family with the birth of Lisa in October 1962. She instantly became everyone's favorite, a beautiful, bubbly baby, and a bright star in her father's eyes. The family was living on Bartlett Avenue, a quiet, leafy street in Whitefish Bay. Donald was growing his business, making sales trips around the world, while still traveling to dog shows with Nancy. The Baumgartners' marriage—a misbegotten union from the beginning—was showing signs of strain and disruption. Nancy began drinking heavily, often leaving the care of baby Lisa in the hands of her oldest child, Sally. Donald and Nancy argued bitterly, and finally Donald moved out, rented an apartment, and started divorce proceedings.

As he gathered some of his possessions from the house, Nancy grabbed hold of a trophy that contained the ashes of his favorite Great Dane, Jody, his first championship dog. He thought he would have Jody's remains buried at his feet when he died. And as he walked out the door, Nancy hurled the urn at him, along with a vicious farewell: "And don't forget your goddamned dog."

Other spiteful stunts followed. One day, in front of her children, Nancy intentionally slammed a drawer on her hand, breaking a couple of fingers. She called police to report that her husband had assaulted her, and Donald was arrested at his office. Summoned to court weeks later, Donald listened while Nancy tearfully testified before the judge, her hand wrapped in a huge bandage, presenting a series of x-rays of her damaged fingers to the court.

Charged with a felony, Donald faced jail time if convicted, and it seemed as if the judge was sympathetic to Nancy's lamentable story. But as the judge weighed the claims of the two sides, Nancy suddenly broke into hysterical sobs, screaming for a long prison sentence for her alleged abuser and cursing her husband for destroying her life.

Seizing upon Nancy's irrational outburst and lack of evidence, Donald's attorney, Alex Rubin, argued that Nancy had deliberately injured herself and falsified the attack. The judge agreed, and the case was dismissed.

"Alex Rubin was a godsend, a scrappy trial lawyer who eventually became my friend," says Donald. "I met him through my cousin, Kenny Storm, who hired Alex to defend him on a DUI. Kenny had been pulled over by the police, and he was so drunk that when the cops opened his door, he fell half way out of his car. Just half way. Kenny's right foot got stuck in the steering wheel, the horn blaring away, and his left foot was out in the street. When the case went to court, Alex got him off. He got Kenny's DUI reduced to a charge of 'public drunkenness' in the street because his left foot was on the street pavement when he was arrested. This was my guy."

Nancy's gambit was one of many witnessed by her kids. "She was acting crazy," says Sally, who was a teenager when her parents separated. "My mother became an alcoholic and went right off the wall. My dad would try to come and see us, and she would have us hide in the basement. There was just so much drama. She'd take the telephone cord and wrap it around her neck a few times and then call the police and say 'My husband tried to strangle me.' I was right there, and he didn't try to strangle her. She just had all this revenge. It went from her being obsessed with the dogs to being obsessed with the divorce. It was like, how to get back at Donald."

The contested divorce dragged on, and Nancy's aberrant behavior worsened. Donald, meanwhile, had been introduced to a woman named Camille Brock by his father in Fort Lauderdale. Camille, known as "Cam," was a stunning six-foot tall Georgia beauty queen who had moved to Miami in her early twenties to become a Playboy Bunny. She and Donald began seeing each other whenever he traveled to Florida.

When Nancy and Donald's divorce finally reached a scheduled resolution in family court, Nancy pulled no punches. She had learned about Donald's newfound romance and wasted no time describing him in open court as a heartless father. Her estranged husband, she told the judge, was a successful businessman who was presently lavishing his twenty-four-year-old girlfriend with a luxurious apartment and expensive restaurants while his children went hungry.

Nancy's dramatic claim made both the morning and the afternoon newspapers in Milwaukee. "Executive Deprived Children, Wife Says," screamed one headline. "While her husband was on a yacht 'cruising the West Indies with a Playboy bunny,' Mrs. Baumgartner had to tell her youngest child there was no milk in the house," read a front-page story in the *Milwaukee Sentinel*.

Her woe-is-me narrative struck a nerve with Circuit Court Judge Leander Foley. He granted Nancy the divorce "on grounds of cruel and inhuman treatment," said the *Sentinel*, and ordered Donald to pay child support and alimony. From the bench, he admonished him for being a bad father. "If these were my children, I wouldn't be living in an apartment with some woman," said Judge Foley. "I'd be on my knees for them."

Less than four months later, Nancy sold the house that had been granted to her on Bartlett Avenue, sold all of Donald's possessions at a garage sale, packed up their three children, and fled the country for Jamaica.

Neither her addiction to alcohol nor her parental responsibilities improved on the sunny Caribbean island. To the contrary. Nancy and her children arrived in Jamaica in the spring. By late summer, the kids figured out that their mother had made no arrangements to enroll them in school.

"We missed our friends, we missed our life," says Sally, who would have been entering her senior year in high school at the time. "Everything was taken away. I mean, the beach was beautiful. Of course it was beautiful. But I wanted to go back."

She called her Aunt Jean in Florida for help arranging a flight home for herself and brother, John. Five-year-old Lisa, though, remained in Jamaica in the care of her alcoholic mother.

"We left her with my mother, who was out of control," says Sally, a retired registered nurse. "It was bothering me a lot. Sometimes I couldn't even sleep. I would be all worried because I was like the mother role for Lisa from the time she was born."

As soon as Sally was out of high school, she made plans to rescue her baby sister. "Lisa's in trouble," she told her father. "I have to go get her." Without hesitating, he bought her a plane ticket to Jamaica.

Accompanied by a friend, Sally landed in Jamaica without telling her mother she was coming. "We found Lisa at my mother's house just outside of Kingston. She was all alone, no electricity, no food. She was living on cans of meat they call 'bully beef.' My mother was on one of her drunken binges. The neighbors told me she used to leave Lisa all the time and would go on these binges. So we dragged her out of there, and I took her home."

Soon after Lisa arrived, Nancy caught a plane to Milwaukee to get her child-supported meal ticket back. The child protection system intervened, ordering psychiatric tests of Nancy and Donald and Lisa to determine who was suitable to care for the child. When Nancy's next-door neighbors in Jamaica heard that she was fighting for custody, they flew to Milwaukee at their own expense to testify against her, telling the judge that they had witnessed Nancy's habitual neglect of her daughter.

The court sided with Donald, granting him full custody of Lisa. In addition, the judge ordered that Lisa never go to Jamaica and denied Nancy visitation rights.

Lisa moved in with Donald and Cam in Wisconsin. Cam and Donald by then had married. The girl had been deprived of proper health care and education, and could speak only Jamaican patois, the dialect used by native Jamaicans. "She didn't know the days of the week. She didn't know the months," Donald says. "She was ill prepared for first-grade or even senior kindergarten."

"I think I've got a house for you," Peggy said to him.

"What? Where?" Donald asked.

"Well, you remember the Wirth house?" she said. "You told me you used to play there as a kid. How would you like to buy that house?"

"For Christ's sakes, Peggy. The guy was just shot there yesterday."

"His wife won't want to go back to the house. She was wounded as well."

Peggy Barrett hurried over to the hospital where Mary Wirth lay injured "and she asks Mary Wirth if she'd like to sell the house," says Donald. "She says yes. I put an offer in. I bought the house for $50,000. And Cam and I and the kids moved in straightaway. There was still yellow police tape in the living room. There were gunshot holes in the drapes and in the wall. On the floor there was a perfect layout in chalk of where Russell Wirth's body had been.

"Augie Bergenthal had come to the house. He was disgruntled. He was part of the family that owned Red Star Yeast, and he felt that he'd gotten a bad deal. I guess he wanted to settle the score. Russell's last words were, 'But Augie, that was such a long time ago.'

"And that's how I came to that white house on Terrace Avenue."

Donald's Terrace Avenue house on Milwaukee's east side.

The Swingin' Seventies descended upon the Baumgartners with a bang. The white house on Terrace Avenue became a whirlwind of activity, the go-to spot for hip and happening parties. The décor was opulent. A crystal chandelier hung in the fourteen-by-twenty-six-foot foyer. A grandfather clock occupied a stairway landing. Oriental rugs padded the hardwood floors.

Amid the clamor and the glamour, the Baumgartner parties reflected the multi-cultural attitudes and freewheeling styles of the times. The music boomed loud, the champagne flowed freely, and the doors swung open to people of all backgrounds, from artists and university professors to African Americans and openly gay couples.

"They welcomed everyone to their house," says Molly Abrohams, a friend who worked for Donald at PMC when she was in high school and college and later tutored his daughter, Lisa. "When Donald and Cam entertained, they entertained lavishly. Donald befriended everyone. And Cam was an artist and knew lots of artsy people in Milwaukee. She was a fascinating woman. She was beautiful, and she was a wonderful home-maker. Cam could cook, and her household was organized. And every day at three o'clock, she poured herself a scotch on the rocks in a huge, beau-tiful, crystal glass. That was a daily occurrence." Molly remembers taking her husband, Ben, to a Baumgartner dinner party when they first started dating. "My first impression of Donald was, this is probably the coolest guy I've ever met. Fun, and smart," says Ben, who worked for years as an attorney with Foley & Lardner and became Donald's personal lawyer. In 1972, after they married, Ben and Molly moved a block away from Cam and Donald.

Molly was especially close to the Baumgartner family. "I first met Molly when she showed up at my office to interview for a job," says Donald. "She had been sent by her mother, Rosemary, who had a wig shop in White-fish Bay. Rosemary had become friendly with Cam, who was a regular customer. Eighteen-year old Molly showed up for the interview all flirty, dressed in a micro-mini school uniform. I should have charged her with sexual harassment, but I hired her instead. Molly and I have since that day been lifelong friends." Another newfound friend at the time was an Olym-pic track star named Ted Wheeler. A graduate of Evanston High School

Donald's Terrace Avenue home was
known as a party house. His long-time
friend Molly Abrohams, lower right,
and sister, Jean, lower left, were
frequent guests.

near Chicago, Wheeler was an All-American at the University of Iowa and competed in the 1500-meter run at the 1956 Summer Olympics in Melbourne, Australia. He returned to the University of Iowa as head coach of men's cross-country and head track coach, one of the first black coaches at a major university. Wheeler also was active in the civil rights movement.

Donald met him through friends in his neighborhood, Marquette University English professor Strother Purdy and his wife, Janet. "Ted hung around the house, came to our dinner parties," says Donald. "I had a fortieth birthday party, and Ted brought forty presents, all crazy stuff. Another time, he called me from Iowa and said he was coming up and he was bringing a pig. He showed up in front of the house with a crate strapped to the top of his car with a live pig in it, a 180-pound pig that he bought from a farm. He said he was going to barbeque it. I said, 'Ted, do you have any

Donald's friend Ted Wheeler, grilling a turkey, loved to barbeque. Most memorable was when he arrived at a Baumgartner dinner party with a live pig strapped to his car. Donald butchered the pig and, with Ted's help, grilled it for his guests.

idea how the hell you're going to barbeque this pig? It's alive, for Christ's sakes.' He says, 'Well, I figured you'd help me. You said you used to dress out meat at your mother's restaurant.'

"So I got a gun out of the closet and shot the pig, hung it up by its back feet, slit it open, dropped everything that didn't look right onto the floor of the garage. Then I took it down to a bathtub we had in the basement, filled the bathtub with scalding water, and shaved the damned thing with a straight razor to get the bristles off. I butchered it in the tub and presented Ted with half a pig. He put on the grill, slow-smoked it all afternoon, and by late in the day, everybody in the neighborhood had come by. We had this enormous pig smothered in barbeque sauce. It was awfully damned good."

Donald's children lived at home amid the hubbub. Sally had just moved out to attend nursing school after rescuing Lisa from her alcoholic mother's neglect in Jamaica and delivering her to his father and Cam to raise. John was in his mid-teens when his father bought the house on Terrace and moved in. He was very much into horseback riding and equestrian competition, and got swept up in the hippie culture at the end of the 1960s. John would go to work for his father at PMC in 1971. By then, he had a young wife and a baby on the way. The child, a girl, would be named Jessica, Donald's first grandchild.

In April 1971, Donald and Cam became parents of a baby girl. They named her Elizabeth Keller "Kelly" Baumgartner, or Kelly for short. "My mother named me Elizabeth, after the queen; Keller, after Helen Keller, a reported distant relative; and Kelly, after Kelly Collins, the Playmate of the Century," Kelly says. "My mother had high aspirations for me. She covered all the bases." After going to the private University School of Milwaukee, Kelly graduated from the University of Rochester magna cum laude and Phi Beta Kappa. She went on to receive a master's from Harvard Divinity School. Today, after founding several technology business—the first at age twenty-five—she runs a virtual reality production company in Milwaukee with her husband, Jeff Fitzsimmons, and a friend, Brad Lichtenstein, both filmmakers. Her father calls her the proudest achievement in his marriage to Cam. "I gave her mother a gold Rolex watch and I engraved on the back of it, *Thank you for Kelly.*"

Lisa and Kelly cuddle up together at home.

One of Kelly's earliest memories is of sneaking downstairs from her bedroom and peeking through the staircase balustrade to watch the parties. "It was a crazy time," she says. "My parents were at the heart of the whole social scene. They were amazing human beings that had a wide group of friends, and it was just a big party scene."

At someone's suggestion, most likely Cam's, *Playboy* had come to the Baumgartners' Victorian mansion to do a photo shoot for the magazine, starring Cam and Playboy Bunny Bebe Buell, the November 1974 Playmate of the Month and then-girlfriend of rock star Todd Rundgren. In one photo, Buell is perched on the trunk lid of Donald's sable brown Jaguar XKE convertible—one of two Jaguars that he owned at the time. She is holding a sparkling glass of champagne and wearing nothing but knee-high suede boots and a full-length fox coat draped very loosely around her shoulders. Donald, meanwhile, sits behind the steering wheel wearing a Cheshire-cat smile and a Geraldo Rivera moustache.

Bebe Buell would go on to become a fashion model and rock 'n' roll recording artist. A brief relationship with Aerosmith's Steven Tyler produced a daughter, Liv Tyler, now an internationally known Hollywood actress.

The so-called sexual revolution of the 1960s played out in a number of ways among Donald and Cam and their friends. Cam, after all, had no hang-ups about disrobing in public. And many people at the time tossed asunder societal restraints and attitudes about sex and nudity, adapting something of a libertine philosophy: Let the fun begin!

"He was like a playboy for awhile," says his half-sister, Roberta Axelrod, the youngest daughter of JR and his wife, Thelma. "That was his persona. He just gave off that vibe. Very friendly, talkative, good-looking, tons of friends. That's just the way he was."

In another sign of the anything-goes attitude, Donald and Cam vacationed with friends at a clothing-optional Club Med on the Caribbean Island of Martinique. "There wasn't a stitch of clothing in the compound," he says. "It was like a nudist colony, people playing beach ball in the nude, volleyball in the nude, swimming in the nude, body painting in the nude."

His son, John, meantime, had sailed to the island with his grandfather and grandmother on JR's fishing trawler. "In the summer of '78, I took a sabbatical of sorts from Paper Machinery and I took my girlfriend, who later became my wife, Terri," John says. "We crewed for my grandfather and my Grandma Thelma. The four of us took his yacht, an Alaskan trawler, an all-wooden beautiful boat—also called *Trenora*—from Fort Lauderdale, Florida, all the way to Trinidad, Tobago, South America, and back through the Windward Islands. It was a three-month trip. We stopped at all these beautiful Caribbean islands. By that time, my father was in Martinique with his second wife, Cam. They were staying at the Club Med. His dad and I, and Thelma and Terri, pulled up at the Club Med to meet my dad.

"Grandfather and I are in the pilot house," John says, "and we're coming up to the Club Med. I have the binoculars, and I look ashore, and no one has any clothes on. And my grandfather grabs the binoculars, and he takes a good look. And then Thelma. You couldn't pry the binoculars away from her eyes. We're looking at all these nude people. Of course a couple of the nudists we see are my father and Cam. There's my step-mom, at the end of the dock, doing jumping jacks buck naked. That's a sight I won't forget."

Bebe Buell, November 1974 Playmate of the Month, starred in a Playboy photo shoot at Donald's house. She bared it all on top of his Jaguar convertible, with Donald grinning behind the wheel.

As Donald expanded his business, Cam did her best to raise daughters Kelly and Lisa while following her artistic muse. She painted, oils and watercolors. She designed clothes, and made costumes for her daughters' Halloween and birthday parties. As another outlet, she heartily volunteered at the Milwaukee Public Museum, painting murals, dioramas, and totem poles of Native American tribes. "Her signature was to paint the Native American women with ample, Playboy-worthy bosoms, making her work easy to spot," says Kelly.

But Cam's deeper dreams were unfulfilled, and her unconstrained personality was discontented, out of place, says her daughter. "She wasn't raised with money. She was raised quite poor," Kelly says. "She wasn't from Wisconsin. She wasn't from the north. The north was the enemy. When we watched *Gone With the Wind*, my mother was horrified that I would root for the North. It was just not her culture, not her people."

To mask her frustration, she drank. Heavily. "I'd never known her sober. She had a very small window, between 12:00 and 3:00, where she wasn't hung over and she wasn't drunk yet. She would be in a sort of pleasant place. And I remember as a kid fantasizing that I could stretch this out."

One day, after he returned from a business trip to Japan, a book about open marriage appeared on Donald's nightstand. It was placed there by Cam, a not-so-subtle sign that she had been involved with other men. "I asked her, 'What the hell have you been up to?' and that changed the direction of our marriage. She was a seductress," he says.

Her friendships with Molly and Ben Abrohams became strained. "She asked me to lie to him for her, and I wouldn't do it," says Molly. "I was much more loyal to Donald than to Cam. And I lost touch with her. We lost our friendship."

Adds Ben: "Cam was so far down the road with her drinking issues, and there was no turning back. She had no desire to change."

Donald could see that his marriage to Cam had run its course, marked by infidelity and Cam's failing battle with the bottle. As with his first wife's addiction, he felt powerless to change Cam's behavior. "She had a serious drinking problem that I didn't recognize at first. When we met I thought, God, she can drink better than I can. She's really one of the boys. Well, it turned out to be more than an ability. It turned out to be a handicap."

In December 1977, while Donald was on a business trip, Cam loaded up her Chevy Blazer and took off for Everglades City, Florida, with a red-headed poet named Scott and her daughter, Kelly, who was nearly seven. "She told me we were going shopping," Kelly recalls.

In a series of events that mirrored the demise of Donald's first marriage, Cam continued to drink, sometimes as much as a half quart of whiskey a day, and, worse, neglected the needs of her daughter. Some years later in the Everglades, when Kelly was around ten, Donald received a call from Luni, a friend of Cam's in Florida. Luni was concerned that Kelly wasn't being educated, that she couldn't read. Donald never wanted to go through another ugly custody battle. "Cam was not malicious, she meant well but she was not capable of raising Kelly," he says. To preserve Cam's self-image, and for the sake of both mother and daughter, Donald and Cam agreed that the school system in Wisconsin was far superior. By sixth grade, Kelly had returned to Milwaukee to live at her father's home.

Flying in from Florida, Cam showed up unexpectedly one day at the Terrace Avenue house when Donald's cousin, Donna Flaxman, was visiting. Asking for forgiveness, she told Donald she was in treatment and asked him to take her back. "I told her absolutely not," he says. "It was too little too late."

Ten years after leaving him, Cam wrote Donald a letter of apology. It read, in part:

> I realize so much more about the disease of alcoholism and the chaos it causes in all the other people who are in the life of that sick person. . . . I've hurt an awful lot of people with my disease. I can't change your feelings or anybody's beliefs, and I'm not attempting to do that. What is important is that I make the effort to apologize for all the years of pain. I am greatly sad about it and want you to be aware of that fact.

Donald looks back on the marriage with some ambivalence. "Her drinking problem only got worse in the ten years we were married, not better. I thought that was something I could handle, and I couldn't. I thought maybe I could rein her in a little bit because she had so much raw talent, but I couldn't. I thought I could fix her, but I didn't. I was caught up in the classic Pygmalion complex. . . . All in all, I'd like to look back at that time as a mostly happy period, what with my business success and the addition of Kelly to the family, rather than as a negative period."

CHAPTER 6

The Third Time's the Charm

Donald was out of town when his soon-to-be-ex-wife Cam lit out for Everglades City with their daughter, Kelly. When he returned home to Milwaukee, he walked into an empty and cold house. Extremely cold. It was the middle of winter. The pilot light on the furnace had gone out, and the radiator pipes had frozen and cracked, spewing black, syrupy sludge throughout the house's interior. There were thirty-two busted radiators stacked up like cordwood on the lawn.

Donald called his cousin, Donna Flaxman, in Chicago, to see if she could help him out.

Donna had known Donald all her life. She was the youngest of the eight first cousins. Donald was the oldest of the cousins, born sixteen years before Donna, almost to the day. They shared the same grandfather and grandmother, and aunts and uncles. Their mothers were sisters. Donald's mother, Mae Lucille, was the eldest of the four Hayes sisters. Donna's mother, Geraldine—the rebellious convent runaway—was the youngest.

"I was born on the 21st of November," Donald says, "and Donna was born on the 22nd of November." As he tells it, Donna was named after him. When Geraldine got pregnant, she and her husband, David, expected a boy and picked the name "Donald," out of affection for their nephew. When Geraldine delivered a girl—on the day after Donald's birthday—"baby Donald" became "baby Donna."

With his second marriage in shambles, Donald lived alone in his spacious east side mansion. With his four children no longer living at home, his parenting responsibilities were negligible. Donna, meanwhile, infatuated by a life of travel and discovery, was open to adventure and eager to explore the world. Unencumbered as they were, Donald and Donna set off in search of new horizons. Sharing more than a bloodline, the two adventurers began exploring the world. And in the end there was love.

Growing up in Highland Park, Illinois, Donna Flaxman knew Donald all her life as his cousin. Their relationship changed significantly in 1978.

"It all started with my mother," Donald remembers. "Donna and my mother were always close, just like I was always close to Donna's mother, Geraldine. My mother said to Donna one day, 'You've got to get yourself a man. You've got to get married. My God, you're almost thirty. It's time to settle down.' And Donna said to my mother, 'Alas, if only I could find somebody just like Donald.' Well, my mother passed that on to me, and it must have stuck."

Their travels took them to places remote and less traveled, such as Haiti and Sri Lanka. Yet the fact that this traveling duo was an item did not immediately register with their family.

"In the meantime," Donald adds, "the family was saying, 'Isn't it nice that these two are traveling together. Donald has taken such an interest in Donna. He took her to Japan, Korea, and Thailand. He's taking her to Europe. Now he's taking her to Sri Lanka. My goodness. They're such good friends.' Actually, nobody in the family suspected. They thought we just had so much in common, exploring the world."

As they traveled together "it was all playtime," Donna says. "My only obligation was to have fun. There was never any pressure or expectation or gun to my head. I could exit at anytime. It was free spirit and adventure, and by the end I was hooked. He was my sidekick. I popped the question on the Algarve coast of Portugal on the road to Lisbon: 'How would a girl like me go about marrying a guy like you?' A couple days later he suggested

Donna and Donald began traveling the world in the late 1970s, from Africa to the Holy Land and points beyond.

marriage. I assumed we would be together one way or another but it wasn't until we were back in Milwaukee and I was moving stuff into his house that Donald hatched a plan: 'Since the family is coming to Milwaukee for Christmas, why don't we throw in a wedding?' he said. Life was very uncomplicated then, or at least he made it seem that way."

Although they didn't exactly swear each other to secrecy, the revelation of their love affair was more a slow burn than spontaneous combustion. They let their story find its way to the grapevine on its own. The first one to suspect something was Mae's husband, Elmer. Then one of their cousins said, "I think Donald has his eye on her."

"Eventually, they all caught on, one by one," says Donald.

As the news spread, Geraldine confronted Donna. Protective of her daughter, she was not happy. Far from it. "What the hell are you doing?" she asked, incredulously. "Donald? Once a playboy, *always* a playboy."

Wary of Donald, she was concerned that the relationship would hurt Donna and tear the family apart. "My mom thought Donald would never settle down," Donna says. He had two broken marriages, four kids, and a reputation. A reputation well earned. It was well known that Donald had had many girlfriends.

Geraldine's initial shock and apprehension passed as soon as she was included in their adventures. After all, she had known Donald since he was born and had stayed with his family as a teenager after fleeing the nuns. And he had an infectious personality—he was as irresistible as he was irrepressible.

In the end, the family welcomed the relationship as a positive thing for everyone. "Donna was terrific for Donald," says Jean McGrath, Donald's sister. "It was a perfect pairing. Everybody took it as an enormous plus. Everybody loves Donna. She's a loving, caring person. I couldn't have been happier that the two of them got together."

Bill Modahl, Jean's cousin (and the cousin of Donald and Donna), agrees. "Donald's about as free of pretensions as anybody you could ever meet. He's a very engaging guy, full of enthusiasm and a lot of fun to be around. He and Donna have made a very good pair. They're very down-to-earth. And I think she kind of quiets him down a bit, which is useful."

Eight first cousins, left to right: Donna Baumgartner; her sister, Nancie Flaxman; John Hoche; Hort Soper; Bill Modahl; Jean McGrath; Henry Hoche; and Donald Baumgartner.

Donald's daughter, Sally, says she was surprised when she heard about the romance but saw it as a good match. "After what my father went through with his other wives, I was just glad he was happy. I think the two of them are closer than any couple I've known in my lifetime."

Bonnie Bockl Joseph and her husband, Leon Joseph, are longtime friends of Donald and Donna. The two couples travel together, they socialize together. "I once said to Donald, 'You're very good to Donna,'" says Bonnie. "And he said, 'Look, when two wives take off, you're going to be very good to the third one.'" For Donald, the third time was the charm.

Donald Baumgartner and Donna Flaxman were married on December 23, 1979, at his house on Terrace Avenue in Milwaukee. It was a small, intimate ceremony, bedecked with dozens of candles and white poinsettias. Forty-nine guests attended. Donna entered the living room from the dining room alone, wearing an off-white satin, knee-length tuxedo dress, with a cummerbund and hand-painted roses. Donald and the groomsmen wore tuxedos. His son, John, was the best man.

Because Donna was only in her thirties, Donald's grandchildren would come to know her by the Yiddish term of endearment "Bubbi," a winsome alternative

Donald and Donna making a wedding day toast, "Till death do us part."

to the more traditional "Grandma." If anyone had questioned Donald's choice of partners in the past, his marriage to Donna promptly dispelled those doubts. She shared in Donald's adventurous spirit and general lust for life, and presented a steadying influence on their marriage and on the lives of his children.

Donna was born on the south side of Chicago. Her sister, Nancie, was eighteen months older. When Donna was in first grade, her family moved from a house near the Tam O'Shanter Golf Course in the town of Niles to the lakeside community of Highland Park, home of the Ravinia Festival and several houses designed by Frank Lloyd Wright. She graduated from Highland Park High School in 1964.

The girls' father, David Flaxman, was Jewish. He worked for his sister Sally's husband, Morris Eiseberg, making seventy-five dollars a week at Universal Cocoa. When Morris died suddenly, David took the reins. Sally gave him a 48 percent stake in the company, and they changed the name to Universal Foods. The company—sometime in the mid- to late '50s—merged with Red Star Yeast. They kept the Universal Foods name until 2010, when it changed to Sensient Technologies.

written personally for the four of them, the Irish eyes of the Hayes sisters are indeed smiling, joyous, vibrant, mischievous, and carefree.

To his mother, Donald of course could do no wrong. "Mae was crazy about him. He was her guy," says Donna. "If Donald caught a fish that was this big, she'd say it was *this* big," she says, gesturing with her hands. "She adored him. He lit up her life. After his dad left, his mom would say, 'Your father left us. You're the man of the house now.' He was only about nine years old." She took him everywhere and asked his opinion on everything.

The oldest of the four, born in 1907, his mother was at the top of the pecking order, the most dominant of the sisters. "Mae Lucille wasn't the most talkative, but she was the oldest one," says Bill Modahl, son of Elizabeth. "The others all deferred to her and sort of regarded her as the senior person." Having graduated from Moser Secretarial School in Chicago and having operated Glenn's Grill, she was businesslike, efficient, and smart.

The next oldest was Betty, also known as Angela, born in 1910. A quiet and sometimes nervous type, she ran Glenn's Grill with her first husband, Glenn Chapman, before Donald's parents took over the business. When she was young, Betty was a manicurist at the Drake Hotel in Chicago. "Errol Flynn was her customer when he was in town," says her son, Henry Hoche, cousin of Donald and Donna. "She always did Errol Flynn's nails, cut and buffed them. He wouldn't have his nails done unless my mother was there."

Following her divorce from Glenn Chapman, Betty decided to go on a cruise to meet an eligible bachelor. According to the family story, she met two men who qualified, and chose a man named Phil Hoche.

The Hayes girls did not always see eye to eye. They were close in age and not immune to sibling rivalry. Idle squabbles would erupt from time to time, well into their later years.

"It was a typical Irish thing," says Hort Soper, the son of Elizabeth and half-brother of Bill Modahl. They would take sides, and then the alliances would change over the years. And it was always sort of cantankerous. For some years, two would be aligned against the others, and then they'd break off their alliance. That's the way it went. Geraldine probably got along well with most of them. But there were years where they wouldn't even speak to each other. These petty, little things would get them all worked up."

Without a doubt, Donald's Aunt Elizabeth made a crater of an impression on him.

Born in 1915 and married seven times, Elizabeth became a bigger-than-life character in the eyes of Donald and virtually everyone she met. "Elizabeth sought and created excitement everywhere she went," Donna says. "She would seek it out. She was enormously engaging, a gifted flirt; smart, funny, flattering—a whirl of glamour."

Even her own children saw her as a live wire. "My mother, Elizabeth, was the third born," Bill Modahl says, "and she was very lively, starting at an early age. She got in trouble with her parents because they found out she had a little business going down at the grade school: She would beat up anyone for a dime, including people who were several grades older and bigger than she was. But she was very Irish and she would take on the job gladly. She was constantly fighting with the nuns and so forth. She was very feisty as a child and as an adult."

Elizabeth was "a real character," agrees Hort, five years younger than his half-brother Bill. "She was the kind of person that would walk into a room and just light it up. People used to call her 'Auntie Mame,' you know, like the play. She had that type of personality. All of the Hayes sisters were very witty. They had a very dry sense of humor."

Elizabeth stood out in a crowd, dressed in colorful dresses and hats of the latest styles. In the 1940s, when living in Bloomington, Illinois, she hosted a talk radio show call "The Gypsy Winks," part gossip and part fashion show. With an on-air clue, or "wink," the Gypsy would tip off listeners on fashion and beauty.

"Elizabeth also had valuable tips for women about flirting and being assertive and catching men," says Donna. "When Geraldine and Elizabeth were young girls still living at home, Elizabeth would run and answer the phone. If it was a suitor for Geraldine, Elizabeth would run downstairs to grab the guy at the front door and run off with him before Geraldine got to the door."

Elizabeth's last husband proved to be a particularly good catch. She was living in South Florida when she met a man named Stephen Calder. Born in rural Georgia, Calder made his fortune in Fort Lauderdale real estate

Donald's Aunt Elizabeth was a major influence in his life.

after World War II. He brought summertime thoroughbred horse racing to North Miami when he opened a racetrack in 1971 that would bear his name to this day, Calder Race Track. Elizabeth married Calder in 1973. They lived in Hallandale, a small beachside enclave near the racetrack.

The Calder track became a playground for celebrities, and an obsession for Elizabeth.

Along with the racetrack, Calder owned two jai alai frontons, 23,000 acres of timberland in Costa Rica, thoroughbred race horses, and a couple of hotels in Florida. He bought up and developed most of the ocean front property from Fort Lauderdale to Pompano Beach called The Galt Ocean Mile.

"He built Elizabeth a big house in Port Antonio, Jamaica," says Donna. "She painted it blue and called it 'Heaven.' It still bears that name today. You can rent it online. It's a lovely vacation spot. She also operated one of Calder's hotels along the beach in Long Bay, Jamaica."

Calder built her a house in Hallandale made of marble—weathered marble slabs on the outside and all polished marble on the inside: the walls, the floors, the exposed winding staircase to her bedroom that cantilevered over the sunken living room. It was all over-the-top Hollywood glamour.

Donald remembers visiting her marble house in Hallandale. "She had a vault in her bathroom. I mean a real vault. I walked in and it was stacked with gold bars, from the ceiling to the floor. Her husband kept great quantities of gems in his desk wrapped in tissue paper. He was a peculiar guy. He lived in his office in Fort Lauderdale and slept on a cot and would only visit the marble mansion for dinner and a short time, always returning to his office for the night."

"It was kind of an interesting thing," says Hort, reflecting on the lives of the Hayes girls. "Back in the days when they were growing up, I don't think women got ahead very often. A lot of them had to rely upon husbands. And I think the Hayes sisters were like that. They were all very attractive and they married guys who were very successful. When they started out, I don't think they had much of anything, and they all wound up doing very well."

If Elizabeth was the most outrageous—and most wealthy—of Donald's aunts, Geraldine was the closest. Although she became his mother-in-law after he married her daughter, Donna, their relationship didn't change much.

"She ran away from the convent and came to live with Mother and Dad when Donald was a youngster," says his sister, Jean. "So she bonded with Donald during that time. She was very tight with Donald, always."

Separated by just twelve years, they had shared experiences: He was a young boy living at home when she knocked on his parents' front door. She had run away from the convent and hitchhiked from Ann Arbor, Michigan, seeking refuge from the Catholic Church. He waited counters and flipped hamburgers at his mother's diner when Gerry was a carhop. They both did stints at the family dairy farm in Minnesota, where Gerry learned how to milk a cow. (Donald, however, never could get the hang of it.) When she married and became a mother, she would make the short drive again and again from Highland Park to Milwaukee with her husband and their two daughters for family dinners and holiday celebrations.

As he was with each of his aunts, Donald was captivated by the high-spirited personality of Geraldine. Geraldine was the most self-assured of the sisters. She lived to be ninety-six.

With their parents, the Hayes sisters later in life, from left to right: Elizabeth, Betty, their mother, Geraldine, Mae, and their father.

"My mother had impeccable taste, and loved clothes and accessories," says Donna. "She was always smartly dressed. Even when she wore jeans, she was never without her accessories—she was still well dressed. She was known for her humor, her timing, and her acerbic wit. She had a low handicap on the golf course, and was an avid bridge player."

The cast of characters in Donald's life couldn't have been more compelling: His grandfather, John Francis Hayes, "Dad Hayes," master storyteller and biggest fan. His father, "the Skipper," inventor, entrepreneur and lifelong adventurer. His stepfather, Elmer, a natural athlete and a real man's man. The four Hayes girls, enchanting, unique women of the world.

Donald recalls, "All these people, they were a part of me growing up. Every one. They were not your average folks. I saw in them this joy of life, this *joie de vivre*, and this lack of conformity that I was very much attracted to. This was the show I attended, and it was a hell of a show."

CHAPTER 7

The Crossing

A year or so before Donald and Donna tied the knot, Bob Baumgartner bought a fifty-eight-foot long-range cruiser made by Hatteras Yachts, a premier shipbuilder in North Carolina. Having owned dozens of boats, the Skipper was looking for a way to get his newly christened pleasure craft *Trenora* (Sea Witch) across the Atlantic Ocean to southern Europe, where it would be docked for future cruises, in unexplored playgrounds.

The yacht had a range for a trans-Atlantic voyage. But the Hatteras LRC-58 model had not been tested for a "blue water" ocean crossing. On paper, the boat had seaworthy communication equipment and the fuel capacity to traverse the ocean. But could it make it safely and comfortably?

The idea for the crossing was hatched around Christmastime, 1978, at the Chicago steakhouse Gene & Georgetti, where Donald and Donna were having dinner with Bob. "My dad had bought the boat, and he said he wanted to get it to the Mediterranean for the summer. He was going to ship it over by deck cargo, and it was going to cost him $60,000. I said, after perhaps one too many martinis, 'Well, for Christ's sakes. It's a long-range cruiser. If it has the capability of crossing the ocean with fuel, why don't you just sail it across?' He said, 'Don't be ridiculous.' And I said, 'Well, hell, if you won't, I will.' That's when the extra martini kicked in."

Donald's father had never crossed the Atlantic, but he had been on the water since he was a boy and had withstood weather conditions of all sorts while at sea. In one of his most perilous journeys, he found himself in the eye of a hurricane off the Florida coast in September 1965.

JR had been on a pleasure cruise from Fort Lauderdale to Nassau in the Bahamas on his ninety-foot power cruiser, also called *Trenora*, with two crewmen and a honeymoon couple from Puerto Rico. A hurricane named Betsy had been tracked as a Stage 4 Storm heading toward the Carolinas, hundreds of miles north of their destination. But when they were about fifty miles off the mainland, the crew got news that Hurricane Betsy had suddenly reversed course and was bearing down on the Florida coast and the Bahamas.

Bob steered the yacht south toward Bimini, looking for safe harbor, and anchored off Gun Cay for the night. The next day, with the hurricane closing in, he piloted the boat to the Bahama Banks, anchoring in water just twelve feet deep, thinking the storm's swell would be smaller and tamer. But Betsy seemed to be stalking *Trenora*. "We got the full brunt of the storm there, and ran aground on a sand bar," he later told a newspaper reporter.

As the eye of the hurricane edged closer and closer, gusts of 140 miles an hour tore the boat from the sandbar and yanked it into the deeper waters of the Gulf Stream, which flows parallel to the East Coast, tossing the helpless vessel like a toy boat in a bathtub amid swells of thirty feet. JR ordered everyone into life jackets and tied them together. According to a sequence of events JR related to his grandson, John, waves flooded the top of the boat and killed both diesel engines. "He had no power," says John. "Grandfather needed to get an engine started, and there was no way to get to the engine room without going up on deck and into the wind. He stepped into the wind, and the it blew him against the rail and he broke a couple of ribs."

By the time the storm passed, the yacht was dead in the water, its electrical power, radar, and both engines knocked out. The next morning Bob managed to repair the generator long enough to send out a distress message by radio, and under the watch of a U.S. Coast Guard plane, *Trenora* hobbled into Port Everglades. All five passengers were safe and—except for a couple of broken ribs, a few smashed fingers, and a sprained ankle—sound.

The three-day drama at sea made headlines. For riding out a Stage 4 storm, the Skipper earned another nickname, "Hurricane Bob."

Before they left the Chicago steakhouse, Donald and his father had firmed up plans for the Atlantic crossing. Donald would assemble a crew and chart a course, Donna would be the cook and provision the boat, and they would set out on Easter Sunday.

"I thought it sounded like a great adventure," says Donna. "I was totally in a state of love. You know, 'wherever he goeth, I will follow.'"

For Donald, the crossing would be a personal challenge. At age forty-eight, he was nearing the half-century mark. Having just read a biography of Gen. Douglas MacArthur, *American Caesar* by William Manchester, he was pumped with bravado and not content to live in the shadow of his hurricane-hardened father. So Donald took his midlife crisis and his girlfriend on the high seas for a high-stakes adventure.

The first leg of the journey was from Fort Lauderdale's Pier 66 to the British territory of Bermuda, about 900 miles. "The ocean crossing," explains Donald, "is from Bermuda to the Azores, off Portugal, because geologically

Donald and his father chart their course in the wheelhouse of Trenora *on the first stage of the Atlantic crossing.*

Bermuda is still on the continental shelf of North America and the Azores are on the edge of the continental shelf of Europe."

The longest leg would be from Bermuda to the Azores, another 1,780 miles. At an average cruising speed of nine knots, burning 8.5 gallons of diesel fuel per hour, and with a fuel capacity of 2,400 gallons, Donald calculated *Trenora's* maximum range to be about 2,400 miles. "We felt that gave us an adequate safety margin to detour around bad weather or fight the seas if we were hit by a storm we couldn't avoid," he said at the time.

Meanwhile, Donna stocked the yacht's galley with meals prepared and packaged individually by a gourmet chef in Fort Lauderdale, then stored onboard in a large freezer. The servings, including entrées such as beef Wellington, would be microwaved and paired with fine wines and champagne, leading one boating magazine to dub the cruise "the Champagne Crossing."

Trenora left Port Everglades at 6 p.m. on April 15, 1979, Easter Sunday, in smooth seas. On board were Donald and Donna; Donald's father, Bob; Nate Root, the soon-to-be husband of Donna's mother and Donna's second stepfather; Donald's son, John; John's girlfriend, Terri Hayes; and Eric Lindboldt, a young deckhand.

By the third day out, the swells had grown to a moderate three to five feet, according to a daily log kept of the crossing by Terri. John trolled for fish from the stern as Donna and Terri fished and sunbathed on the fly bridge. The crew watched in delight as three dolphins danced in the waves alongside the boat.

Later that night, on the boat's high-seas radio, the New Jersey-based weather service WOO broadcast a storm warning: A massive weather system was moving southwest off the Grand Banks of Newfoundland. Two freighters had floundered as far south as New Jersey's coast. (The onboard radio was a single-sideband high seas radio, an expensive piece of technology that allowed boaters in the middle of the Atlantic to communicate ship to ship or ship to shore and receive weather broadcasts through a Weather Routing subscription service. The radio was bought as an incentive based on a bet Bob made with his son: If you quit smoking, I'll get you the radio. Otherwise, you can smoke all you want and find your own damned way across the Atlantic. "I quit cold-turkey, right on the spot," Donald says. "Never had another cigarette.")

Donna tries her luck at deep-sea fishing.

As they approached Bermuda, the wind had kicked up to twenty to twenty-five knots, with gusts of thirty knots and seas eight to ten feet breaking over the boat's beam. Motoring toward the island of Bermuda, the passengers tried to relax in the main salon after a gourmet dinner and a few bottles of wine. Donald sat leaning in a chair that was lashed with a bungee cord to the sidewall. Donna was seated on a barstool that was bungeed to a pad eye, a closed hook, while John was at the helm with a cup of coffee. Suddenly, from out of nowhere, a huge rogue wave slapped *Trenora's* port side, sending her into a sudden, forty-degree roll to starboard.

The wave knocked Donna to the floor. It sent John sailing toward the pilothouse door, and catapulted Donald across the breadth of the salon, like he was propelled from a slingshot, face first.

"I remember grabbing the pilothouse door with all fours, like a cat," John says. "I'm hanging on as the boat goes over and I'm looking into the sea. And out of my right eye I see my father. He's stretched out like Superman. He's flying. Literally. Horizontal. I swear to God, he is in the air, his hands out in front of him."

Donald was heading straight for an open window. But just before he went into the ocean, he made contact with a lamp that JR had bolted to the furniture so it wouldn't get damaged in rough weather. Unfortunately, it was Donald's face that suffered the damage, but at the same time, saved him.

"When *Trenora* righted herself," continues John, "we see that Dad would have gone out the salon window. But he hit the lamp and it stopped him cold."

Donald wrapped his face in a bath towel to stop the bleeding. "I had a couple of black eyes and a twisted nose," he says. "And I bled like a stuck hog for a while."

A broken nose is no laughing matter to Donald, as Donna applies first aid after rough seas sent him headlong into a cabin lamp.

"I think I helped soften the blow for him, aside from the lamp, as I was all black and blue," says Donna. "He wouldn't let anybody look at his face so we could see what was left of it. His father wanted nothing to do with it."

The next day, the storm hit full force. Twenty-foot waves, "as big as condominiums," says Donald, pounded *Trenora*, sending gear and bodies dancing across the deck and bouncing off the bulkheads. Despite the constant commotion, the crew never missed a meal, dining in style on gourmet cuisine and fine wine every night. As the boat rolled up and down, Donna would crawl on her hands and knees in the galley to fetch an extra helping or more condiments.

On the fifth day, *Trenora* anchored in Bermuda's St. Georges harbor. The crew cleared customs the following morning and docked at the Royal Bermuda Yacht Club, battered and bruised and thankful to be standing on *terra firma*. Socked in by bad weather and in need of some hard-earned R&R, the crew explored Bermuda for a few days. Donald took a quick flight home to Milwaukee for business dealings, and then returned to join the party. The Beach Club became a favorite hangout for dinner and drinks, and Club Disco was the perfect spot for burning off energy and downing colorful rum cocktails. It was an easy routine to follow, as confirmed by a succinct entry in the daily log: *Stayed up late partying.*

During the day, the crew wandered along sandy, cliff-side beaches, checked out island artifacts in the hills, and went spelunking in a hidden tunnel. They rode horses, toured a botanical garden, and rented a small fleet of Mopeds.

Riding the motor scooters turned into a competitive sport between Donald and John. "Every day my dad and I would ride to the weather station in Hamilton, Bermuda," John says. "We'd check on the weather, looking for a good window where we could cast off and head for the Azores. Well, every day Dad and I decided to go a little faster and try to shave off a little time on the way to the weather station. Mind you, it *was* a race. One day after the rain, I came around a hairpin turn a little too quickly and the bike went out from under me. I'm tumbling on the asphalt and my father's right behind me, and instead of running me over, he grabs the front brake and then catapults over me. He didn't hit me, but, in saving his son, he managed to skin up his knees and elbows pretty good. Now, let's just be clear: The guy who's mostly beat up on this trip before we even left Bermuda is Dad, who already has had a lamp try to readjust his face, and now his knees and elbows are all messed up from road rash."

When he wasn't challenging his son to a road race or buying drinks for his crewmates, Donald spent a day rigging up a safety harness so Donna wouldn't be thrown around the galley in rough seas. "When we got into Bermuda, she was so bruised and beat up, people thought I'd been abusing her. So I bought a strap and a harness that she could wear, and I put screw eyes all the way around the galley. As she walked around, she could snap herself into the counter from the refrigerator to the stove to the sink, unsnapping one and re-snapping the other, so she wouldn't go flying."

After eleven days, the skies finally cleared and the holiday came to an end. It was time to set sail. As planned, Bob Baumgartner, at age seventy-one, and Nate Root, in his late sixties, had flown home to the States, leaving Donald, Donna, John, Terri, and Eric to board *Trenora* for the next leg of the voyage.

The crew bid Bermuda farewell on Monday, April 30, 1979. The sky was blue and the weather was fair. The calm wouldn't last long. Weather Routing had alerted them to a storm that was building over the Grand Banks, the massive underwater section of the North American Continental Shelf southeast of Newfoundland. A rich international fishing ground, the cold-water Labrador Current meets the warm-water Gulf Stream at the Banks, often spawning cyclonic storms in the North Atlantic.

> We're in the middle of the Atlantic now! We are going
> farther south to avoid gale storm north of us.
> —From *Trenora* log entry, May 1.

The shortest distance across the Atlantic is not a straight line but an arc, called a Great Circle Route. Rather than following a constant heading, ship captains adjust their course periodically to stay on the arc. But, heeding the warning from Weather Routing, *Trenora* was forced to deviate from the arc.

"The weatherman sent us farther south. He kept pushing us south," Donald says. "And so we couldn't take the shortest route. We were way above the equator in the north latitudes, an area referred to by sailors as "the Roaring Forties." So, by going south, it increased the distance rather considerably, and we had to use up more fuel, which was nerve-wracking because we had allotted only so much fuel per day."

Before the voyage, Donald had taught himself how to navigate by the stars. "Knowing at Christmas that we were going to take the boat over, I was concerned about navigation. We had bought a primitive satellite navigation system for the yacht. Compared to today's satellite navigation systems that give you a constant readout of your position, this thing would read maybe once every twenty-four hours. The SAT/NAV back then was a miracle,

Trenora leaves the port of Bermuda on the second leg of the trans-Atlantic journey.

but by today's standards it would be a joke. This was 1979. There were not many satellites up there back then. It was not dependable. We would go for hours or even days without a fix. Never knowing how it would perform caused me to study celestial navigation. I had about four months to train myself how to do it. I bought a sextant along with several navigation books.

"A sextant measures the angle between the Earth and the celestial object that you're looking at," he says. "Then you put that figure into what they call a sight reduction table. In the old days, you'd have all these tables and you did the math by hand. I bought a calculator that allowed me to input that data, and then it did most of the math for me. I would go down to Beach Road along Lake Michigan during the day and take sun sights, and at night I'd go take moon shots and star shots.

"When I could locate myself within about a mile of where I was stand-ing, I figured, well, that's close enough, because if I can get within a mile, I can pick it up on the boat's radar. I wanted to make damned sure I didn't miss the Azores of course because if I missed, I'd be adrift for God knows how long. We would just go with the currents, and who knows where we would wind up. Maybe South Africa." To check the accuracy of *Trenora's* satellite navigation system, he made sightings with the sextant wherever possible to plot its position on the crossing.

Combined with Donald's sextant readings as a backup, the satellite navigation system, or SAT/NAV, proved to be a reliable instrument. As he told *The New York Times* shortly after the crossing: "The most important piece of equipment we added was a Magnavox satellite navigator connected to a gyro-compass and speed log. It worked flawlessly and was invaluable in allowing us to determine precisely our position, course, range, distance traveled over the bottom, and set and drift."

Despite the threat of a storm, the crew of *Trenora* didn't interrupt the Champagne Crossing. There was plenty of sea life to observe, delicious din-ners, and late night dance parties to enjoy *Saturday Night Fever*, with John Travolta and the Bee Gees.

While Donna was stretched out on the top deck, she realized she was staring into the eye of a giant sperm whale. It was clearly surveying the boat and maintained eye contact for a measurable time. "He was clearly checking me out, giving me the eye," she says.

> Saw tons of squid, and big ones. Saw whales, more
> dolphins too. . . . Disco dancing tonight!
> —From *Trenora* log entry, May 2.

Trenora crossed paths one day with a U.S. Navy research vessel. When Donald tried to confirm *Trenora's* position by radio, the captain of the Navy ship wouldn't oblige him, leaving Donald to wonder if the ship was on a spy mission, or if the captain was just being rude.

On Day Six en route to the Azores, things got more serious. The weather service advised *Donald* that the Grand Banks weather system was developing into a cyclonic storm—a potential hurricane—and moving their way. Donald ordered a lifeboat drill and the inspection of all life jackets as a precautionary measure. He also came up with a brilliant idea: flood the empty keel fuel tanks with seawater to provide more ballast. Thousands of pounds of diesel fuel had been drawn from the tanks in the course of the cruise from Bermuda. This gradually reduced the ballast in the very bottom of the yacht. Pumping water into the tanks replenished the ballast and helped prevent the boat from rolling.

"It was a very top-heavy boat," says Donald, "and as we emptied the tanks, the boat kept getting higher and higher out of the water and rolling more and more. So I filled the tanks with seawater. So as we used fuel, I put sea water in the empty fuel tanks to help keep the boat stable."

> Pretty rough. Wind west on our stern. Boat tipping 20-25 degrees. . . . Starboard generator quit. Now on one generator. Can't use air conditioning or water. . . . We're all filthy.
> —*Trenora* log entry, May 6.

> John finds solenoid to be problem of the generator and he fixes it. . . . We clean the boat and ourselves today. . . . Had steak & champagne party to celebrate.
> —*Trenora* log entry, May 7.

As luck would have it, while they veered south to avoid the northern storm, another storm system was coming at them from the south. "We're six or seven days at sea and we now have to make a decision," says John. "Based on fuel consumption, you cross the point of no return. You no longer have enough fuel to turn around and go back to Bermuda. We now have to both adjust our course and go for the Canary Islands, south off the western coast of Africa, or go for the Azores, off Portugal. We make the decision to continue our course to the Azores. We're getting a rough ride. We're no longer into a nice pleasure cruise. The waves were maybe ten feet but they were what you call 'peaking seas,' because it's real slop. It was just a sloppy sea that's meeting from the north and the south. The boat is getting bounced around, and at this point we have our next major injury."

Donald offers to help Donna prepare beef Wellington in the boat's galley.

Donna was making coffee for John, who was on watch. Piloting the boat was divided into two shifts: John, from after dinner to sun up, and Donald, from morning until dinnertime. Eric and Donna would take the "dog watches" (4 p.m. to 8 p.m.) and sub when needed. Donna also brewed killer coffee, strong enough to melt a spoon and keep everyone on watch wide-eyed for hours on end. The sloppy seas were throwing the yacht side to side, and as she was pushing the French press coffee pot's plunger through the grounds and boiling water, the glass pot exploded, drenching her with scalding coffee.

"I had second-degree burns all over my lap and legs." Donna covered her burns with zinc oxide and dampened the severe pain with the only shot of morphine from the medical kit. The accident put their situation in stark relief. In the middle of the North Atlantic Ocean, with near-hurricane winds bearing down on the yacht, things were getting rough for the crew of five.

> No radio contact. . . . Boat rolling to 40 degrees. Squall
> coming 20 knots behind us. Waves breaking over the bow.
> . . . Finally got radio contact to weatherman.
>
> —*Trenora* log entry, May 9.

"This was not a boat that was meant to bear the force of a million gallons of water slamming into it with the might of a runaway freight train," says Donald. "We knew we had bitten off a lot more than we could chew."

Trenora was fifty miles from its destination, the town of Horta in the Azores, when they finally regained contact with their weatherman, Mike, at Weather Routing. His report was not encouraging: "Grand Banks system still building. Serious depression from the south. Suggest you head directly for Horta and make the best of it." He signed off wishing us "Good luck!"

As Donald would later say, the entry to Horta was a nightmare, with the winds gusting at forty to fifty knots. "We were three miles from Horta, and due to the wind and spray, we couldn't even see the island with binoculars. I've never heard winds howl like that."

The crew caught sight of Horta on May 9. The Horta marina was in a narrow cut between two islands of the archipelago, Faial Island and Pico Island. At first sight, it appeared *Trenora* could cruise straight into the channel to Horta from the west. But it wasn't as easy as it looked. "We get to this spot, it's late afternoon, and we're tired," recalls John. "We've been at sea for ten days. The weather service tells Dad that we should just go in the lee side of Horta and come right up close to shore, drop an anchor and rest, and then in the morning make the run to the harbor. We get right up to shore; you could throw a baseball from the bow of the boat right to the island. But we can't drop a hook. It's too deep, like 500 feet. We don't have enough anchor chain."

As midnight approached, John heard Portuguese being spoken on the VHF radio. When he put out a call asking for assistance, the reply came back in English. The captain of a 300-foot inter-island ferry, the *Ponta Delgada*, was in the vicinity, and he offered to guide *Trenora* into Horta. But to get there, the boat would have to go around Faial Island and through the cut between the islands from the east.

"He held his position for us to come up on his stern," says John, "and we would follow him into the port. We could see his masthead lights and everything, we were so close. At this point we're thinking, *we're there!* But this is where we almost didn't make it."

Funneled into the channel between the islands, the breakers exceeded twenty feet. "The wind was blowing now at seventy knots, and we were rolling up to forty degrees," Donald says. "The bow of the boat was so far down in the swell that the propellers were out of the water just turning in the wind. I was at the helm and did all I could do to keep the boat from broaching—its side to the wind and sea."

Donald and John kept their eyes fixed on the freighter's lights. "He went up, up, up, up, up, and we're in back of him," Donald says. "Then, all of a sudden, it's like he just disappeared, vanished over the top of the wave. Seconds later, we came up behind on the same wave he was on. And we surfed into the harbor totally out of control on a giant breaking wave in the middle of the night."

"We pretty much kissed the stone quay," says John. "*We're alive! We made it!* It's a huge deal. Had we come in from the west and hit that wave on our nose, we would have capsized. We met Captain Armando, who had guided us in." A colorful, handsome character, wearing a cape over his shoulder, he had been written up in *National Geographic* in 1976 as "Black Beard."

Donald's father rejoined the crew with his wife, Thelma, in the Azores. Boarding *Trenora* and leaving the memories of their stormy arrival behind, the crew sailed to the Portuguese island of Madeira, then on to the Algarve Coast of Portugal and the city of Vilamoura, where, on the morning of May 28 —forty-two days after shoving off from the coast of Florida, they finally entered the Mediterranean through the Straits of Gibraltar. The final leg of the crossing was complete.

According to records kept by the crew, the Hatteras LRC-58 traveled 3,818 nautical miles while underway for 460.8 hours (nineteen days and four hours), at an average speed of just under eight knots.

"They called our boat a long-range cruiser, but it wasn't meant for a long-range crossing of the ocean," says Donald. "No, it's strictly a pleasure yacht. It was not a boat that was built to do what we did. The Hatteras people were quite impressed. They put us on the cover of their magazine. We were the only Hatteras that had ever crossed the ocean. *Boating Magazine* even included us in an article titled "10 Who Dared."

Tying up the boat in Vilamoura, they rented a car and drove north to Lisbon to pick up Donna's mother, Geraldine, and Geraldine's boyfriend, Nate, who rejoined the group on *Trenora* for a leisurely cruise of the Mediterranean.

Trenora *sails into the port of Vilamoura, Portugal, after a long, storm-beaten crossing.*

After passing through the Straits, they docked in some of the north coast's most picturesque ports: Calpe, Savilla, and Cadiz in Spain; the Spanish island of Mallorca; Antibes and Nice in France. "I remember going to San Tropez," says Donna. "As luck would have it, they were just wrapping up the Miss Nude Riviera contest, and we were sort of the beneficiaries of that. Donald took off his trunks and went skipping down the beach. And then there was his father, the big mustached sea dog with his Greek fisherman hat and his black turtleneck sweater—he was quite a sight."

Compared to the harrowing adventure they'd just been through, sailing the pleasure yacht in the Mediterranean was a breeze. "This is where you'd want that boat to be," says Donald. "My father's idea of shipping it over was a better idea, no question about it. I mean, we risked our lives doing this thing. And we saved him at least $50,000." As it turned out, Bob would sell *Trenora* before Donald and Donna would return to the Med again.

A satisfied captain in the pilothouse at dusk.

The Gourmet Crossing was the cruise of a lifetime, something for the record books, something to tell the grandchildren someday. The bumps, the bruises, the burns, the unrelenting storms and unforeseen diversions—all were more than the crew had bargained for, but counterbalanced by their display of vigor and nerve, and sense of sheer awe as they conquered the breadth of the turbulent Atlantic.

For Donald, the adrenaline-fueled triumph surpassed any feelings of regret. Nearly four decades after the trip, the experience still resonates. "It was more than a crossing, it was a passage for me. To paraphrase the explorer Edmund Hillary: It's not the mountain or the ocean we conquer, but ourselves."

The voyage also sealed the future of Donald and Donna. "That's when we knew we were going to get married," says Donna. "After we survived it all, we felt we could survive anything, even marriage."

Storm tested, cyclonic tough . . . or as Donald puts it: "It was one hell of a date, wasn't it?"

CHAPTER 8

The White House, the Berlin Wall, and a Rocky Mountain High

The fast-food revolution was a stroke of luck for Paper Machinery Corporation. Customers wanted a beverage with their Big Mac. And for every Coke or Sprite or hot coffee they ordered, a paper cup was needed.

The fast-food chains had become household names across America in the 1960s. In an on-the-go society, disposable containers were synonymous with speedy service and convenient meals. The trend was irreversible. In less than a decade, the Golden Arches, Colonel Sanders, and "Have it your way" slogan spread to markets around the globe.

Meanwhile, overseas very few companies were manufacturing paper cup-forming machines. This was a golden opportunity for Donald and his company. By the late 1970s, Donald and his sales reps were making sales calls on nearly every continent in search of new customers. As the demand for paper cups grew, these new customers, particularly the Japanese cup makers, demanded speed and reliability from the cup-forming machines they ordered, which pushed PMC's engineers and machinists to design and build machines that ran much faster and much more efficiently.

Then something surprising happened. As PMC made steady advancements in the performance of its machines, the old-line cup fabricators—the five "majors," Dixie, Lily-Tulip, Continental Bondware, Sweetheart, and, eventually, Solo—began buying machines from PMC. Since the early decades of the twentieth century, when paper cups became commonplace, the long-established majors had built proprietary cup machines, using them exclusively to make their own cups, and never selling to third-party interests. But the majors had not kept up with the technology, and fell behind.

"They quit manufacturing their own machines, recognizing that their own were far inferior to what we were offering," Donald says. "We were dedicated to building machinery. They were dedicated to making cups. Their focus was on marketing and producing cups, and as an afterthought, they had a machine-building program. We had our full, 100 percent concentration on making the machine better and better and better. By placing machines with so many different customers, who found fault with our machines and complained about this and that, we had an opportunity to continually improve."

Building a better mousetrap, so to speak, was an evolution of technology that had boxed in the major cup makers. As John Baumgartner explains, the construction of an ordinary paper cup is more complex than people realize. For the engineers and machinists and assemblymen who design and build the machines that make the cups, innovation is a necessity. "The world had been producing two types of cups, a hot cup and a cold cup," says John. "Hot cups for mostly coffee and tea, cold cups for mostly soda water or drinking water. In the 1960s, '70s and into the '80s, all hot cups were constructed using a polyethylene coating on the inside and raw paper on the outside. Cold cups had no plastic on the inside, just paper. The cold cups were glued together and then run through a wet waxing machine that would apply a coating of wax. The wax was heated to permeate the paper, creating a sticky, waxy feeling to the touch.

"In the 1980s, somebody came up with the idea of using a double lining of polyethylene for a cold cup, and once you had double poly cold cup—inside and outside—you got rid of the glue sealing and waxing. Without wax, you had the ability to do a much better job printing." Cleaner and smoother, the cups were sealed by heating the polyethylene to a molten consistency. The bottom was folded in and then pinched to create a leak-proof seal.

The next-generation paper cup caught the attention of cup makers and the press. Trade magazine *Paper Sales* gave it a glowing review in its July

1987 issue: "Manufacturers have responded to the demand for quality and the rise in the cost of materials for making plastic cups by offering a double-side, polyethylene-coated paper cup. The cups have the advantage of high luster, bright graphics, durability, and protection of drink flavors."

And *The Milwaukee Journal's* business page gave the story of polyethylene-coated cups a colorful PMC hook:

> Here's a word of warning for the slow, slow drinker: Stay away from McDonald's sodas. After three hours with liquid inside, the cups start buckling on the sides, and the wax begins to feel, well, very waxy.
>
> All this hardly matters, of course, to the ordinary consumer. . . . What it illustrates, though, is a change sweeping through the paper-cup business, a change in which Milwaukee's Paper Machinery Corporation plays a key role. It's the move from wax-coated cups to those coated inside and out with polyethylene.

"The Dixie Cups, the Lily-Tulips, and all these guys had been building machines for glue sealing and waxing for fifty years or more," says John. "Now these machines were obsolete because the market was going to double poly."

John began working at Paper Machinery at age nineteen, the third generation Baumgartner to join the family business. "At the time I started in '71, we were a very small company, two dozen employees in total. I was an apprentice at that time for guys that had worked for my grandfather, JR, and had come over from Mercury Engineering. I started in the spray booth, spray-painting, and I got very good at it. I would paint cars in the shop after hours. The mechanics would do the mechanical work and I'd do the bodywork, and between this collaboration, I was able to always have a used car that looked great and ran great.

"I then went over to the machine shop and was an apprentice on the engine lathes and milling machines," he adds. That lasted for a number of years. Then assembly, and, somewhere around '77, '78, I moved into the office into purchasing. By 1982, I had packed my briefcase and spent the next twenty years traveling the world, opening up more of the global, international business for us. I've gone the whole nine yards."

When the company began to fabricate its own machine parts as a way to run a self-sufficient shop, John was part of the transition. "We started buying some expensive machine tools from overseas to build parts," says Donald, "and John went overseas and found really good suppliers in Taipei and in Italy. And then, with all his foreign contacts and his experience in negotiating, he got involved in sales. From sales, into management, and from there he stepped up as president in 1999. He had a very thorough and complete knowledge of every part of the business, perhaps with the exception of our accounting department. But he went to school to study finance, and he learned about that as well."

PMC moved quickly to design and build machinery that made the new, double-lined poly cup. At the same time, it ramped up the speed of its machines. "Dad hired an engineer named Darryl Konzal, who brought new thinking to our engineering department," John says. "With Darryl, we developed a better mechanical drive, and we moved our speeds up incrementally from 200 cups per minute to 225 cups per minute, then to 240, then 275, then 300. And today, we're up to 330 cups per minute." The faster machines of course pleased their customers, old and new.

Donald and the PMC-1000, the company's workhorse machine.

Leading up to the 1980s, the paper cup industry saw multiple changes of ownership. With the rapid advancement of the machines that made the cups, the new generation of owners of the old-line paper cup companies finally saw the light: they were years behind. "The business people were now in charge," says Mike Kazmierski, senior vice president of sales at PMC. "And the business people said, 'This is lunacy. We're building the same machine we built in 1960. PMC has got a product that's faster, safer, more efficient, produces a higher quality product.'"

Abandoning their machine-building programs, Lily, Sweetheart, and the other majors started buying PMC machines in large quantities. "That," says Kazmierski, "was really when the floodgates opened for us."

While inking new deals with the biggest cup makers in North America, Paper Machinery also locked up a substantial share of markets overseas, installing machines in Europe (England, Spain, Italy, France, Finland, Poland, Turkey), Asia (Japan, South Korea, Taiwan, Thailand, Singapore), the Middle East (Israel, Saudi Arabia), South America (Columbia, Venezuela, Chile, Brazil, Argentina), and Central America (El Salvador, Honduras, Costa Rica, Jamaica), as well as Australia, Canada, Mexico, China, Cuba, and even Russia.

Around 1972, when PMC began focusing hard on foreign markets, about 90 percent of all paper cup-forming machines sold outside of North America were made in Germany. By the mid-1980s, PMC had sold some 550 machines to customers in twenty-six countries. Exports accounted for nearly one half of its sales.

Its workhorse machine, the PMC-1000, cost $325,000. It could turn out drinking cups and ice cream containers up to sixteen ounces at a speed of 200 per minute. According to numbers collected by the company for an ad campaign, a single PMC cup machine, in an eight-hour shift, could produce a nested stack of cups nearly twice as high as the Empire State Building.

"Don pioneered the growth of this company," PMC Vice President Ray Bonkoski told the *Milwaukee Business Journal* at the time. "He persisted through tough times with the idea of developing a commercial cup machine that could be sold to anyone, not just the handful of giants controlling the market."

On May 5, 1986, Donald received a Western Union Mailgram from Alfred H. Kingdon, the Cabinet Secretary and Deputy Assistant to President Ronald Reagan. "On behalf of President Reagan," it read, "I wish to extend to you an invitation to attend a ceremony in observance of World Trade Week and for the presentation of 'E' and 'E-Star' Awards. The ceremony will be held in the Rose Garden on Monday, May 19, at 11:30 a.m."

Paper Machinery Corporation had been selected as a recipient of the prestigious "President's 'E' Certificate for Exports." The national award was given each year to companies who had made "an outstanding contribution in the Export Expansion Program of the United States of America." As chairman and chief executive of PMC, Donald would be presented with the award personally by President Reagan, only the second time since 1961 that a sitting President would present an "E" Award personally to a Wisconsin company.

The awards date back to World War II, when the United States government presented the Army-Navy "E" Award to war plants in recognition of "Excellence in Production" of war equipment. The famous red-white-and-blue pennant bearing a big "E" was seen as a badge of patriotism. In 1961, President Kennedy revived the World War II "E" symbol as recognition to outstanding business exporters. The "E Star" was introduced in 1969 to honor past "E" Award winners for their continued export expansion.

The morning of May 19 was sunny and warm in Washington. Sitting on folding chairs next to Donald on the Rose Garden lawn were his wife, Donna, sister, Jean, and daughter, Kelly. Presiding over the ceremony was Malcolm Baldrige Jr., the U.S. Secretary of Commerce, who introduced the President.

"Good morning to all of you, and welcome to the White House," Reagan said to the small group of businessmen accepting the award. "It's an honor to have you join us to help celebrate World Trade Week. Together, we can underscore the significance of international trade to our nation and the world."

Never one to miss a chance to relive his Hollywood days, Reagan departed briefly from his proclamation. "By the way," he said, "I can't help but recall that in my former career, I had something to do with exporting for overseas markets myself. In those days, American motion pictures occupied more than 75 percent of the playing time of all the screens of the world. Unfortunately, the

President Ronald Reagan presents Donald Baumgartner with an award recognizing PMC's expanded export business. The May 1986 presentation in the White House Rose Garden was a crowning achievement in a string of awards for the company.

movies that we sent overseas sometimes, well, they weren't always successful. I had one called *Cattle Queen of Montana*. It lost something in Japanese."

Returning to his script, the President addressed the recipients. "The enforcement of our trade laws, vigorous trade talks with Japan and other nations—it is only right that we in government should make those efforts. But in truth, our nation would be nowhere without you—you who've shown such initiative in opening new international markets. You're proof that American business has never been afraid to compete, that our business community is as innovative, efficient, and competitive as any on Earth. My friends, for setting such high standards, I thank you."

The event was a thrill for Donald. "That was more damn fun. We were certainly not the only recipient of an award for foreign trade. But I got a chance to have Ronald Reagan hand me the award and shake hands with Ronald. He said a few words, and I thanked him and said a couple words back to him."

After the ceremony, the President returned to the Oval Office as the recipients and guests mingled in the Rose Garden, posing for pictures and drinking ice tea and lemonade (alas, served in glass tumblers, not paper cups). Commerce Secretary Baldrige stood for a snapshot with Donald, who wore a blue Armani suit, white shirt, and red silk tie. Donna, meanwhile, posed with the framed award in her arms.

It was all a too brief for Donna. She wanted to bask in the majesty of the moment. "There we were, after going through all the required security and name checks, in the Rose Garden," she says. "We were very titillated to be there, looking out at the expanse before us and the wrought iron fence excluding everyone else. We're seated, President Reagan arrives, says a few things. Names are called. Donald is called. He springs to his feet and walks briskly to the podium. Shakes hands. "Nice tie," says Ronald. Donald beams. Jean takes photos. And Donald says, let's go. I'm like, 'Huh? We just got here! When will you ever be on this side of the fence again?' He said he didn't want them to reconsider! We were out of there in a flash, the first to leave. I was waiting for my ice tea."

For Jean, though, the experience was more routine; she had been very active in Republican politics for years. "I had met President Reagan on several occasions," she says. "And one thing about Reagan, he was extremely

Attending the White House reception were, left to right, Donald's daughter, Kelly, sister Jean, and wife, Donna.

personable. I mean, he'd shake your hand and look you in the eye like he had all the time in the world to visit with you. He was quite the charmer."

More awards followed. In 1990, Paper Machinery was honored for its worldwide marketing in the annual Wisconsin Manufacturer of the Year awards, sponsored by Wisconsin Manufacturers & Commerce and the Virchow Krause accounting firm. The following year it received an award for "Competitive Excellence in International Business" from Price Waterhouse.

The year 1992 was particularly gratifying. PMC was named "Export Success Story of the Year" by the Packaging Machinery Manufacturers Institute. The World Packaging Organization gave the company its Worldstar for Packaging award, and the James River Corporation, a giant international paper company and packaging fabricator, presented PMC with a "Gold Key Award for Product Development" for designing and building a machine that made a Breyers ice cream package.

Paper Machinery had been moving into different sizes and shapes as companies came up with new ways to package their products. Retooling its existing machines, PMC produced containers with rounded corners, packages for M&Ms, Sunsweet Prunes, and Quaker Oats. Rectangular, oval, elliptical, or round, PMC's machines could turn out three-ounce mini-cups, ten-pound chicken tubs, and dozens of sizes in between. "It's a niche packaging business that's supported us over the years," says Kazmierski. "Sometimes it's been 15 percent of our business, and sometimes 5 percent of our business. But it's certainly been important to us, because it helped us develop different markets."

The highlight of the award season, however, was winning the Wisconsin Manufacturer of the Year Grand Award, the state's highest honor for a manufacturing company. Given Paper Machinery's recent achievements, the recognition was well-deserved and garnered dozens of letters of congratulations—letters from U.S. Congressman Tom Barrett, Milwaukee Mayor John Norquist, university professors, fellow manufacturers, law firms, and many others. The following spring Mayor Norquist signed a public notice proclaiming April 7, 1993, "Paper Machinery Corporation Day" in the city of Milwaukee.

Soon after, another letter showed up in Donald's mailbox. In a handwritten note, JR Baumgartner congratulated his son for his accomplishment.

> Dear Don,
>
> Just returned from a cruise to the Bahamas and found a letter from your office enclosing a copy of a Proclamation recognizing Paper Machinery Corporation as "Wisconsin Manufacturer of the Year."
>
> You have taken PMC far beyond anything I envisioned when we organized the company back in 1946.
>
> I want you to know that I am very proud of you and all your achievements as only a father could be. Thelma and I will return to our home in Wisconsin in May and will call you then.
>
> With love,
>
> Pop

The kudos kept coming, including two awards in 1993 that were personally satisfying to Donald—the Wisconsin's "World Entrepreneur of the Year" award, sponsored by Ernst & Young, *Inc. Magazine*, and Merrill Lynch; and the President's "E Star" Award for Excellence in Exporting, recognition given to past "E" Award recipients for their continued contribution to the Export Expansion Program. Donald would not attend a White House reception this time around.

The awards banquet for Entrepreneur of the Year was at the Pfister Hotel in downtown Milwaukee. Donald's father, JR, who was eighty-six, sat with his son at his table. Accepting the award, Donald gave a nod to JR. "He has been my mentor all my life."

In his hometown, his alma mater Shorewood High School honored him years later, for his achievements and services to the community. The high school devoted a day-long event in April 2018 to recognize Donald and four other "distinguished alumni" at a school assembly, luncheon, and awards ceremony. "We are very proud of their accomplishments and grateful for this opportunity to recognize them, as they help our students understand the importance of service to their community," said Shorewood School Superintendent Bryan Davis. Past honorees included U.S. Supreme Court Chief Justice William Rehnquist, U.S. Congressman and Secretary of Defense Les Aspin, and filmmakers Jim Abrahams,

At his alma mater, Shorewood High School, Donald is honored in 2018 as a "distinguished alumni" for his service to the community.

David Zucker. and Jerry Zucker, creators of the popular *Airplane!* and *The Naked Gun* series.

Months later, in recognition of his business acumen, he would be inducted into the Milwaukee organization BizStarts' Entrepreneur Hall of Fame. "The goal of the event," said Glenn Margraff, executive director, "is to celebrate entrepreneurship and communicate to generations of our citizens the importance of those who had the determination, persistence, and willingness to take the risks to start and grow a great company."

Impressed by PMC's Presidential "E" award and its foray into overseas markets, Milwaukee Mayor John Norquist asked Donald to co-chair his Advisory Council on International Trade. Donald traveled to Europe with Norquist several times to discuss trade options with business executives and government officials. Each time he paid his own way.

Donald had gotten to know the mayor shortly after his election in 1988. Donald had been scouting locations in the Milwaukee area for a new PMC headquarters, and Norquist was pitching industrial-zoned properties inside the city limits for PMC's plant.

One of their first trade missions was an eleven-day trip to Europe in December 1988. The itinerary included stops in France, Amsterdam, West Berlin, and East Berlin. The entourage consisted of Donald Baumgartner; John Norquist; Carl Mueller, the mayor's chief of staff; and Shirley Krug, a state senator from Milwaukee.

"They took me along as a token capitalist," Donald smiles.

Their visit to the Netherlands was to shore up support for Time Insurance, a Milwaukee company that had been recently acquired by a Dutch corporation. The Dutch firm was considering plans to move Time Insurance to Minneapolis. Meeting at the corporation's headquarters in the ancient city of Utrecht, the Milwaukee group appealed to the firm's executives to keep the company in Milwaukee. The executives apparently were impressed—Time Insurance and its employees stayed put.

The next stop was the town of Mulhouse in northeastern France, a designated Sister City to Milwaukee. Norquist was a train enthusiast, so his trade group traveled by train. "We don't need any reservations," he said to his trade ambassadors. "When we get to the station, I'll look at the schedule and figure out how to get us from the Netherlands down to France."

Norquist booked an overnight train to Mulhouse with sleeper cars, recalls Mueller, now a public relations executive in Milwaukee. "We figured, what the hell, we can sleep overnight and arrive fresh in the morning. Well, the trouble with that was, John picked a local by mistake, so it stopped every five miles. It stops, the brakes are screeching, and the cars are banging together. You're jostled around and wake up. People get off and on. It takes off. And you fall back asleep. Five minutes later, bang. It stops again. So we get up in the morning and we go to the dining car for breakfast. Everybody looks awful, and Donald is smiling. John turns to him and says, 'Donald, how did you sleep?' Donald says, 'Oh, I slept like a baby. I woke up every half hour and cried.'"

After two days in Berlin, the group was escorted by United States officials through the Brandenburg Gate into East Berlin. They stayed for five days. The date was December 17, 1988, a time of paramount historical significance, eleven months before the Berlin Wall would be torn down, allowing free access between the East and the West. East Berlin was in turmoil. The old Soviet Union was crumbling. The days of East German leader Erich Honecker were numbered. Norquist, Donald, and the rest decided to take a look at what the wall was like before it fell.

Norquist had been invited to East Berlin to visit the Mildred Harnack School, named for a Milwaukee native who had joined the Nazi resistance as Hitler came to power. When he was in the Wisconsin State Senate, Norquist had sponsored legislation honoring her courage as a Nazi resistor. He was invited to visit the school by the East German mayor.

Harnack met and married a German national in Wisconsin, then moved to Berlin with him in 1930. They became part of the famous resistance group the Red Orchestra, and were arrested by the Gestapo during World War II. Her husband was hung, and a few years later, Hitler himself ordered Harnack's execution.

Carl Mueller recalls a young student from another country approaching Donald in an international hotel, asking if he could exchange East German marks for U.S. currency. "We had been warned not to do that," Mueller says. "This guy was offering like fifty marks to the dollar. Don exchanged $100 worth. So the next day he asked this East German official, who was our official guide, to take us to a workers' bar. He wanted to see how the average workers lived and where they went to have a good time after work. Don asked the waiter how much a beer cost, and the waiter said two marks. Donald looked around the room and said, 'Well, give everybody in the bar a drink on me,' and he took out this big wad of East German cash.

"After he got done buying the round, it hardly put a dent in the wad, so he said, 'Now ask them what they want to eat. Give everyone something to eat.' So Donald became kind of famous in that workers' bar as a friend of the working man."

In essence, Donald had negotiated his own trade agreement, trading dollars for deutsche marks and boosting the local economy, buying food and beer for his newfound East Berlin comrades.

Paper Machinery's reputation as the best in the field was known internationally. Its awards got a lot of press in the industry, and PMC's own aggressive marketing and sales campaigns effectively edged out most of its competition. PMC's only serious competitors were two or three long-standing cup-machine makers in Germany.

So maybe it wasn't a surprise when a paper cup-forming company in Korea copied PMC's technology and started building and selling the cloned cup-making machines.

In 1992, PMC learned through a South Korean trade magazine that the paper cup manufacturer Hyun Jin in Seoul had introduced the HIC-150 paper cup-forming machine. The Korean machine was an exact duplicate of the PMC-1000, right down to the shape of the safety guards and the location of the controls and emergency stop buttons. The Korean company copied more than the machine itself. "The Hyun Jin sales literature and technical support information are direct lifts of our materials," Kazmierski said at the time. "PMC symbols and various shapes are used on their floor plans. I remember them well because I drew the plans myself back in 1982. They're exact copies, right down to the millimeter."

Paper Machinery had sold five PMC-1000s to Hyun Jin between 1979 and 1985. By reverse-engineering the machines—disassembling them, reproducing each part, and then building new machines that were precisely the same—the Korean cup maker sold their knockoffs at a price $100,000 less than PMC's in Singapore, Taiwan, Australia, Belgium, and other European companies.

Adding insult to injury, the magazine reported that the Korean government sponsored the reverse-engineering project with a $650,000 grant to Hyun Jin to help start up an export market for paper cup machines in South Korea.

Donald was furious. "We have factory workers right here in our plant whose families fought in the Korean War so that South Korea could have a democratic government," he said then. "I might expect this behavior from the North Koreans. But I can't accept it being sponsored by the South Korean government—our allies."

With its PMC-1000s selling for $700,000 apiece, Paper Machinery stood to lose millions of dollars in business if the Koreans continued to poach their customers. Immediately Donald and John put together a battle plan. They instructed their engineering team to upgrade the PMC-1000's technology and increase its speed. They shortened their production schedule and cut the cost of the machine to undercut the Korean's price advantage. They informed their customers about Hyun Jin's actions. And, through the Wisconsin Department of Development, they lodged a complaint with the South Korean government.

Within a month, Korea's assistant minister of Trade, Industry, and Energy responded, saying an investigation had been launched. Although the Korean government questioned Paper Machinery's intellectual property rights to the PMC-1000 and denied subsidizing Hyun Jin with a $650,000 grant (it claimed it was a development loan from a commercial bank), the ministry said it recommended that Hyun Jin halt production of its PMC knockoff, and the company agreed to no longer make the HIC-150.

Mike Wallace with the CBS news show *60 Minutes* caught wind of the Korean controversy and set up an interview with Donald to discuss that and steel tariffs. He arrived at PMC with a camera crew one day and recorded the segment, but it didn't air, scooped, evidently, by some bigger news event. Wallace, though, was impressed with Donald's performance. "They told me you'd be good," the newsman said, "and you were. You spoke in perfect sound bites."

The Korean concession was a half-hearted victory. "The United States government got the Korean government and Hyun Jin to agree that they would only build the machines for internal use at their own cup factory, but a year later I'm at a machine tool show in Hong Kong, and who's advertising their machine? Hyun Jin. All they did is change the name of the machine. They called it the HC-1000."

Although the Koreans are bit players in the international market, they're still an aggravation to John and Donald—perhaps the cost of doing business in an international market when you're at the top of the heap.

"They are to this day still offering cup machines based on our stolen design," Donald says. "They're the same as our old design, not our new design. From a technical standpoint, they're way behind us. But they do exist."

In the early 1990s, as the American public embraced public recycling programs, the paper-versus-plastic debate reached the executive offices of PMC. Foam and plastic cups had become popular a decade earlier in fast-food restaurants, convenience stores, hospitals, schools, and workplaces. Extruded polystyrene foam, or Styrofoam, was thin, light, and a good insulator. It could be colored or clear, didn't sweat with cold drinks or condense with hot drinks.

Paper Machinery started making plastic cups in the '80s for Amoco Foam Products, altering its paper cup-forming machines to process Styrofoam instead of paper. "Their marketing theme was 'one cup' for hot and cold," says PMC's Kazmierski. "And they went to McDonald's and said, 'You don't need two different cups in your system.' But because this cost more than the paper cup did at the time, it really never took off the way they hoped it would. So they used it in their food shops at Amoco gas stations. We gave them a worldwide exclusivity on the technology in return for buying a number of machines per annum."

Amoco and others in the plastic packaging industry claimed foam plastics were better for the environment than paper or glass. According to the Polystyrene Council, the production of foam requires less energy and water than paper or glass. Foam can be made with waste chemicals instead of trees or minerals, and without chlorofluorocarbons (CFCs), which contribute to global warming. By comparison, the production of paper, said the council, requires large amounts of fossil fuels and chemicals that leach into landfills.

On the other side of the debate, opponents of plastic argued that paper could be more efficiently recycled or reused, and would degrade in landfills, unlike plastic products. Environmentalists decried the ever-expanding landfills and poor waste management practices, pointing to the debacle of the garbage-laden barge called *The Mobro* that cruised up and down the East Coast in 1987 looking for a place to unload.

By the late 1980s and early '90s, public opinion began to shift away from the use of plastic containers. In 1988, the first ban of polystyrene foam was enacted in Berkeley, California. Two years later McDonald's stopped using containers made with CFCs. Other companies soon followed suit.

"Foam cups are not environmentally friendly, so a lot of people are switching from foam to paper," says Scott Koehler, PMC's chief financial officer. "But if you think about it, it's not just the environmental end of it, it's also the aesthetics. Starbucks isn't going to sell a five-dollar cup of coffee in a white foam cup. It's not going to work. They want a nice, colorful paper cup with their logo on it. That's a product feature. As drinking coffee becomes more of an experience, it's about way more than the coffee. There's a marketing aspect to it as well."

While it built several machines that formed foam plastic cups, Paper Machinery was true to its namesake. "The foam cup that was ubiquitous in all of the fast food operations was not ours. We had nothing to do with it," says Donald. "Even though the foam plastic cup was cheap, and had good insulating qualities—you could pour scalding hot coffee in it and hold it—it had the major disadvantage of being a nightmare to dispose of. With a lot of help from the environmental people, we moved plastic cups out of fast foods and got into paper."

The anti-foam sentiment brought millions of dollars of business to Paper Machinery. Says Kazmierski, "We've developed technology to form two-piece paper cups that are wrapped with an insulated sleeve. So the cup has the thermal properties of a foam cup but it's 100 percent paper. If you go to McDonald's and buy a coffee, you'll get that cup, produced on our machines."

For bucking the foam plastic trend, Donald was presented with the honorary degree of Doctor of Public Service by Northland College, a small, liberal arts school on the shore of Lake Superior in Ashland, Wisconsin. On the diploma, college president Robert Rue Parsonage applauded Donald for his "high environmental standards" and devotion to community. "We celebrate the entrepreneurial abilities and the ethical judgment you exercise in promoting low-impact appropriate technology over more wasteful materials and methods."

Standing at the podium in a black graduation gown, Donald accepted the honorary degree with humor and grace, imparting a measure of common sense to the Class of 1991:

> One of the things that pleases me most about this recognition is that it cuts against the grain. It runs contrary to expectations. How has it come to pass that Northland College, with its strong dedication to environmental protection, is honoring a Milwaukee industrialist?
>
> What am I doing near the shores of this beautiful lake, standing in front of a large contingent of what many of my business associates would term tree-huggers?
>
> I have learned that things are not always what they seem. What passes for conventional wisdom, as often as not, is simply a lack of imagination.
>
> I am standing before you today because I have not hesitated to choose what Robert Frost called "the Road Less Traveled." And, as he said, "That has made all the difference."
>
> The Grateful Dead would put it differently: As they say, "What a long strange trip it's been."
>
> I am an entrepreneur who made my fortune by focusing on paper at a time when plastics was clearly identified as the way of the future. I began by trying to perfect machinery to manufacture paper cups.
>
> Everyone else in my generation had seen "The Graduate" with Dustin Hoffman, and heard that the future was clearly in plastics. I must have missed the

movie, so I kept working with paper. My competitors focused their research and development on plastics—and created a great opportunity for me.

We marketed our products aggressively. Today, nearly 600 of our machines are in operation, literally around the globe. . . . We have worked hard, we have challenged popular misconceptions—and we have become known to the world in our field.

Finally, let me address the idea that business people and environmentalist are natural enemies. Members of both groups are guilty of harboring that kind of attitude. I've heard business people claim that if environmentalists had their way no one would have a job, our factories would all be idle, and our standard of living would be set back fifty years.

I have heard environmentalists denounce all corporations and business people as being motivated solely by profit and having a callous disregard for what tomorrow may bring for their employees or our environment.

I like to think that you can be an industrialist and an environmentalist. At a time when the populace at large is finally beginning to focus on our fragile eco-system, I am proud that for forty years my company has been in the forefront of promoting an environmentally sound, renewable resource.

There is a place within society that needs your skills and know-how. Find that place, defend your actions, and make this world a better place.

In 1995, Wisconsin became one of the first states to prohibit recyclable materials from being added to landfills. The ban included all plastic containers, including those made of polystyrene foam.

After nearly forty years doing business in the same brick and concrete-block building, Paper Machinery Corporation was ready to move. It had been a long time coming. Going back to the start of Milwaukee Shipbuilding, the plant on Lancaster Avenue on Milwaukee's northwest side was overcrowded with machinery and employees.

"We kept growing at that location," says Donald. "We bought the buildings on either side, and built an addition in the back. We kept adding to it." By the late 1980s, there was no more room to expand. More than 100 employees worked in the plant.

"It was hot down at the old place. We didn't have air conditioning," says Craig Johnson, who worked as an assemblyman, assembly foreman, and then plant supervisor from 1972 through 2013. "Everybody would be sweating, and Don would come in around 2:30 and say, 'Put a quarter-barrel of beer on.' So we put a quarter-barrel of beer on. The guys wouldn't have to punch out until 3:30, so they got the last hour of the day drinking beer and cooling off."

Paper Machinery outgrew its longtime plant on Lancaster Avenue.

Construction of a new corporate headquarters and manufacturing plant began in 1989 on a vacant parcel in the Bradley Woods Industrial Park. Situated at the corner of 91st Street and Bradley Road, the building was finished in February 1990, open for business. At 90,000 square feet, it was nearly double the size of the former plant. Yet in coming years, the plant would be expanded three times as PMC continued to grow. Nearly thirty years later, the red brick building retains a timeless quality. The west side of the building, which houses an atrium entryway and suite of offices, echoes the design of Frank Lloyd Wright's "prairie style" architecture. A low-slung roof over a horizontal row of adjoining windows overlooks a rolling parkway along the Little Menomonee River. The landscape was brilliantly designed, conceived by Brian Gore, whose father, Don, was a former employee of PMC. Donald's spacious office, with a fireplace and wall of glass, faces south onto an outdoor fountain and reflecting pool.

In the massive, newly air-conditioned production facility, a bank of windows just below the ceiling allows for natural light, while a colorful, hand-painted mural by Milwaukee graphic artist Richard Taylor wraps around the entire upper part of the wall. Despite the constant whir of the cup-forming machines, spitting out samples of paper cups faster than a major league baseball pitcher, the production floor is quiet and clean.

In the office suite, a curated collection of fifty-nine early twentieth century stone lithographs and models of early-1900s steamships bedeck the hallways and create a nautical theme, a nod to the early days of Milwaukee shipbuilding. Nearby a display case holds a small collection of drafting tools, historic photographs, and articles of the company's beginnings. Included is a photo of John Robert Baumgartner, with a quotation: "In your business as in ours, to stand still is fatal—to rest on past achievements is to invite others to move in and take over."

As construction of the new PMC headquarters neared completion, Donald was having a hard time finding a buyer for the plant on Lancaster Avenue. It was old, and the neighborhood around it had degenerated. One day, while in the weight room at the Milwaukee Athletic Club, another club member, a local businessman, struck up a conversation.

Paper Machinery's newly constructed headquarters opened in 1990, a modernized, spacious facility for the expanding company.

The PMC building included landscaped grounds and a fountain.

"This guy told me he was looking for storage facilities, but he didn't have any money to spend. I said, 'Well, I have a building.' And he said, 'Well, I have an empty lot. Maybe we can work out a deal.' It turns out he had fifteen acres of undeveloped land near Vail, Colorado. Donna and I flew out there. I looked at his lot, and I said to myself, *Let me see: The building on Lancaster Avenue, or fifteen acres on the top of this mountain, a few minutes from some of the best skiing in the world? I'll take the fifteen acres on top of the mountain.* So we traded even up. He even threw in $400 in cash to sweeten the deal.

"That property on Lancaster was not really saleable. I was lucky to get rid of it at all. But he needed a loading dock and storage place for all these containers of novelty items he was selling. He was stuck for a spot, and he was glad to get it."

Around the same time, Donald and Donna purchased a 9,000-square-foot house in the Village of River Hills. Although the trend at the time was to downsize, the Baumgartners decided to move to the quiet, green grandeur of a fifteen-acre estate.

The house had been built in 1929 by architect Thomas Van Alyea, Sr. Its previous owner had moved to California, leaving it in the hands of caretakers for nearly three years. So while living in their home on Milwaukee's east side, the Baumgartner's newly acquired, two-story, lannon stone mansion became a major remodeling project.

"It was a nightmare," he said. "We had to re-plumb everything. We had to rewire everything. We had to do a whole new heating and central air-conditioning system. All the mechanicals were redone 100 percent. The furnace ducts in the basement were filled with asbestos. What a mess. I had no idea what I was getting into when I bought the house. It looked nice, but nobody had done a damned thing to it." A general contractor and an interior designer, John Schlanghaft, was hired to oversee the renovation on the inside.

Outside, the house's red-tile roof, as brittle as potato chips, was replaced with a slate roof. "The house was surrounded by grass and a few evergreen hedges," says Donna. "Donald looked at this and in his mind, he saw something completely different—an Italian *palazzo*. He created a lannon stone terrace with columns and sitting walls that connect and descend to the pool terrace. I had no frame of reference for what he was doing. This was entirely his vision,

The Baumgartners remodeled their 9,000-square-foot home top to bottom and added a rose garden labyrinth, gazebo, and interconnected system of creeks and ponds on the grounds.

and it was perfect. It was absolutely grand. We added a fountain in a reflecting pool. Several rooms were reconfigured, and a few interior walls torn out. But the house's original footprint remained the same.

"We worked with a Belgian landscape architect named Francois Goffinet," she adds. "The main terrace was defined by twin knot gardens at the base of two Bartlett pear trees. The terrace opens up to nearly five acres of manicured lawn. We planted a rose garden, with seventy rose bushes, and a continuous flowering 'Kitchen Garden' enclosed by a maze of boxwood hedges planted with dahlias, phlox, penstemon, cosmos, delphinium, and allium, of all varieties and colors." An iron gazebo from the 1850s, discovered by Donna on the roof of a building in New York's Soho neighborhood, was installed to anchor these parterre gardens.

Today the estate is dotted with sculptures, antique garden statuary, bronze planters, and benches and is comprised of a system of interconnecting pathways that circumnavigate the property. A natural overflow was converted into a recirculating water feature creating two ponds, which are in turn used as irrigation.

The remodeling project took close to two years to complete.

As if Donald didn't have enough to do, he and Donna decided to build a log house on their Colorado lot to use as a ski lodge and vacation retreat. "Donald was very frustrated with the lack of progress remodeling our house," says Donna. "In order to divert his energies, we focused on the Colorado project to keep him from pulling his hair out. We both loved skiing and, with the kids, had been just about everywhere from northern Wisconsin to the Rockies to St. Moritz, Switzerland. This was a natural."

Plans called for a three-story, 10,000-square-foot house with views of the snow-capped Gore and Sawatch mountain ranges to the east and the south. As part of their design scheme, they instructed their builder to use materials native to the Rocky Mountain region when possible. The final design included rocks from local rivers, fieldstone from a nearby creek, Colorado buff sandstone, Engelmann spruce, and lodge-pole pine.

The property is not far from the picturesque ski town of Vail and abuts the White River National Forest. The logs themselves—culled from dead standing timber—were milled in Montana. It took seven tractor-trailer loads to haul the logs to the site, and a crew of fifteen to assemble them into the shell of a house.

A log home built near Vail, Colorado, is a mountain haven and ski lodge for Donald and Donna's family and friends.

Inside, contemporary conveniences and modern technology, including a pool table, home theater room, and Jacuzzi, blend with Western native themes and authentic Germantown Navajo rugs, antique Indian artifacts, a collection of late nineteenth century stone lithographs of Buffalo Bill Cody as well as other late nineteenth century cowboy-themed stone lithographs, and a collection of mid-nineteenth century Tramp Art. A twenty-five-foot river-rock fireplace anchors the vaulted-ceilinged great room, a giant elk head mounted on the stone, the inspiration for the name of the house, Elkhead. The saloon on the lower level was furnished from old, shuttered ranches. Many of the treasured finds were acquired by Claire (Stanley) Van Hee, an interior designer who was originally from Milwaukee.

"The opportunity to have a home in Colorado was perfect timing," Donald says. "It allowed us to house the whole extended family at Thanksgiving and Christmas with enough ceiling height to accommodate a fourteen-foot tree. Skiing with the family was one thing, skiing with our 'Family of Choice' was another. The FOCs included Suzy and Ron Walter, Kathy and Robo Brumder, Lori and Bruce Gendelman, Jamie and Joan Hummert,

The Baumgartners hosted a group of close friends, their "Family of Choice," every year at their Colorado home.

and John and Andy Grant. We would gather every third week in January for our annual love-and-ski fest year after year. That was always the highpoint of the season for us."

"We rebuilt our house on Dean Road, we built from scratch the house in Colorado, and we built the factory on Bradley Road all in the same year," he adds. "I had my hard hat on the whole time."

He wouldn't retire his hard hat for very long. In 1990, in the midst of his construction projects, Donald had joined the Milwaukee Art Museum's board of trustees, and already there was talk about expanding the museum into something much more grand and notable.

CHAPTER 9

Encore Performance

onald saw his first opera when he was a teenager. He had a friend named Dolores Anello, whose father happened to be the founder of Milwaukee's first opera company, the Italian Opera Chorus. "Dolores and I were buddies," says Donald. "She dragged me down to see Verdi's *Il Trovatore* when we were in high school."

Dolores' father, John-David Anello, conducted the Italian Opera Chorus. Established in 1933, it was renamed the Florentine Opera Company in 1950, a nod to the birthplace of opera.

Donald recalls the night of the performance. "I'm sitting in the theater, practically in the first row, and I fell asleep during *The Anvil Chorus* in the second act. It's also known as the *Gypsy Chorus* when the Gypsies strike their anvils singing the praises of hard work, good wine, and Gypsy women. It's a very famous chorus, and very boisterous. John Anello knows where his daughter is sitting. He looks over his shoulder at her and he sees me conked out. Afterwards, at the end of the performance, we go backstage, and he says to me, 'I have never seen anybody sleep through *The Anvil Chorus*.' I got better at staying awake as I learned more about opera, and I came to enjoy it."

"Enjoy" is an understatement. Within a few years after attending his sleep-induced first opera, Donald had become a full-blown opera enthusiast and a fixture at Florentine's performances. Anna Netrebko, who was once his dinner companion in Vail, tops his list of favorite divas. Certain arias move him to tears; *Madame Butterfly*, for one, with the tear-jerking soprano aria "Un bel di vedremo" (One Fine Day). He had the pleasure of chatting with and escorting Beverly Sills when she was in Milwaukee, and a few years ago flew with Donna to Vienna to see Elina Garanca perform a favorite opera, *Carmen*.

After Donald and Donna married, their interests in the arts began to converge. Donna, an early lover of the ballet in Chicago, started volunteering at the Milwaukee Ballet, and through Donald, she became acquainted with the world of opera. Donald joined the Florentine's board of directors, and the two of them began to sponsor events and then performances.

Florentine Opera Company

Bill Florescu ran the Florentine Opera Company beginning in 2005 as general director. A former operatic singer and arts administration in Columbus, Ohio, he met the Baumgartners when he was still new to the Florentine.

"My first opera would have been Beethoven's *Fidelio* in the fall of 2005," says Florescu, who resigned in May 2018. "We had a pre-opera dinner for board members and friends. Donald and Donna came in a little bit late. They had just returned from a trip to Vietnam. Donald was waxing eloquently about all the fantastic food they'd had, and he was very exuberant and jazzed about the trip. I remember telling my wife that this was somebody who takes a bite out of life. You come across people in that strata sometimes who seem unapproachable. You feel they're talking to you from their level down to where you are. Never once have Donald and Donna made me feel that way. They're just incredibly friendly."

Asked to cast Donald as an operatic character, Florescu chooses Figaro from *The Barber of Seville*, another of Donald's favorites. "Donald's very charitable. And he likes the good things in life. I sometimes kid my wife and say, If I was ever going to be a wealthy person, that would be the model of who I'd want to be. I have no danger of that happening, by the way."

The oldest professional performing arts group in Wisconsin and the sixth oldest opera company in the country, the Florentine Opera has staged hundreds of performances in Milwaukee, from the best known—*Aida, Carmen, Tosca, Rigoletto, La Traviata*—to the esoteric, *Of Mice and Men, The Crucible, Wuthering Heights,* and *Sister Carrie,* a 2017 world premiere.

A lifelong opera fan, Donald met one of his favorite singers, Anna Netrebko, in Vail.

More than 150 featured artists have performed with the company over the years, and several international superstars have sung with the Florentine, including Jose Carreras, Placido Domingo, Marisa Galvany, Luciano Pavarotti, and Beverly Sills. Its mainstage performances are accompanied by the Milwaukee Symphony Orchestra (since this writing they are now working with the Milwaukee Ballet Orchestra) in Uihlein Hall at the Marcus Center for the Performing Arts. A company chorus of forty-five artists performs in mainstage productions as well as community events and education programs.

A few years ago, Florescu and his wife, Roberta Ricci, started a "mini-tradition" of meeting Donald and Donna in Italy every summer for the annual Verona opera festival at the Arena di Verona, constructed in the first century AD. "The Florentine does a gala every year, a fundraiser," Florescu says, "and I was going to do a master class in Italy in the summer of 2014. We decided it would be neat to have one of the gala items be a trip to the opera in Verona with my wife and I hosting. Well, Donald and Donna won it, so we did it and they loved it. They love the big, traditional operas. I was going back there for a second year and said to them, 'You know, if you'd like, we're going go again,' and so we did it again. Then in 2017, it was really on a whim. I called Donald. I said, 'Hey, look. We love Verona. We're going to go back. Would you like to go?' And they said, 'Sure,' like I was asking them to go to Bartolotta's for dinner or something.

"It just evolved," Florescu adds. "We've been three times. The first time we went we saw *Turandot* and *Aida*, and the second time we saw *Nabucco* and *Aida*, and this last time we saw *Tosca* and *Aida*. The festival does *Aida* every year. It's like their *Nutcracker*. So I take care of getting the tickets, we figure out where to meet, and then Donald gets dinner. We have a restaurant we love where the amarone and branzino is fabulous. It's called Nastro Blu, which is 'Blue Ribbon' in Italian. It became an annual dinner for us."

Under the direction of Florescu, and with some financial backing from the Baumgartners, the Florentine began recording performances that were staged at the Marcus Center. The recordings were then produced into studio-engineered CDs and released internationally by Naxos Records, one of the largest classical record labels in the world. Remarkably, in 2012, the Florentine won two Grammy Awards for its CD, the soundtrack of its production *Elmer Gantry*. The recording won top awards for Best Engineered Classical Recording and Best Contemporary Classical Composition, by composer Robert Aldridge.

The two couples—Donald and Donna, Bill and Roberta—flew to Los Angeles for the Grammy presentations. Awards for classical music and less splashy awards were held at noon at the Convention Center downtown next to the Staples Center, where the top awards would be televised and handed out in the evening.

"As it turns out, they have two red carpets," Donna says, "one for the Hollywood stars, and then one for everyone else. The pre-televised awards were at the Convention Center, black tie. It was a free-for-all, no assigned seats. But we scrambled and got front-row seats. We saw Taylor Swift and

The Baumgartners met Florentine Opera's general director, Bill Florescu, and his wife, Roberta Ricci, in Verona, Italy, for the annual opera festival in the ancient Arena di Verona.

Bon Iver, Foo Fighters, Ed Sheeran, Joyce DiDonato, Lady Antebellum, and Tony Bennett perform. We were sitting right there when we found out we won. They had a screen drop down with the list of nominees. When it scrolled down to *Elmer Gantry*, it listed the Florentine Opera as the winner. So we found out on the spot. It was a great moment. A while later, opera star Joyce DiDonato sang, and the audience jumped to their feet in a standing ovation. It was if they had never heard a voice of that quality." The Florentine's recording was nominated in three categories; it won two out of the three. "It was one of the coolest, coolest moments of my life," says Florescu.

Following the afternoon show, the couples walked next door to the Staples Center for the Big Event, the internationally televised 54th Annual Grammy Award. It was the year of Whitney Houston's sudden death the day before. Adele and Taylor Swift had big wins, as did Kanye West, Swift's nemesis. (She won in the Best Country Song category for her composition "Mean.") The band Bon Iver from Eau Claire, Wisconsin, got the Grammy for the Best Alternative Music Album.

Donald and Donna support the Florentine's production of live operatic recordings into CDs. In 2012, the Florentine won two Grammy Awards for its recording of Elmer Gantry. *The Baumgartners attended the awards ceremony in Los Angeles.*

After capturing two gold-plated statutes, the glitzy Hollywood event was a bit of a letdown for the Baumgartners. "We lost our front row perch," says Donald. And the Staples Center was no Arena di Verona. "It's an NBA basketball arena," Donna says. "You could get chips at the counter, but there was no place to sit and eat. There was this little ledge to lean on, and we were eating nacho chips and dribbling all over ourselves. It was very funny. It was like we got all dressed up, Donald in a tuxedo and me in a red velvet dress, to go to a basketball game. And there we sat, up in the nosebleed section. The lighting guy was from Milwaukee, and we were texting about the upcoming acts and what not to miss. Jennifer Hudson ended the program singing Whitney's 'I Will Always Love You.' It was a very cool moment."

In 2012, the Florentine Opera moved its administrative offices from a glassy downtown office building to a nineteenth-century industrial complex in Milwaukee's revitalized Riverwest neighborhood. Several of the cream city brick buildings, occupied by a high-end furniture manufacturer, La Lune Collection, were eventually renovated for the Florentine's rehearsal studio and production center. Meanwhile, around the corner is a remodeled, two-story neighborhood house named Casa di Opera, home of four emerging opera singers enrolled in the Florentine's Studio Artists Program.

Donald, having been involved with the opera since 1991, is now a life director on the Florentine's board. In November 2017, he and Donna gave $1.5 million to support the Donald and Donna Baumgartner Studio Artists Program. Every two years the program selects four young operatic singers from hundreds of applicants around the country to train and perform at the Florentine's center.

"The company was transformed in my time there," Florescu says. "We were the traditional opera box company, 'opera box' meaning you rent sets, you do a big, great opera at the Marcus Center, and the rest of the year you pretty much aren't heard from. Now they are really part of the neighborhood. They rehearse next door and also have a whole concert series there. The administrative office is there." In addition to mainstage productions, the Florentine offers programming in the community and in schools, reaching about 40,000 people a year with free and reduced-cost programming.

In addition to spreading the voice of opera around the city, the Florentine Opera Company in September 2017 released its fourth recording, a CD of Robert Aldridge and Herschel Garfein's Sister Carrie, produced from performances in October 2016 by Naxos Records, aiming for yet another Grammy or two.

Milwaukee Ballet

Before moving to Milwaukee and marrying Donald, Donna had been following ballet in Chicago. She wept at one of her first ballets with her mother, the American Ballet Theatre's performance of *Giselle*, with special guests Margot Fonteyn and Rudolf Nureyev. Since the late 1980s, she has been a board member of the Milwaukee Ballet and has served on its executive committee.

Donna, a Milwaukee Ballet board member, met at the Ballet studios, with Wendy Whelan, a legendary dancer with the New York City Ballet. Whelan retired from the company in 2014 after dancing for more than thirty years.

Donna and Donald also support the Vail International Dance Festival, where they have sponsored some of the country's top ballet stars, such as Tiler Peck with New York City Ballet and Herman Cornejo with American Ballet Theatre. They have attended the festival nearly every summer since they first acquired their mountain property.

Donald's support of the Milwaukee Ballet started when he was living on the east side in the 1970s. He was approached for a donation by a board member and neighbor, Pat Van Alyea. "I think I gave $3,000, which to me at the time was like $3 million," he says. "It was actually the first major contribution I made to the arts. So after that I had to follow my money. I had to go see what the hell I was buying. I started going to the ballet."

Like Bill Florescu, Michael Pink, the artistic director of Milwaukee Ballet, has grown to know and admire the Baumgartners as personal friends and benefactors. They're in his corner, and the Ballet is enriched by their involvement. Their friendship stirs new ideas, and occasionally inspires collaboration within the city's rarefied arts community.

"I met them as part of my interview process when I came here in the middle of 2002," says Pink, a native of England. "I went to an event at their house. To host an event like this was a wonderful way to network and for them to introduce visiting artists and new employees of the Ballet. I'd just come over from England to do my interview, and literally four days prior to that, my third child had been born. We lived in the country in an old English farmhouse. We'd elected to do a home birth and so, my daughter, Georgina, arrived two weeks early—and very, very efficiently. My wife, Jayne, is a former dancer, so she's very fit. We actually delivered Georgina at our home by ourselves. When I arrived here, I shared this story with Donald. He looked at me and—this is rather crass, but—he said, 'Well, it makes sense. You put it in. You should take it out.' I knew I was going to like him immediately. Not one person in the room batted an eyelid."

To be effectual philanthropists, hard choices are required. How do you say no? How do you say yes? How do you keep to your mission? "For Donald and Donna, so much of it is about personal taste and preferences. I think if they were an established foundation it would be very much a different scenario," Pink says. "I've always felt I can go to them and ask

Used with permission of the Milwaukee Ballet

Donna and Donald with Michael Pink, artistic director of Milwaukee Ballet.

specifically for one-off gifts for something. It could be a small amount or a large amount, and they really will just think about the impact of that gift to the organization, to the recipients, to the artists."

Beginning in 2015, three consecutive seasons have been presented by Donna and Donald Baumgartner. Their donation was substantial. Yet, as active sponsors, they're mindful of what it costs for a local arts group to keep the lights on. Literally. On one occasion Pink asked Donald if he would chip in $5,000 for lighting in the rehearsal studio. "Just a few electrical bits and light rigging and away you go. It's very low key and just gives us an opportunity to do things in house. Donald understood the benefit of it. He and Donna have sat in that room year after year, watching little performances of the up-and-coming dancers in our training academy, these young hopefuls taking the first major steps into their careers."

Since it was founded in 1970, Milwaukee Ballet has become one of the city's principal performing arts groups. Along with its crowd-pleasing yearly productions of *The Nutcracker*, its bold interpretations of "story" ballets under Pink's directorship have been lauded internationally as vanguard presentations, as demonstrated in his adaptions of classics such as *Peter Pan*, *Dorian Gray*, *Snow White*, and *Beauty and the Beast*.

The Ballet presents more than forty performances to more than 50,000 people each year, and is one of the few dance companies in the country to maintain its own symphony orchestra. In 2018, the Ballet's resident company includes twenty-four professional dancers along with twenty trainees in its Nancy Einhorn Milwaukee Ballet II program, a second company of "next generation" dancers. The Milwaukee Ballet's School & Academy is the only professional ballet school in the Midwest that is fully accredited by the National Association of Schools of Dance. It trains more than 600 students a year.

Donna and Donald rarely seem to compete. Instead, they complete each other as partners and as companions, challenging while accommodating each other's opinions and choices. "They are a perfect couple that complement each other," Pink says. "Initially, I thought Donna was very much silently behind Donald," Pink says. "Donald is a larger-than-life character, and Donna is this beautiful woman who's there by his side. Donald has these one-liners and Donna is very thoughtful, quiet, and just seems to understand how to facilitate things, how to make things work. I find her direct and honest, and that's really helpful, because you rely on people to give you straight and honest answers. Which comes back to Donald. That's what you get with Donald: There's no pulling the punches. He's kind of sage, very wise. He's not telling you what to do, but he's giving you pearls of wisdom."

Donald and Donna ham it up with Milwaukee Ballet's cast and crew during the 2015 production of Dracula.

Both used with permission of the Milwaukee Ballet

Donald and Donna have toured the world, soaking in different cultures, visiting world-class museums, attending performances in beautiful opera houses and concert halls. "They bring that wealth of cultural experience back to Milwaukee," says Pink. "For the Baumgartners, their world truly is *the* world. To some degree, when we first came here, you could argue, 'How much does Donald really know about ballet?' But actually, the more you get to know him, the more you see he has such a wealth of knowledge about art, photography, his wines, his cars. He has a real, heartfelt knowledge of these things.

"Donald loves all things that are very beautiful, and there are no more beautiful things on two legs than ballerinas, as a physical art form. He has a keen eye to seeing what is quality ballet, what is accomplished. He appreciates real artistry."

As its programs progressed over the years, Milwaukee Ballet outgrew its storefront headquarters on the city's near South Side, and in August 2017, plans were released for the construction of a new center. The company purchased a site for a reported $2.4 million in Milwaukee's historic Third Ward, a vibrant, commercial-residential neighborhood bordering the Lake Michigan shoreline just south of downtown. A two-story, 52,000-square-foot brick building will house the Ballet's offices, seven rehearsal studios, the School & Academy, and Community Engagement outreach programs. Performances would continue at the Marcus Center. Deeply committed to the Ballet, Donna and Donald contributed an extraordinary gift of $10 million toward the new building—named the Baumgartner Center for Dance—their largest philanthropic gift to date.

"There's no question, the Baumgartners are among the circle of people who are the heartbeat of the arts and philanthropic giving," Pink says. "Donald and Donna like to also connect people. They join people together in their home."

Steadfast and straight talking, Donald seldom lets his ego get in the way of relationships. He unquestionably enjoys his role as humanitarian. "I sat with Donald not too long ago when he and Donna did an Open Gardens event for the National Garden Conservancy," Pink says, "where people could wander around the gardens at their home. Donald sat there all day on the patio at the back. I sat with him. We just sat and talked about anything and everything. There were dancers who danced around the garden making everything look alive and beautiful. He was making it all a pleasure, not standing up and saying, 'This is my house, rah, rah, and welcome to the manor.' It wasn't Lord Grantham from *Downton Abbey* or anything like that. He was just enjoying people, enjoying what he had done."

Milwaukee Film Festival

Donald considers himself a film buff. He watches movies of all kinds—features, documentaries, shorts, foreign films. "I go from director to director and just go through Amazon or Netflix or whatever's available. I look at several movies a week. I always have," he says. Preparing for a trip to Spain once, he watched several movies by the Spanish filmmaker Pedro Almodóvar.

Film runs in the family. Donald's son-in-law, Jeff Fitzsimmons, has studied film production and worked in the industry in Dallas and Seattle. He sits on the board of Milwaukee Film, which presents the Milwaukee Film Festival each fall, and, with Donald's daughter, Kelly Fitzsimmons, and filmmaker Brad Lichtenstein, runs a virtual reality filmmaking company, Custom Reality Services.

Donna likewise is into films. She and Donald were members of Milwaukee Film, the parent organization of the festival. In its early days, they were not sponsors.

Jonathan Jackson was hired to run the Milwaukee Film Festival in August 2008. Raised in Cleveland "on a diet of blockbuster movies," he says, his tastes evolved in college when he discovered independent and foreign films. He transferred to the University of Wisconsin-Milwaukee's film department in 1998, and worked as program manager for the UWM Union Theatre for three years before signing on with the Milwaukee International Film Festival in 2003 until its demise in 2007.

His first interaction with Donald and Donna in early 2012 was eye opening. Jackson had met the Baumgartners briefly at Milwaukee Film Festival events, introduced by Bill and Carmen Haberman. The Habermans co-founded the Festival with Chris Abele, Milwaukee County Executive. They remain on the festival's board of directors and suggested that Jackson ask the Baumgartners for a contribution.

"So I arranged a meeting alone to go visit them at their house," Jackson says. "I was still pretty green as a fundraiser and a leader of a nonprofit. I come up to their house. One of the nicest homes I've ever seen. And Donna greets me at the door with their dog, Lola. I laid out my plans to them for the short term and long term of the festival. I explained that I understood their great support and leadership with the Milwaukee Art Museum, the Florentine, and the Ballet, and how we at Milwaukee Film thought that we could benefit greatly from not only financial support, but also engagement at the board level."

Donald and Donna had given a relatively minimal donation of $1,000 to Milwaukee Film. "So I presented a few opportunities to them. The highest was jumping from $1,000 to $20,000 in support. At that time, Milwaukee Film didn't have many supporters at that level."

The Baumgartners were interested. "And the piece I remember most from that meeting is the phrase Donald used: 'We'll do $20,000 this year to sort of dip our toes in.' Here I am, overjoyed and overwhelmed that they are choosing to donate $20,000, an enormously generous gift for us at the time, and yet Donald's referring to it as 'dipping his toes in.' That sort of reframed my thinking about potential fundraising in Milwaukee and the capacity of supporters to donate to Milwaukee Film." Donna joined the board later that year and took a seat on its executive committee.

The largesse of the Baumgartners rose exponentially since that $20,000 toe-in-the-water gift. The following year they agreed to contribute $50,000 for three years. When that agreement ended, they committed a total of $600,000 spread out over five years. "That was the biggest, longest commitment to Milwaukee Film at the time," says Jackson. By 2015, the Baumgartners were named recipients of the annual Abele Catalyst Award, which recognizes change agents who have made a long-lasting impact on the community through film.

Jackson has been enamored with Milwaukee's venerable Oriental Theatre since he first walked through the doors of the 1927 "movie palace," named as one of the top 10 theaters in the country by *USA Today* and *Entertainment Weekly*. Weeks after seeing his first film there—Darren Aronofsky's Sundance winner *Pi*—he began working in the concession stand, selling tickets, and cleaning the theater's floors after shows.

Jonathan Jackson has run the Milwaukee Film Festival since 2008. He spearheaded the drive to have Milwaukee Film renovate and operate the revered Oriental Theatre.

"There is something magical about seeing a movie at the Oriental Theatre," Jackson wrote in the online publication *Urban Milwaukee*. "It's a true palace of cinema. The main house looks like a temple: the elegant drapery, larger-than-life Buddhas, ornate ceiling, and gigantic screen combine to create a transcendent cinematic experience."

In June 2017, Jackson announced publicly that a long-held dream of his had come true: Milwaukee Film had signed a thirty-one-year lease to operate and maintain the Oriental Theatre as of July 1, 2018. The film organization would revitalize the movie house and book screenings year-round in the Oriental's three theaters, essentially replacing national chain Landmark Theatres.

On the opening night of the 2017 film festival, Jackson announced that the Baumgartners had contributed $1.5 million for the theater's transition. "It's an unrestricted contribution," says Jackson. "Again, it was more than I thought they were going to do," Jackson says. "As part of this, they'll receive recognition in the theater's lobby."

In its goal of raising $10 million for the project, Milwaukee Film also received $2 million from Abele, $1 million from the Herzfeld Foundation, and $1 million from Milwaukee philanthropists Marianne and Sheldon Lubar.

The Baumgartners, Donna in particular, have been very actively involved with Milwaukee Film. "Jonathan has great vision and passion for creating a film culture in Milwaukee. The Oriental fits perfectly into that scheme," she says. "He is an effective leader. As an impassioned visionary he keeps his board engaged and enthused. He is constantly reaching out to his board for their views. Many members refer to the festival as their favorite two weeks in Milwaukee—they look forward with great anticipation to this time of year. Everybody's happy to see the Oriental survive and evolve."

Unlike any other event in the city, the Milwaukee Film Festival is as close as it gets to the excitement and glamor of Hollywood. Limos line up at the curb in front of the Oriental, chauffeuring VIPs to opening night. Long lines of enraptured moviegoers snake for two or three blocks outside of each of the festival's fives venues, waiting for admission. Spotlights shine, after-parties go on into the wee hours, and excited people let their hair down.

In nearly ten years, the Milwaukee Film Festival has grown to become one of the ten largest film festivals in the country, says Jackson, overshadowing the Chicago Film Festival. Attendance for the fifteen-day 2017 festival was up 9 percent from the previous year, with nearly 300 films, a record 84,072 attendees and 101 sold-out screenings.

"Jonathan has got a lot of enthusiasm. He gets things done," Donald says. "He sure as hell has gotten a lot done with Milwaukee Film. It's become one of the major film organizations in the country, thanks to him and his drive. People in Milwaukee just jumped into this. He put a program together that people care about, and it adds to the quality of life. That's why we give to it."

Having the Baumgartners as major contributors and someone like Donna on the board helps validate the integrity of any arts group. "Donna has been directly engaged in organizing and leading the planning for events," says Jackson. "She's opened her Rolodex, advocated for us, helped me pinpoint individuals that might like to engage with the film festival.

Used with permission of the Milwaukee Film

Milwaukee-born director and scriptwriter John Ridley, center, met Donald and Donna, and Kelly and Jeff Fitzsimmons, at the Milwaukee Film Festival. Ridley won the Academy Award for Best Adapted Screenplay in 2014 for 12 Years a Slave.

"They've made an epic contribution to the arts landscape in Milwaukee," he adds. "We wouldn't be where we are today without their generosity and commitment. I doubt we'd have a Calatrava addition at the art museum. I doubt we'd have the ballet or Michael Pink in Milwaukee without them. I doubt we'd have as strong an opera company as we still have with the Florentine. And the film festival wouldn't be what it is today without their support."

Jackson remembers talking to Donald about a documentary film he'd seen with Donna at the festival a couple years ago called *Landfill Harmonic*. It's the story of students in Paraguay who play musical instruments made entirely out of garbage from a landfill. As seen in the movie, their story went viral on the Internet and began to tour the world.

"I found out from Donald that he made a donation to this organization after seeing the film," says Jackson. It was uplifting, he says, to hear that one of Milwaukee Film's benefactors was so moved by a movie that he'd made a donation to the movie's subjects.

"It's rare and exciting for donors to choose to focus on the arts. All the other causes in our community are just as worthwhile, if not more so, but I think if the community doesn't have the arts, it doesn't have its soul."

The Baumgartners have helped out dozens of local schools and nonprofit organizations—including the Boys & Girls Club, United Performing Arts Fund, Milwaukee Repertory Theater, Renaissance Theaterworks, Danceworks, Present Music, Milwaukee Symphony Orchestra, Milwaukee Public Museum, First Stage, Next Act Theatre, and more. For thirty years, Donna and the Baumgartner family have supported the Next Door Foundation, an early childhood education program in Milwaukee's inner city, through fundraising events and financial backing.

Kelly's daughters, Brynn and Reiley, have spent time at Next Door reading and cooking with the kids, says Donna, "Bubbi" to the two girls. "They love going out there, and the kids love them. Reiley often asks when she can go back again. In 2015 and 2016, I asked that Sally, Kelly, and John designate a portion of their trust money to the Baumgartner Family Reading Room there. Milwaukee Mayor Tom Barrett came to speak at an event the same day the room was revealed. When Donald and I created a trust for the kids in 2012, we stipulated that a certain percentage had to be donated to a not-for-profit or charitable organization. It's one of the best things we've done."

The Baumgartners' concentration has been on the arts. "The arts are what separates us from everything else. It's the highest level, high human achievements that mean so much," says their friend, Carmen Haberman, who, with her husband Bill, runs the Richard and Ethel Herzfeld Foundation in Milwaukee, which makes grants to arts, education, and cultural groups. "Creating something is just so important. To write a symphony, to play a symphony, to play an instrument, to understand music, to draw art— it tells us who we are. It's our history. It gives us perspective. It's about our humanness, and elevates our culture."

For Donna, who spent her early years as a potter, championing the arts has been personally gratifying. "We are giving to the arts simply because we can," she says. "It has been rewarding to see artists have an opportunity to do what they love and to see the audience embrace them. The arts are a bedrock for so many people. I believe the community is truly excited and appreciative to have the high quality of art we have in Milwaukee. I've heard that some people wouldn't want to live in a city that didn't have a Saks Fifth Avenue. For me, I wouldn't want to live in a city without the arts. So in that sense, it's self-fulfilling."

Front row, left to right: Brynn and Reiley Fitzsimmons, Donald and Donna's grandchildren, volunteer at Next Door Foundation, an early childhood education program. With Donna, left, and their Aunt Sally, right, the two sisters are commended by Milwaukee Mayor Tom Barrett.

Support like the Baumgartners has lifted the city's thriving arts groups to a national standing, says Donald: "I'm just proud that Milwaukee has an arts group like the opera, like the ballet. We're a small city, and a lot of cities the size of Milwaukee do not have ballet companies or opera companies. It's just not done. It's unheard of."

Donald doesn't pretend to have an artistic bent himself. "I don't sing. I don't dance. I don't paint. I don't sculpt. I don't give myself any credit for having any talent in any of the arts." Although his father liked to sing and enjoyed musicals—Yul Brynner and Rex Harrison were favorites—there were no artistic talents or interests passed down from his parents.

"There were no artists in my mother's or father's life, no poets, no singers, no dancers. There was little or no culture in the home," he says. "But I've always been interested in the community that I live in and the benefits that the community receives from the arts. So when I had the means to do it, I was happy to help support them. They need the help of people such as myself."

CHAPTER 10

The Making of an Icon, Part One

The Milwaukee Art Museum was running out of room. To celebrate its centennial anniversary in 1988, a series of special exhibitions had to be installed in what essentially was a big, empty all-purpose room appropriately nicknamed "the bunker" on the east side of the building.

When it first opened in 1957, the museum's collection occupied 40,500 feet of gallery space while sharing the site with the Milwaukee County War Memorial Center in a building designed by American-Finnish architect Eero Saarinen. With its wide and windowed two-storied rectangular boxes of exposed concrete cantilevering out thirty feet in three directions, the building garnered international attention for its bold form.

An expansion in 1975 added 175,000 square feet to the museum. Designed by Milwaukee architect David Kahler, the utilitarian addition—a massive two-story structure, in the style of brutalist architecture, that swept out from under the Saarinen to Lake Michigan's edge—vastly increased the space for the permanent collection and provided at long last a wing for 600 pieces of modern artworks bestowed years earlier by Peg Bradley, wife of Milwaukee industrialist Harry Lynde Bradley.

Yet despite the new home for the Bradley Collection, the museum lacked a permanent gallery area for big touring exhibitions. MAM at the time had

The original Saarinen-designed building above Kahler's vast addition to the Milwaukee Art Museum, circa 1985.

developed a well-regarded reputation under its dual directors. Russell Bowman was hired as chief curator in 1980 and was named director in 1985, sharing the leadership role with Christopher Goldsmith, who had come aboard in 1982 as executive director. While Goldsmith oversaw the museum's finances and operations, Bowman supervised the collections and touring exhibitions. Both coordinated fundraising.

Russell Bowman

The drawbacks in presenting the centennial celebrations got the new directors thinking about adding exhibition space and the very role of the museum itself, says Bowman. "In exploring this with staff and consultants and the board of trustees, Chris and I decided what we really needed was to build an extension."

It wasn't simply a question of more square footage, though. Goldsmith and Bowman and a few

Christopher Goldsmith

board members believed a whole new floor plan was needed, a whole new appearance. The museum's configuration itself was problematic. It had no front door to speak of, and getting to the artwork was confusing. Many collections, including the Bradley, were located somewhat remotely on the second level or on the first floor near the temporary exhibition space, far removed from the main entrance and parking lot on the building's south side.

Moreover, the art museum had no physical connection to the city. Downtown Milwaukee was up above on a bluff to the west. Down below stood the museum, severed from downtown by a major boulevard along the lake. The museum needed a more eye-catching physical presence, something identifiable and inviting that would draw not only members of the community but would put the museum on the map nationally and beyond.

"Museums were changing from temples of art to community centers," Goldsmith says. "We didn't have any space for that. We had a tiny gift shop. We had virtually no food service. When we did a public event, we had to take all the art off the wall in that east entrance gallery. So we tried to get something going."

The board of trustees, however, responded with one big yawn. "No interest whatsoever," Goldsmith says. "There was just no vision." Board president Susan Jennings leaned on members for contributions and asked them to solicit donations for an expansion. "But we couldn't get donors. You needed a lot of money behind it, and nobody in Milwaukee had raised a lot of money, frankly, for eons. There was nobody stepping forward. So it died."

Then, a few years later, opportunity came knocking. A patron named Richard Flagg stopped by the museum on one of his regular visits to chat with Goldsmith. Flagg was a Jewish refuge from Nazi Germany who had made his fortune in the tannery business. He and his wife, Erna, were passionate about art and had donated substantially to the art museum. Two noteworthy collections bear their name: The Flagg Collection of Decorative Arts and Sculpture, and the Richard and Erna Flagg Collection of Haitian Art.

Goldsmith mentioned to Flagg how hard it was to win support for a much-needed expansion. "I think this needs to be done, and I'm going to help you," Flagg told him. "What I'm going to do is get you a lead gift."

Days later, Flagg made a cold call to Walter Annenberg, Milwaukee native, multi-billionaire media mogul, one of the country's biggest philanthropists, and owner of a world-class art collection. Annenberg had lived in Milwaukee for twelve years before moving to New York and eventually taking over his father's company, Triangle Publications, which started as a newspaper distribution business in Milwaukee and reportedly was sold to Rupert Murdoch in 1988 for $3.2 billion.

Walter Annenberg did not know Richard Flagg, but he invited him to his home in California to meet, says Goldsmith. "And Richard came back with a check for a million bucks. He said Annenberg told him, 'I now have fulfilled my duty to Milwaukee. Don't try anymore. This is it!' All of a sudden we had a million dollars."

The groundwork was laid for what would be one of the most consequential building projects in the city's history.

Donald and Donna Baumgartner, meanwhile, had become more and more active in the museum's functions. They helped plan and co-chaired the Friends of Art's annual Bal du Lac fundraising events, and attended art auctions. Bowman met the Baumgartners through one of the art "support groups" that he led. "There were support groups for different areas of the museum's collection," he says. "So there was a Fine Art Society, a Print Forum for the prints and drawings. I met Donald and Donna through the Contemporary Art Society art auctions." Donna tells the story that she got a cold call from Bowman inviting her for a tour of the upcoming auction. "It wasn't just a tour, it was an education." It turned out to be the ultimate cultivation. "Russell could be very seductive," she adds.

The Baumgartners had been collecting art since they were married. "I didn't get really serious about it until Donna hit the scene in 1977, '78," Donald says. "She was a potter and had a major interest in the visual arts. We bought art first in Haiti, then France. We bought art in Italy. We bought art wherever we traveled. When we went to shows, we bought art. The art museum's Contemporary Art Society has an auction every couple years. And we bought a lot of pieces at the auction."

"The first really expensive piece we bought cost $10,000," Donna says. "It was a painting I saw in Chicago at a gallery. The artist was a teacher from Michigan, Stefan Davidek. He had a figurative piece that I liked, but it wasn't available, so I got an oil painting of paint cans instead. Green and blue paint dripping over the sides. I was really quite drawn to it. We had it hanging as a centerpiece in our living room when Bob Forrest came to the house. He was Milwaukee's premiere interior designer years ago. He used to date Peg Bradley. Bob came in, took one look at it, and said, 'That's brutal.' Well, I was quite excited about it. It was my first real painting."

Donald was less enthused. "We paid ten grand for those paint cans. They were horrible."

"They were vibrant. Painterly!" she counters.

Donna finally conceded. "The local newspaper came out to do a story on our house, and that was the main painting in the photograph. We moved, and after Bob put the jinx on the painting, I agreed not to hang it in the new house."

With Bowman's guidance, Donald and Donna's tastes grew more discriminating, yet not without the whimsy and curiosity that had led them (or Donna, at least) to Davidek's paint cans.

"They've simply responded to things as they've seen them," Bowman says. "Their collection is more figurative than abstract, including drawings by Picasso and Richard Diebenkorn. And there's an emphasis on photography, which developed starting with the museum and then very much on their own." Donald was an amateur photographer with an impressive collection of Leica cameras and lenses, so it was a natural segue for him.

The Baumgartners offered a glimpse of their collection in the MAM's 2017 exhibition *Milwaukee Collects*. Individual works owned by major local collectors were selected by museum curators and borrowed for display. Among the Baumgartner pieces were a landscape watercolor by Milton Avery; a pencil drawing, *Seated Female Nude*, by Marsden Hartley; and a black-and-white photograph of a woman sitting in a chair wearing a sheer robe, by Eugene Von Bruenchenhein, a prolific, self-taught artist from Milwaukee; and a small, black-and-white photograph by Cindy Sherman.

In December 1989, Bowman asked the Baumgartners for help landing a major acquisition. For well over a year, he had been trying to purchase an American folk-art collection that was considered one of the finest of its kind still in private hands. Assessed at $2.3 million, the 273-piece collection was owned by Michael and Julie Hall, collectors in Michigan.

Bowman's discreetly unpublicized fundraising effort was a struggle, however. Faced with a contractual deadline, he solicited support right up to the last minute in some cases, finally raising enough money to close the deal. The Michael and Julie Hall Collection of American Folk Art was sold to the museum for $1.55 million; the remainder of its value was a gift from the Halls. It stands today as one of the museum's prized collections.

The Baumgartners contributed $50,000 for the Hall Collection at the urging of their friend, Joe Checota, their first serious donation to the museum. Using Donald's phrase, they had "dipped their toes into the water."

The purchase of the mother lode of folk art was a coup for the museum, and personally gratifying for the Baumgartners, who share an appreciation with Bowman for self-taught and outside art, artworks that typically are made by people living out of the mainstream. "They're artists, sometimes street people, who for most part have no formal training, yet create things that are of interest," Donald says. Donna liked them precisely for that reason—they were raw, less formal, and immediate.

Several years later Donald and Donna, at the request of Bowman, gave the museum a piece of outsider art titled *Dog and Pups* by Morris Hirshfield. A Polish immigrant who had settled in New York, Hirshfield began painting after retiring from his clothing manufacturing business in 1937. He received recognition almost immediately and was hailed as one of the major folk artists of the twentieth century. A retrospective of his work was exhibited at New York's Museum of Modern Art in 1943. "Hirshfield is a very important artist," says Margaret Andera, the

Dog and Pups by Morris Hirshfield.

Milwaukee Art Museum's interim chief curator and curator of contemporary art. "Paintings by him are rare, as he only painted seventy-six known works. MAM has three."

Following the acquisition of the Hall Collection, Donald became president of the Contemporary Art Society and then accepted a seat on the art museum's Board of Trustees in 1990. With a newly purchased home in River Hills under renovation, and construction underway of a new headquarters for Paper Machinery Corporation and a log home in the Colorado mountains, he needed something else to keep him busy, he was on a roll. In his sixtieth year of life, he was laser focused with energy to spare, full of "piss and vinegar," as he has said, and looking for his next ocean to cross.

Earmarked for the selection of an architect, the $1 million gift from Annenberg lit a flame of enthusiasm in the museum's boardroom. With the trustees' feedback, Goldsmith and Bowman began to shape the vision of the MAM's next phase and laid out a plan of action.

An Architect Selection Committee was formed, made up of 21 trustees, an extraordinarily large group of extraordinarily diverse, dynamic, and resourceful individuals, including Betty and Harry Quadracci, owners of Quad Graphics and *Milwaukee Magazine*; Sue Selig, an art collector and wife of Baseball Commissioner Bud Selig; Robert Greenstreet, dean of the School of Architecture and Urban Planning at the University of Wisconsin–Milwaukee; Ray Krueger, an environmental lawyer; Wayne Lueders, a business lawyer and CPA; Michael Mahoney, a banking executive; David Uihlein, Jr., president of an architecture firm; Frederick "Eric" Vogel, an architect and interior designer; Marianne Lubar, a board director of numerous nonprofits and wife of businessman Sheldon Lubar; Richard Pieper, an entrepreneur and business executive; Margaret Chester and Marianne Epstein, both grand dames of Milwaukee and ardent supporters of MAM; plus many others.

Donald was on the Architect Selection Committee. With his eye for detail—simultaneously put into practice as he oversaw the designs of his new business headquarters, his new home, and his new Colorado getaway—he was a perfect fit. Although he was a relative newcomer to the board, he would play an oversized role in making the final choice.

"At the first meeting, everybody said, 'We've got to buy American. We're not going to do anything other than an American architect,'" says Goldsmith. "By the second meeting, it was, 'This is a little shortsighted. We exhibit art from around the world. We have to look worldwide.'"

The selection committee invited seventy architects with international reputations to submit examples of their work. The committee received fifty-five applications. "We had been advised by other museums to choose your architect, don't choose a design," Bowman says, "because you'll get something that doesn't look at your needs completely, and then you're kind of stuck. Choose your architect and let him design it for you. And that's what we did."

The selection committee narrowed the list to eleven, including internationally celebrated architects such as Frank O. Gehry, Cesar Pelli, and Robert A.M. Stern from the United States; Norman Foster from Great Britain; Arata Isozaki and Fumihiko Maki from Japan; and, to a lesser degree of renown, Santiago Calatrava from Spain.

Calatrava, in fact, was not among the initial fifty-five applicants. He was considered for the project only after Bowman happened to read an article about him in an architectural magazine. Impressed by Calatrava's work, he was compelled to persuade the selection committee to add him to the pool.

Except for a glass atrium in Toronto, Calatrava had not designed a single structure in the Western Hemisphere. He was best known in Europe, for his bridges, rail stations, and airport terminals. But the fact that he was relatively unknown in the United States ultimately worked in his favor. And when the committee pared the list to three finalists, Calatrava was one of them, along with Arata Isozaki and Fumihiko Maki from Japan.

"When we were looking for an architect, we wanted someone who was emerging to international recognition," says Bowman, "We wanted an architect who was early in his career and would give all the attention to our project that we thought we needed."

Eero Saarinen had been an eager young architect when he designed the first stage of the MAM and War Memorial Center, one of his first projects in the United States. Likewise, local architect David Kahler was young and in the early phases of his career when he was tapped to build the 1975 addition.

The Calatrava-designed train station at the airport in Lyon, France.

To best judge the three finalists, several members of the selection committee traveled abroad to view the architects' work. They began in Zurich, Switzerland, Calatrava's home and base of operations, where they toured the railway station he had designed years earlier. But it was their next stop, Lyon, France, that caused a flurry of excitement.

Calatrava was completing the construction of a train station at the Lyon international airport, the first airport to be served by high-speed rail. The triangular superstructure of steel, concrete, and glass spanned 394 feet and measured 120 feet tall, an imposing symbol for the city of Lyon. From the sky, it resembled a huge bird with its wings extended from an arched spine, protecting the terminal. As their plane landed, committee members stared in awe through their windows at the structure. Their excitement was palpable. No one had seen anything like it. "I think I'm in love," commented one member.

They were greeted in Lyon by the architect and his wife, Tina. It was the first time Donald and Calatrava met. "I remember he was perfectly dressed and had wonderful olive green shoes," Calatrava says. "I had never seen such elegance. I thought, *Here is a very special person, a person with taste.* I also remember his enthusiasm. He was very enthusiastic, interested in everything. And what happened was, this first impression grew in the most positive way during the years."

After seeing the winged building, the final leg of the trip was anti-climactic for Donald and others on the tour. The Japanese architects were among the top in the international field. Arata Isozaki had designed the massive indoor sporting arena for the 1992 Olympics in Barcelona. Fumihiko Maki had built the National Museum of Modern Art in Kyoto, and won the esteemed Pritzker Prize for his work. But their buildings were no match for the ingenuity and sheer spectacle of Calatrava's.

"None of us had seen architecture as art," says Goldsmith. "We saw architecture as a building, not as a piece of art. Lyon was the first exposure to Calatrava, and then we went to Japan, and it was far less dramatic."

Initially opinions among the selection committee were divided. Some leaned toward the more established Japanese architects, while others were wowed by the beauty and excitement of Calatrava's designs. For a time, Goldsmith and Bowman were on opposite sides of the ledger. "I was concerned that Calatrava's architecture maybe was a little too different from the Saarinen and Kahler building, and maybe a little flamboyant," says Bowman, who, ironically, had brought Calatrava to the attention of the board. "Eventually I was persuaded by Chris and Donald and others that Calatrava ought to be the selection."

Donald lined up solidly in the Calatrava camp. Calatrava was his guy. "Donald made his mind up when he saw Calatrava's architecture in Lyon," Bowman says. "And so did many other members of the selection committee. But Donald was the most vociferous."

In the end, Calatrava prevailed. Taking a leap of faith, the committee recommended Calatrava as the expansion project's architect. The board announced the hiring of Calatrava in December 1994; the firm Kahler Slater was named the local architect of record. David Kahler and Calatrava would become working partners and good friends.

"What we wanted was a dramatic building, and, obviously, Calatrava does that in spades," says Bowman. "We wanted an architect whose work we would be introducing into this country. Calatrava fit the bill. We felt we were getting a young architect at the beginning of his emergence to wide recognition."

The entire selection committee was convinced they would get all of Calatrava, his artistic talent, his architectural vision, and his engineering brilliance—his heart, his soul, and his mind. The museum by the lake would become his signature project in the United States.

In early 1996, the Board of Trustees launched a year-long, $35 million capital campaign—which included an $8 million endowment—an amount that would triple over the course of the venture. Weeks later Calatrava presented his designs to museum officials and potential donors in Milwaukee, walking his audience through his thought process and making sketches on the spot to elucidate his ideas.

As many have since pointed out but few fully appreciated at the time, Calatrava was not only an architect, he was also an artist and engineer. He had studied drawing and painting in Valencia, Spain, beginning at age six, and continued art education in secondary school in Paris. After receiving a university degree in architecture, he studied civil engineering. His genius is

© Lila Aryan

Calatrava presented his three-dimensional design of the addition to the museum's Board of Trustees in 1996.

in applying these skills and talents in his designs, says Ray Krueger, a member of the selection team. This was particularly evident when faced with the site challenges of the Milwaukee Art Museum project.

"How do you design a museum next to an architecture icon, the Saarinen Building?" Krueger says. "How do you design a museum that has to relate to the lake? And how do you relate this museum to the city? He had these vertical and horizontal planes and references, and he understood and talked about how difficult that is."

For example, says Donald, he was quick to resolve the spatial divide between the museum and downtown Milwaukee. "Calatrava was the only one that came up with the idea of bridging to Wisconsin Avenue and connecting the top of the city to the museum. That concept was one of the major considering factors of choosing him." Drawing on his expertise for designing extraordinary bridges, he would link the city bluff and the museum's reception hall with a 230-foot, cable-stayed footbridge over the lakefront boulevard, Lincoln Memorial Drive.

"I worked a long time to answer the question of connectivity to the city," says Calatrava, "proposing the bridge, proposing the relation to Wisconsin

© Lila Aryan

Donald discusses the Calatrava model with MAM board member Laurence Eiseman.

Avenue and to the lake, proposing the relation between the two museums, the Saarinen and David Kahler buildings. All those things were discussed a long time. Then suddenly I came up with a small model to propose the opening roof. Donald and Russell Bowman and Chris Goldsmith, they were very enthusiastic from day one. They just opened their minds. They were pushing to have a very special building.

"This moved me to have the courage to make such a proposition, a roof that opens," he continues. "I did not arrive with a project like that. It grew in different conversations. And certainly the client, in this case Donald and the two directors of the museum, they were very much willing to have something special, a landmark place that would give a new character to this area."

Calatrava also understood the museum's urgency in redefining its physical identity, starting with a new entryway, says Goldsmith. "Essentially we wanted an entrance pavilion that could be readily identified as the art museum that could contain both a major changing exhibition gallery and a major meeting space—a hall that didn't have art in it but was artful."

Based on Calatrava's preliminary designs, the addition—which ultimately would add 146,000 square feet to the museum—would house the temporary exhibition space that it sorely lacked and free up space in the Kahler building to expand the permanent collection by 30 percent. And, it would create a new entryway to the art museum that was airy, pristine, and bathed in light. As Calatrava would often say, he wanted the structure to be "transparent." Most dramatically, the reception hall would be topped by a pair of moveable wings—referred to by the French term *brise soleil*, or "sunscreen." When completed, the brise soleil, as it opened and closed, was an emotion-rendering wonder, a uniquely recognizable symbol of the museum, and an icon for the city. Donald would one day see to it that every paper cup machine shipped from Paper Machinery's plant was fitted with a small plaque bearing a likeness of the museum's open wings and the phrase "Made in Milwaukee."

Sheltered beneath the wings would be Windhover Hall, with a soaring ceiling and cantilevered glass prow reaching for the water, and flanked by two parallel, glass-and-marble gallerias, a venue for public meetings, lectures, cocktail parties, and even weddings, functions that most museums today require.

"At the time we were planning the building, Betty Quadracci was one of the leaders in saying it needs to be a community meeting space," Bowman says. "That was really a guiding principle for her. And I think it really became a guiding principle for the museum that everybody agreed to."

It was Betty and her husband, Harry Quadracci, who gave the museum the enormous shove into the realm of the possible. Their unprecedented contribution of $10 million, anonymous at the time, kicked off the capital campaign and set the wheels in motion. More donations followed swiftly, and, remarkably, by the end of the year, the campaign goal of $35 million had been surpassed by $1 million.

Planning, building, and paying for a project of this magnitude involved an inordinate number of jurisdictions and entities, each with their own agendas, including: the architect, the architect of record, the general contractor, the engineering firms, the banks, the City of Milwaukee, the County of Milwaukee, the War Memorial Center, the Port of Milwaukee Harbor Commission, and on and on. To take point as its hands-on intermediary between the needs of the architect and the interests—and budget—of the museum, the Board of Trustees formed a Building Committee, a group of ten that would oversee design, construction, and cost estimates. Among the members were an architect, a banker, a marketer, two lawyers, several business executives, and art collectors.

Donald was asked to chair the committee. He was uniquely qualified, having spent years building sophisticated precision machinery to exacting specifications. He was a manufacturer and a CEO.

"He was the right person for all those things," says Calatrava. "Donald is a man who has an industrial background. His machines have been exported

© Jim Brozek

© Jim Brozek

Following the December 1997 groundbreaking of the addition, a construction crew etched the outline of what would become the "prow" of the building into the snow, and the building's interior slowly took shape.

and sold all over the world. You need a person like that, who has a wide vision, who doesn't became nervous, who knows what is possible if everybody works together. He has an enormous capacity to organize. Not only does he have an enormous sensibility for art, but also he has the clarity to make things possible."

Museum Trustee Ray Krueger became Donald's right-hand man on the Building Committee. "Donald has this gregarious, lives-large kind of personality, a good heart, very approachable, and very successful business person," he says. "He had the right personality for the job. He's not one of these CEO types, 'my way or the highway.' He's a good listener."

As a lawyer who includes in his practice laws relating to art and architecture, Krueger's perspective was also shaped by his family roots: He is the grand-nephew of Wisconsin-born artist Georgia O'Keeffe. "Donald was someone who had the stature to take this on, and probably the only person who would volunteer to do it, because it was insurmountable," he says. "But he saw something in the architect and in the promise of this design that captured his imagination. And because he saw it, he helped others see it. It all had to start somewhere in transferring the vision from the architect to the people who will build it, the people who will fund it, the people who will run and operate it. And so that's where I met Donald. We worked very closely together on the Building Committee."

© Jim Brozek

Santiago Calatrava in downtown Milwaukee with MAM trustees, left to right, Ray Krueger, John Burke, and Donald Baumgartner.

There were meetings with the architect all the time. "Donald would pre-
side. We'd go into a room, and three walls of the room would be wrapped
in paper six feet high, just blank paper. And we'd sit down with Calatrava.
Issues would be brought up, people would be debating: Do we need this?
Do we need that? Donald's response might be, 'Well, Santiago, what do you
think of this? Could you give us some ideas?' Calatrava would get out his
watercolors, and he'd go to the wall that was wrapped with paper, and he
would paint solutions right then and there. And if you didn't like that one,
he'd paint another one. And Donald would sit back and say, 'Well, this looks

pretty good. What do you think, group?' And of course everybody was just mesmerized by Calatrava."

This sort of spontaneity, however, could cause a measure of consternation among board members. The initial design had no plans for the south end of the addition, for instance. More than midway through construction, Calatrava introduced drawings for what would become the south terrace, an expansive brick patio with a view to the west of the city skyline and to the east of Lake Michigan and rows of crab apple trees—a cantilevered canopy, supported by nine bleached concrete arches over a bank of windowpanes. Today the patio is named the Baumgartner Family Terrace, thanks to a substantial donation designated at Donald's request by his father's Charitable Remainder Trust.

As the project drew more interest and support from donors, the building committee increased the scope of the construction, approved by the board virtually every step of the way. "'If you can raise the money, we can spend it' became our motto," Donald says. "Or so some people thought."

Construction managers kept a clay model of the building in their on-site trailer to help them visualize design changes that seemed to occur daily. Occasionally those changes would raise eyebrows. With Calatrava's concept to align the pedestrian bridge and spine of the building's wings precisely with the city's main east-west thoroughfare, Wisconsin Avenue, the engineering challenge was

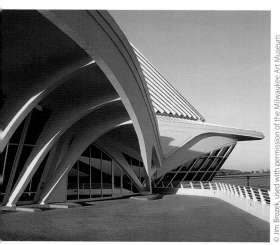

Baumgartner Family Terrace.

Donald and Calatrava became working partners and good friends.

ratcheted up to a whole other level. When he submitted drawings for a deluxe, heated 100-car underground parking garage with skylights and arching white-washed support beams, critics howled. "It's a shame to waste it as a place for parking cars, since it is about as good a space for the display of contemporary art as you could ask for," sniffed *The New Yorker's* architecture writer.

But, as with nearly every design change, the trustees approved it. Says Goldsmith: "Calatrava went down to the Johnson Wax headquarters in Racine to take a look at what Frank Lloyd Wright had done with the employee garage. He said, 'I'm going to give you a better one,' And that was the bar for him personally, to do the most beautiful garage ever built. Because he was going to outdo Frank Lloyd Wright, which is pretty crazy. And very expensive. But, you know, why not? It'll be there hopefully for a hundred years."

The addition would not be an exceptionally large building. It was intended foremost as a new entryway, a pavilion. "A pavilion has a limited dimension," Calatrava says. "The idea was to make something significant, as a sign or a symbol, in this place. This was a strategy and, from the very beginning, understood by the client and supported all the way through. We built a bridge with a mast on the side of the museum. We built a roof to rise up and reinforce the image of the bridge. It's not a bridge and then a roof. Bridge and roof are making a unity. And then the idea of the brise soleil, the movable

Striving to outdo Frank Lloyd Wright, Calatrava vowed to make the underground parking area "the most beautiful garage ever built."

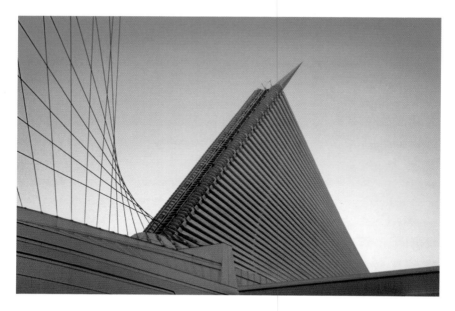

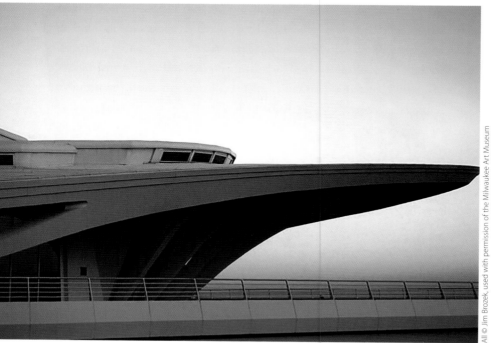

The shapes, forms, and contours of Calatrava's design were nothing like anything else seen in Milwaukee.

part, transformed the whole thing and gave it another dimension. Donald and the building committee, they understood that very well."

Coming up with design changes often was the less difficult part of the equation. The bigger challenge was figuring out how to pay for them.

"I was absolutely determined to not have the project cut back," says Donald. "There was a lot of push to take off this, reduce that. I mean, some people wanted to take the damned mechanical wings off. 'They're too expensive,' they said. Or, 'We don't need a bridge. We don't need the South Terrace.'"

As the design evolved, the budget evolved. In January 1997, a month after meeting its target goal of $35 million, the budget was increased to $50 million. By the fall of 1999, the construction budget was $63 million, as reported by the *Milwaukee Journal Sentinel.* By March of 2000, it clocked in at nearly $98 million, including a $12 million endowment and costs for the gardens and gallery renovations. With a goal of raising $100 million, donors were keeping pace with the ever-mounting expenses. By February 2001, two months before its "soft" opening, with much of the addition still under construction, $83 million had been taken in.

"The push was constantly coming from critics who said you're spending too much money, you're spending too much money," Donald adds. "I became very close with Calatrava. And I was goddamned determined to build it the way he wanted it built to fulfill what he saw as a vision for this museum. I wanted every part of it to be there."

A true friendship developed between Donald and Santiago Calatrava, who would travel to Milwaukee some forty times during the course of the project. He was very accessible. Prospective donors would invite him to dinner. He particularly loved the steaks at Coerper's Five O'Clock Steakhouse. On one occasion, the hotels were booked because of a Harley-Davidson anniversary rally, so Calatrava stayed at the Baumgartners' home. "It was his fortieth birthday," Donna recalls. "We had a little celebration over breakfast while he sketched with his watercolors. He was always sketching. He left behind a pile of watercolors in his room."

"I had had very little relations with the United States," says Calatrava, "and this was effectively the first time that I seriously was involved in a project in the States. And so I came to Milwaukee and I found the people enormously nice. My wife and I, we were enchanted from the welcoming and the kindness and the friendship we received. The consequence of all of this was that in 2000 we decided to send our kids for education to the United States. They all studied at Columbia University, and three of them are now living in the United States. With Donald and Donna, we are in touch, and we are grateful and very honored to be their friends."

Donald also formed a close bond with Jack Pelisek, a member of the Building Committee and president of the board of trustees from 1998 to 2001. A Milwaukee lawyer, one-time University of Wisconsin regent, and civic leader, Pelisek was respected, well connected, and well liked in the community.

"Jack had a canny ability to know where all the money was buried in Milwaukee and how to raise it," says Donald. "He was extremely good at it. First we would meet with Calatrava, and he would tell us what he needed. Then I'd listen to all of the moaning and groaning from the committee and the trustees and the bankers. Then I'd go to Jack and ask, 'Can we do it?' And Jack would say, 'We can do it.' And, by God, we did it.' Many people were so enthused with Calatrava and dazzled by his vision that they really wanted to be involved in it." One event held in the Bradley Collection rooms featured display cases that housed small maquettes [small, preliminary models] of the building. It caused such excitement that Bill Teweles, a businessman and museum trustee, tapped on Donna's shoulder and exclaimed, "I want to be part of this!"

As the outline of the building rose along the Lake Michigan shoreline, a collective sense of excitement grew, inspiring a cascade of unsparing donations. It was unlike anything Milwaukee had seen. Some 2,400 individuals, corporations, and foundations contributed to the Calatrava project; twenty-five gifts of $1 million or more were made. Among the contributors: Real estate moguls John and Murph Burke gave $1.5 million for the naming rights of the brise soleil. Marianne and Sheldon Lubar gave $5.25 million to support what would be a state-of-the-art, 265-seat auditorium. Publisher Roy Reiman and his wife, Bobbi, made a seven-figure donation to help fund the cost of the pedestrian bridge. The Walter Schroeder Foundation supported one of two gallerias with a gift of $2.25 million. Pleasant Rowland, creator of the American Girl brand, gave $3 million. Industrialist and philanthropist Michael Cudahy put up a total of $11.4 million to pay for what would become the Cudahy Gardens, an expansive network

© Jim Brozek

The intrinsic attraction of the water wall in the Cudahy Gardens.

of plazas, hedgerows, water walls, and fountains designed by renowned landscape architect Dan Kiley. Included in the Gardens were English ha-has (sunken fences) providing vertical barriers to prevent access by grazing livestock. Not that that was much of a problem on the lakefront.

The Foundation of Jane Bradley Pettit, the daughter of Peg and Harry Bradley, contributed $10 million on top of her original gift of $3 million, and Betty and Harry Quadracci made additional donations to increase their total contribution to $13.7 million.

"It got to a point where the trustees were all committed to fulfilling this vision," says Krueger, who served as president of the board from 2009 through 2011. "This is forever. This is going to be an icon for the city. It would not only provide additional space and function for the museum, but it would extend the reach of Milwaukee Art Museum nationally and internationally."

Donald and Donna Baumgartner made initial contributions of, first, $2 million, then $1 million, and then added another $1 million to help satisfy the museum's debt. In coming years, they would create an endowment of $8 million, placing them among the top-tier benefactors of the Milwaukee Art Museum.

CHAPTER 11

The Making of an Icon, Part Two

The museum scheduled the grand opening of the main entrance for the middle of September 2001. The brise soleil, the museum announced, would be completed (hopefully) in early October. Members of the public looked forward to finally getting an up-close look at the expansion. But for those who had been long involved with its construction, the run-up to those approaching deadlines was a white-knuckle ride that could not have been more tense or more bittersweet.

Donald had been elected president of the board of trustees in early 2001, succeeding Jack Pelisek. Existing galleries were being renovated, and fundraising was in high gear. Then, on June 20, Pelisek lost his ongoing bout with cancer. He died months short of seeing the doors open to the city's new architectural wonder.

"Jack was in the hospital," Donald remembers. "I'm at his bedside and I've got my hand on his shoulder, I said, 'You can't leave me, Jack. Not now. We've got to raise more money here.' But that was the end for Jack. He never left the hospital."

Months later, on a Tuesday morning, another blow, this one impossible to fathom. Terrorists attacked New York City and Washington, D.C., throwing the country into chaos and uncertainty, upending any sense of normalcy. The opening of the museum addition was days away.

Museum officials decided to open the doors a few days early, allowing people to visit free of charge for the weekend. And beginning on Friday, September 14, in the face of the 9/11 attacks on the nation, thousands of people treaded across the suspended pedestrian bridge and filed into Windhover Hall to gawk at its peaked ceiling, gaze through the glass of its cantilevered prow at the Lake Michigan waters, and ponder the very probability of its creation. Throughout the day, the sunlight of late summer streamed in from all sides of the "transparent building," washing across the Italian marble, white and pure.

The building took on the appearance of a modern cathedral. Bouquets of flowers were placed inside to honor the victims of 9/11. Chris Goldsmith suggested placing a book on a pedestal for people to sign and share their thoughts. The new hall became a place of consolation. Shielding the visitors from the construction of the unfinished sunscreen overhead, a huge, translucent curtain hung, an unintended veil of mourning. Displayed along the galleria were huge glass sculptures by artist Dale Chihuly, beautiful shapes and colors. Visitors passed within inches of the fragile glasswork in awe.

Two long concourses or Galleries—entirely white, from floor to ceiling—led patrons from the Windhover to the gift shop, the Lubar Auditorium, and the permanent collection galleries in the Kahler building. The concourses acted as promenades, allowing room for temporary art installations and fitted with stone benches. Each was illuminated by a wall of glass, one facing the city, the Schroeder Foundation Galleria, and one facing the lake, the Donna and Donald Baumgartner Galleria.

The finishing touches were still to come. Calatrava's design called for the moveable wings to be formed by seventy-two fins, thirty-six for each wing, made of a carbon fiber composite, a light and durable material. The size of the fins would vary, from twenty-four feet to 105 feet, and when fully opened, the brise soleil would extend nearly as wide as a Boeing 747. The general contractor, however, had trouble finding a firm to make the fins.

"Nobody knew how to fabricate a piece of carbon fiber that size. They couldn't find anybody to even try it," says Donald. "So our building committee went directly to Calatrava, and he said we could use steel instead." A

Top: Windhover Hall. Left: The west Galleria. Right: A glass sculpture by Dale Chihuly on opening day.

tube-like fin of thin steel would be much less expensive than carbon fiber and as strong or stronger.

Calatrava contacted a manufacturer he knew in Zaragoza, Spain. Although fabricating the seventy-two fins could take months, the manufacturer assured the museum the job would be done in time to meet the October deadline. Getting the pieces to Milwaukee, though, proved to be a much bigger problem. Transporting them by ship would take far too long, and chartering a plane large enough to fly them across the Atlantic seemed like an iffy proposition. Following the horror of 9/11, business stopped and travel stopped. Air space over the United States was restricted, tens of thousands of flights were grounded. There was no way to know whether the terrorist attack would derail the debut of the sunscreen.

As the dust began to settle, Michael Cudahy came up with an idea. He phoned his son-in-law, a pilot for FedEx, who suggested that the museum hire a couple of Russian Anatov 124s—the largest cargo planes in the world—to transport the steel parts from Europe to the United States. The narrow fins were carefully stacked onto long, wooden racks, similar to wine racks, in the belly of the two cargo planes, and the unassembled sunscreen was flown from Spain to Milwaukee in ten hours. To truck them from Mitchell International Airport to the museum in the dead of night took another sixteen hours.

With the opening fast approaching, construction crews scrambled, working overtime to build the wings. Days before the October deadline, a series of test trials were scheduled to see if the wings would open. Late in September, a small group of engineers and construction managers gathered inconspicuously on the bridge. A switch was thrown, everyone held their breath, and slowly, slowly the wings began to rise.

Days later, another test. "It was Chris Goldsmith and me and the building committee," says Russell Bowman, looking back. "Finally resolving the design of the brise soleil, getting it built in Europe, getting it transported here, and having it work. Seeing it lift for the first time was a very emotional moment."

October 14, and the time had come to show off the wings to the public. Donald and Donna Baumgartner co-hosted the gala grand opening with

Fireworks bathe the Milwaukee Art Museum in color, as the wings of the Burke Brise Soleil swing open.

Donald and Donna with the Calatravas, above, and with Harry and Betty Quadracci, below.

Harry and Betty Quadracci. The reception was held during a downpour under a tent directly across the Reiman Bridge from the museum. Mahler Enterprise's cleaning crew had been there all day with mops. The rain continued as people gazed into the evening sky, waiting for the magic moment to arrive. The rain turned to a light drizzle and the fog began to lift, and the Burke Brise Soleil gracefully swung upward to trumpeted heraldic music, while streams of fireworks exploded above, bathing the museum in light. A moment forever etched in the hearts and minds of those present.

Dedication of the Reiman Bridge.

Calatrava was in Milwaukee for the opening. "I remember the opening very much," he says, "not only because we were opening a building in particular, but because the moment was very particular, a few weeks after September 11th. A building is a building, but in my mind there was this fact: Here you see a building that opens its wings and it makes a claim that we are still here. It is indeed a testimony of, let's say, my love and my respect for the United States of America and the city of Milwaukee."

The addition would propel Calatrava's professional standing in the United States. More than fifteen years after 9/11, the white elliptical wings of his World Trade Center transit terminal would be unveiled in downtown Manhattan as part of the reconstruction of the Ground Zero site. Designed by Calatrava, the building's skylight is opened on temperate days, and its stationary wings evoke a bird in flight, much like the wings of the Milwaukee Art Museum.

"What architecture wants to be is something more than a pure functional place," he says. "It wants also to become a sign or signal. The wings over Milwaukee you see reflected in the transportation hub. So both buildings for me are in a way related to each other."

Following the opening of what is now popularly called "the Calatrava," the museum received numerous accolades. *Time* magazine named the

Jim Brozek

Earlier phases of the Milwaukee Art Museum as seen through the glass of the brise soleil.

mullion frames for the large glass panels could not be made here; they too had to come from Spain. And in the gift shop, the beautiful pear wood counter display cases were fabricated and pre-assembled in Switzerland, then dismantled packed and flown here, where they were installed by the Swiss. Our theater seats here were made in Spain as well, and so on and so on. I think the message might be if you hire a cutting-edge European architect, you better be prepared to spend some time in Europe.

Let's talk about the brise soleil. It was March of last year and we were fresh out of ideas. The carbon fiber fins we had been pursuing were no longer an option—the cost estimates were more appropriate for a stealth bomber. We were out of time, we were out of money, and had no concept what to do next. It was at that March meeting that we tried to convince ourselves that the building would look just fine without a brise soleil. Just like every other time we got in trouble, we went back to Europe for a solution. This time we went to Santiago himself, as he had as much

The Burke Brise Soleil takes flight as schoolchildren file past the Baumgartner Family Terrace.

or more at stake than we did. A museum without the much-hyped brise soleil just was not an option. Santiago designed and supervised the fabrication in Spain of the fins. They were delivered by Russian jet and installed in time for our Gala Opening. And all of this for less money than our contractors wanted to build and test *just one fin* out of carbon fiber.

Much has been made of the $100 million cost of this addition. We worked hard to contain the cost while holding the design true to Calatrava's vision. We continually went back to the board and back to the donors for guidance, and the message was always the same: "You will only get one chance. Do it right!"

We did our best. The cost was high but the building in almost every way exceeded our expectations. Hopefully in the years to come, as people use and enjoy this building, the problems we encountered and the cost of the construction will be forgotten.

About a year or two after the Guggenheim Museum in Bilbao, Spain, was completed, my wife Donna and I went to have a look. And what a revelation this was. Here, in this decaying rust belt city, about the size of Milwaukee, on the north coast of Spain stood Frank Gehry's masterpiece. The impact his museum had on the community was enormous. Before the Guggenheim, Bilbao had fewer than 100,000 visitors annually and not one first-class hotel or restaurant. After the museum opened, they were seeing more than 1 million visitors a year with new hotels, new restaurants, a brand new airport, and much more. A true renaissance.

It's too early to say what the Calatrava addition will do for Milwaukee. But I can say what it's done for the Art Museum in the few short months we've been open, and it's impressive. Attendance is at 300,000, way over or best estimate, and the gift shop, with those wonderful pear wood display counters from Switzerland, had sales in November alone of $300,000.

All of us are very proud of what we've built, and we hope you will come often and enjoy this fabulous facility as much as we do. Thank you.

CHAPTER 12

"Who the Hell Ever Thought It Would Be You?"

I t was January, winter in Wisconsin. The Milwaukee Art Museum was opening its latest exhibition, *Uncommon Folk: Traditions in American Art*. Included in the show was a collection of quilts from the remote African American hamlet of Gee's Bend, Alabama. Sewed by women who were descendants of slaves, the quilts are regarded as some of the most important African American cultural contributions in the history of American art.

With little fanfare, a certain Hollywood celebrity slipped into town for the exhibition. "Jane Fonda came for the opening," says Donald. "She's a longtime supporter of the Gee's Bend quilt project, and the night of the opening, we had a dinner. I sat next to Jane. She was talkative and friendly, and as we chatted, I asked what she was doing in North Vietnam in 1972 sitting on an anti-aircraft gun in a Vietcong uniform. Her response was priceless. 'Donald, that was not a Vietcong uniform. That was Issey Miyake!'"

Donald dined with Jane Fonda when she attended an exhibition at the Milwaukee Art Museum.

The Japanese fashion designer was well known to Donald, which made him appreciate Jane's dodge all the more.

Donald has been mindful of fine clothing since he was a boy. "I discovered cashmere socks in fourth grade, and I've been very fussy about the way I dress since I was in high school," he says.

His fussy tastes reflected a refinement of how he presented himself and a flair that set him apart from the crowd—and still does. "I started with off-the-rack suits, slacks, and coats from designers like Valentino and Armani, which evolved into bespoke handmade suits, first from Oxxford Clothes in Chicago"—rated at one time as the top suit maker in the United States by Forbes— "and then Gieves and Hawk in London, one of the best tailors on Savile Row." When

Donald, sporting a cashmere jacket, valued fine clothing at an early age.

he had outgrown or replaced his suits, he donated them to the former Pennywise resale shop run by the Junior League of Milwaukee. His suits never hit the floor. One well-placed call and they were all picked off by police detectives, who needed suits for court appearances.

He shops for sweaters made from vicuña, a lightweight natural fiber softer than cashmere. "My shirts and sweaters and accessories were from Hermes and Loro Piana, both high-end shops, and shoes from Gucci. Now most everything, including shoes, are from Zilli, a menswear store in Paris. When I first met Santiago Calatrava and his wife, Tina, in Lyon, I was wearing a pair of olive green ostrich shoes, which caught Tina's attention." Also one of his staples are Zilli alligator loafers. "Alligator tends to be pretty sturdy. They're great in swamp water."

To his daughter, Sally, having a father who was a clotheshorse was a matter of course. "As far back as I can remember, he was always a flashy dresser, good looking and flamboyant. And he always had the alligator shoes. He loves good-looking shoes, and you could always see all the women looking at him, checking him out."

As the head of a manufacturing company that became a market leader internationally, Donald was good at making money, and good at spending it on the finer things in life. Suits, shirts, and slacks of the finest fabrics hang in his closets, shoes made from exotic leathers line the racks of his wardrobe. He owns a collection of Swiss-made watches that includes a Breguet Tourbillon and a Ulysses Nardin Blue Cruiser, an unconventional timepiece with a face that might be a little too hard to read. Each watch is kept on an automatic winder to ensure its accuracy.

As he has done when informing himself about opera, fine art, architecture, home design, and everything else that captures his imagination, Donald became a self-taught aficionado of fine wines. He studied the regions producing Bordeaux, Burgundy, Chardonnay, Champagne; he learned about growing seasons and how certain climates and soils impact a vineyard; he had a wine cellar built in his basement out of a former silver vault, and stocked it with over 1,000 bottles of wine from around the world. He's active in three wine-tasting clubs with good friends, sharing bottles of exceptional and rare wines.

Such are the inclinations of a self-made man with an eye for quality. "My tastes are simple," he says, borrowing a line from Winston Churchill. "I am easily satisfied with the very best."

Donald has been fascinated with automobiles his entire life. He bought his first sports car when he was in his twenties, a 1954 Kaiser Darrin two-door roadster—white with red leather seats and a red top—the first American car built with an all-fiberglass body. An unusual car for the times, the Kaiser Darrin turned heads at the red-bricked apartment building where he lived with his wife, Nancy, and their children, Sally and John. "I loved that red interior," says Sally, looking back to when she was six or seven. "He still has the fondness of the fancy cars, going back as far as I can remember."

A 1954 Kaiser Darrin convertible was Donald's first sports car.

From there, Donald's car collection escalated in price and horse-power—first Cadillacs, then Mercedes. "I bought my first serious sports car during my second marriage when I had a little extra cash. I owned a couple of sable brown Jaguars, an XKE convertible, and a Jaguar sedan. And this passion just sort of hung there. I was always looking at everybody else's cars. Then one day Donna and I went to a movie, *Down and Out in Beverly Hills.* It was about a guy who made a fortune making coat hangers. It was a silly movie, but I was so impressed when this guy making coat hangers bought a Rolls-Royce that I went out and I bought a Rolls-Royce myself. I thought, if he can have a Rolls-Royce as a coat hanger manufacturer, I sure as hell can have a Rolls-Royce as a cup-machine manufacturer, because paper cups are every bit as important as coat hangers. Just like the guy in the movie, I bought a Rolls-Royce Corniche convertible, named for the corniche roads along the Mediterranean in the south of France.

"After that, all hell broke loose. I bought a Ferrari Testarossa in 1985."

The red Italian sports car epitomized automotive styling and power. With its low-to-the-ground frame, rear-to-front tapered body, and twelve-cyclinder scream-of-a-jungle-cat engine that embodies the sound of speed itself, the

Top: Owning a Ferrari Testarossa opened the door to auto racing for Donald.
Bottom: His cigarette boat was painted Ferrari Red to match his Italian sports car.

Ferrari was a pure thrill to drive. It was fun, quirky, unique. Named Testarossa, or "red head," for the two red-painted cam covers on the engine, it was the kind of car that draws a crowd when parked. Notable owners have included the likes of Michael Jordan, Mike Tyson, Walter Payton, and Rod Stewart.

Matching the power of the red-headed Ferrari, Donald got hold of a high-performance "cigarette" boat he called the *Gamecock*, much like the one Don Johnson ran on the popular TV show *Miami Vice*. The speedboat was the open-water equivalent of a Ferrari Testarossa.

"The *Gamecock* was a forty-foot cigarette boat, an ocean water racer equipped with three, 454-cubic-inch 'Heavy Chevy' engines that put out 1,200 horsepower, with a top speed of seventy miles per hour. Originally owned by my father as the *Foxy Lady*, it was a plenty hot boat but in dire need of restoration. I took the boat to PMC, where I had some of our best mechanics give it a thorough going over, repainted it Ferrari Red, and renamed it the *Gamecock*. Then I had a graphic artist paint fighting roosters on the hull and foredeck.

It was ready, but for what? High-speed planing hulls on cigarette boats are problematic in rough water. On calm Friday nights, we would take friends to fish fries in Port Washington or Racine. Our most ambitious adventure was a high-speed, nonstop run to Mackinac Island. And our worst adventure was a crossing of Lake Michigan from Grand Haven in high seas. To stop the boat from floundering I had to use enough speed to keep us on plane, which meant about thirty-five to forty miles per hour, jumping from wave crest to wave crest. For three solid hours, we had a wall of ice water in our faces. This wasn't Miami, and I wasn't Don Johnson."

With a fast boat and a fast car, Donald was into speed. So why not try racing, he thought. "I bought the Testarossa from a dealer in Lake Forest, Illinois, and they encouraged me to drive in the historic Road America races at Elkhart Lake, Wisconsin," he recalls. "That was my first experience on the track, and I loved it." Located north of Milwaukee in a park-like setting of rolling hills and ravines, Road America's 4.048-mile, fourteen-turn track was built in 1955. Its original configuration has never been altered. Races run the gamut: from vintage cars to NASCAR pros to "gentlemen racers" who might want to bury the speedometers on their road cars without the risk of a speeding ticket.

"There was everything out there, from high-speed Ferraris like mine to some very ancient cars—everything but a Stanley Steamer. We weren't achieving super high speeds or anything like that, but I had an opportunity to open it up a little bit."

Donna graduated from the Skip Barber Racing School, and both of them joined the AMG Driving Academy offered at Road America. "They had a beginning class and they had an advanced class and then they had a race class. Then we took racing classes with Mercedes-AMG, and then Porsche on a track in Alabama. Donna took additional lessons from Ferrari on a track in the Laurentian Mountains in Quebec Province. And then Ferrari held back-to-back classes at Mont Tremblant near Montreal. Both Donna and I went through all three levels and received our advanced *Pilota's* license. So we went up to Canada and ran around like crazy. In each of these opportunities, we had full use of the track and went flat-out fast, clocking speeds of up to 170 miles an hour."

Also an avid racer, Donna more than once topped her male counterparts on the track.

Students competed among themselves. "We had a long track competition in Birmingham with the Porsches, along with a short track competition," says Donald. "In one of the races on the short track, there were six of us competing. To all of the guys' embarrassment, my son John included, Donna had the quickest time on the short course."

"All these girls were jumping up and down," Donna says, "and I had no idea why they were all so excited until I got out of the car and they told me I had the best time. I was just having fun. Who knew? And then I became totally bloated with myself, and when I did it the second time, I flew right off the track trying to beat my stunning upset."

Over the years, Donald and Donna have driven sports cars through England, Ireland, France, and Germany. They toured Italy with Red Travel in 2007 in a rented Ferrari followed by a guide car that hauled their luggage and charted the course. At the invitation of Mercedes Benz and as owners of a Mercedes-Benz SLR McLaren, they were able to participate in the

Donald and Donna participated in the reenactment of the Mille Miglia, an endurance race across Italy.

reenactment of the classic Mille Miglia, a 1,000-mile, open-road endurance race from Brescia to Rome. "We started at Mercedes headquarters in Stuttgart," Donald says. "We were given our cars and divided into small groups, mine led by Boris Becker, an International Tennis Hall-of-Fame champion with lighting fast reflexes, for the drive to Italy. We drove all night through Switzerland over the Alps through the rain at incredible speeds set by our very aggressive leader, Boris. The event itself was a bit less thrilling, as we were running with vintage cars."

Today Donald's pride and joy is his McLaren P1. With a carbon-fiber body and a 903-horsepower hybrid engine, the British-made McLaren was built with the performance characteristics of a Formula One racecar. Donald bought the car in Volcanic Orange. Since the purchase, the car has appreciated in value to well over $2 million.

The P1 is often described as a "hypercar," a class of automobiles occupied by few, cars such as the Porsche 918 Spyder, Ferrari LaFerrari, and the Baumgartners' Lamborghini Aventador and McLaren P1. Debuted at the Paris Motor Show, only 375 P1s were made in the year of production, 2013. The seven-speed, two-door coupe appears futuristic, with winged

course community in an Atlanta suburb. And as they chatted, Phil gazed out at the splendor of Donald's fifteen acres, tennis court and swimming pool, majestic hardwoods above the manicured lawn, woodland ponds and fountains, statuaries among neatly shaped hedges and rose gardens.

"We're standing out on the terrace," Donald recalls, "and Phil starts giggling. His wife says to him, 'Don't say it, Phil. Don't say it.' And Phil, he's got this big, shit-eating grin on his face and he's laughing. So finally I ask him, 'What is it, Phil?' And he looks at me and says, 'Well, Donald, I was just thinking to myself . . . who the hell ever thought it would be you?'"

Donald didn't have an easy answer to his friend's question. He'd had a sturdy upbringing and a measure of luck in his life, which he freely would admit. But he also possessed an independent nature, an inner steadiness that he drew on to solve problems and withstand adversity without getting shook, whether he was building a family business or sailing a boat through a hurricane-strength storm. With self-confidence and resilience, he had mastered his own destiny, had charted his own course, always. He was captain of his ship.

"I see myself as an optimist," he says now, "not because shit doesn't happen, but because I have the confidence to know I can handle it. Right or wrong, I've always seen myself as capable."

CHAPTER 13

Around the World in Eighty Years

Thousands of photographs taken around the world by Donald are stored in a small room in the basement of the Baumgartner home. Donald takes particular pride in his photos of animals in the wild. "The best shots I have are of tigers, lions, gorillas, black rhinos, zebras, and giraffes."

Along with his cache of photos, a large map of the world hangs on the basement wall, peppered with dozens of colored pushpins. "Donna and I traveled a lot from our first date on. I put a pin in the map wherever we had been, and it really expanded over time. Missing are some parts of Siberia, but practically everywhere else has a pin in it somewhere. Our courtship was all about travel. We went somewhere every weekend. I worked weekdays, and weekends we usually flew to wherever my dad was cruising. He was always on the move, throwing the lines off, heading to the next port, always exploring the waterways. Donna was a great traveler. We covered all the Great Lakes, up to Mackinaw Island, Beaver Island, up the Hudson River, and through the Erie Canal. We were always going somewhere, if not with Dad."

On one of their first trips together they went to Haiti. "I had heard about a very luxurious resort in Haiti," Donald says. "An oxymoron? I suppose it is. Haiti is a country that has seen so much turmoil and destruction, a country of the voodoo spirit, sex, death, and resurrection, a country of revolution and

233

In their travels together, Donald and Donna saw the world from many perspectives, including from above the Namibian desert.

the government's paramilitary group Tonton Macoute. Haiti was then and is today one of the poorest of the Banana Republics."

The resort was called Habitation Leclerc. It was built in the nineteenth century by Napoleon's sister, Pauline, and her husband General Leclerc, who was sent to Haiti to quell the slave revolt that later led to their independence. Years later it was set up as a resort by Katherine Dunham, the well-known American anthropologist and dancer who helped shape the Alvin Ailey dance by including Haitian folklore and introducing African and Caribbean music to modern dance. The resort attracted guests like Jackie Onassis and Mick Jagger. And Donald Baumgartner.

Like most of their travels, the trip to Haiti included an element of adventure—or, in this case, misadventure. "We drove our rented car one day to Jacmel in search of a pristine pool of water at the bottom of a waterfall," Donald recalls. "The only way to get there was a two-hour trek on horseback up a narrow steep trail. We took a young guide with us, a boy about fourteen, fifteen years old. The trail was on a sheer cliff overlooking the ocean. The descent was treacherous. We came to a ditch that the horses had to jump over, and Donna's horse refused to move. So the boy got off his horse to help and promptly slipped and fell over the edge. He's hanging on to a rock with one hand and a branch with the other, screaming '*Au secours! Au secours!*'—"Help!" And Donna says, 'Donald do something!' 'Like what?' I snorted. 'For Christ's sakes, help him!' So I got off my horse, reached down, pulled the kid up, and got him back on the path. I'm standing in back of my horse and in front of Donna's horse, and my horse took that opportunity to kick me with both feet in the chest. I fell backward into Donna's horse, which then bit me on the shoulder. I'm now in pain, but the kid is still moaning in French, scared out of his mind. With all this going on, his horse bolts back to the barn without him.

"Meanwhile, little did I know that my car keys had fallen out of my pocket somewhere on the trail. We got back to the stable, I have no car keys, it's getting dark. What now? Then suddenly, from out of nowhere, comes this parade of Haitians carrying torches to light the path and find my car keys. And that was enough drama for the day. What wonderful people.

"Donna loved Haiti and was not anxious to leave at the end of the trip. She especially loved the art and the food. The French restaurants in Petion-ville were exceptional. Donna had her first taste of duck. There was duck a l'orange, duck with peach Melba, duck with green peppercorns, and duck with cherries. She had duck every night we were in Haiti."

Standing in front of the world map, Donald traces a course with his finger that follows the pushpins from the Hawaiian Islands to Mexico's Sea of Cortez, Cabo San Lucas, Acapulco, and then down into the Southern Hemisphere to the Galapagos Islands; Lima, Peru; and the ancient Incan ruins of Machu Picchu, high in the Andes. "The air is rare at Machu Picchu," says Donald. "They brewed coca leaves for us into a tea to help with the extreme altitude and hovered to make sure we finished the whole pot."

Donna and Donald on a later trip visited the Peruvian port city of Iquitos, gateway to the Upper Amazon River. There they hopped on a small boat to a special lake where they could swim with the pink dolphins. "Instead, we went swimming with the little fish that are supposed to swarm and rip at your flesh, the piranha," he says. "But they're not at all that vicious. Hollywood and the media created these images of piranhas as human flesh-eaters.' Massive Piranha

Donna does the paddling on a leisurely cruise down the Upper Amazon River in a dugout canoe.

Despite the overblown warnings, Donald and Donna swam comfortably with "flesh-eating" piranhas.

Attack,' cries *The New York Post*. Well, we were swimming with piranhas, no problem."

Donna's more memorable moments in the Amazon were the visits to the villages and meetings with the children. Says Donna, "Not just bringing gifts to them—Green Bay Packer gear, pencils, and paper—but asking questions, like what they wanted to be when they grow up. 'A tourist,' one child smartly replied. The tour operators there were very impressive. They have come a long way from their fathers, who hunted exotic birds and animals to earn a living, to learning the value of conservation—as a value in itself, and for the survival of their culture. It has catapulted them from hunters to educators."

"Most of our Third World adventure trips involved kids," she adds. "They were the greeters, the welcome committee. They were very curious and always surrounded and followed us, sometimes looking for money, bonbons, souvenirs, or just to learn English. We often carried Packer T-shirts. On a walking trip through Vietnam, we had a group following us and Donald was teaching them to chant 'Go Pack Go.'" After their trip down the Amazon, they flew to Patagonia, Chile, and were guests on a PMC customer's 200-foot yacht. "The boat had two helipads," Donald says. "Everyday the helicopter would drop us at a remote stream for fly fishing."

Fitting kids in a village in the Amazon with Green Bay Packers garb, Donald taught them how to cheer "Go Pack Go!"

They've been to Rio de Janeiro and Sao Paolo in Brazil for the Formula One races, and went with friends to Buenos Aires and Bariloche in Argentina. "We took Kelly's family to Cartagena, Columbia, for New Year's Eve," he says. "They pull out all stops for New Year's Eve. To say it was an over-the-top, nonstop extravaganza would not be an overstatement. You can see on the map we've also been all through Central America: through the Panama Canal with Dad, Costa Rica for Christmas, and Belize, where Dad retired, many times."

Scuba driving was one of their favorite activities. Donald planned diving trips to some of the top diving spots on the planet. "The greatest diving we ever did was in the Maldives, 1,000 coral islands in the Indian Ocean," he says. "It is unquestionably the most pristine in the world. The water is clear beyond belief. We stayed on a Four Seasons yacht. It was completely outfitted as a luxe dive boat. We were five days with master divers, and twice a day we'd dive with one or two tanks. Clearly the top diving experience of a lifetime.

"Then we scuba dived on the Great Barrier Reef off Australia's east coast. I hired a floatplane to take me out to the reef with Donna and Kelly. I'm sitting in the cockpit with the pilot, and I said to him, 'You take a lot of divers out here. Just between you and me, this place really has a bad reputation for great white sharks. Do you ever see any?' He says, 'Oh, my God, no. That's just a lot of conversation. We don't have any problem with sharks out here. Don't worry about it.'

So we dropped the floatplane next to the reef. I suit up, step down onto the float, put my mask on, put my breathing gear on, drop into the

Donna and Donald traveled to some of the best scuba diving sites in the world, from Australia's Great Barrier Reef to the Maldives, an island nation in the Indian Ocean.

water—and I am face to face with a great white. He's not three feet away from me. We're eyeball to eyeball, and his head is—Christ, it's huge! He looks at me. I look at him. And I jumped straight up out of the water. Donna said she saw me walk on my flippers. We waited until the big guy swam away—we hoped—and then went diving. The reef was filled with marine activity. It was just great."

Although it might have been the spine chilling, his encounter with a great white wasn't his only brush with a shark. Donald was swimming with his grandkids off the coast of Belize in Shark Ray Alley, where swimmers and divers can mingle happily with nurse sharks and stingrays. "The rays and nurse sharks are friendly enough," he says. "The children are paddling around, playing with the rays and hanging on to the sharks' fins. I'm in with the kids too, and as I get out of the water, suddenly an interloping bull shark not familiar with the drill came by and took a big horseshoe bite right out of my flipper."

Their excursions took them to the other side of the world. Their first trip to South Africa was in the late seventies. That included their first safari, to Mala Mala, a huge private game preserve. In the mid-eighties, they went to Central Africa, then the northern coast of the African continent, Casablanca in Morocco. They've traveled to Istanbul to St. Petersburg, and to Moscow with Kelly during Mikhail Gorbachev's perestroika reforms, returning to these places on their own years later to observe the changes after the Soviet Union collapsed.

Their trips to Africa always started or ended with stops in London or Paris. "We were on the maiden voyage of the Queen Mary, traveling in a lavish 'Queens Grill' suite," says Donald. "It was black tie, all very stuffy, all super luxe; if you have the time it's a great way to start a European holiday. A fun way to get from Paris to London is the Eurostar, a two-hour-and-twenty-minute train trip through the Chunnel. We boarded our first-class coach on the Eurostar at the Gare du Nord station in Paris." Donna was helping the only other person in their car put her luggage in the overhead. "You look just like Juliette Binoche," Donna said to her. "I *am* Juliette Binoche, and I have a script to read," she replied, putting an end to their short conversation.

Trips to Africa took Donald and Donna to Victoria Falls, at the border between Zambia and Zimbabwe, and Mala Mala, a private game reserve in South Africa.

Opposite: The couple visited some of the oldest ruins on Earth, including pyramids along the Nile River.

With Kelly along on another rail trip, they boarded one of the most legendary set of train carriages in the world, the Venice Simplon-Orient-Express, from London to Paris to Vienna. "It was all very upscale except they were using the original carriages made by Compagnie Internationale des Wagons-Lits, carriages dating from the 1920s, a time well before today's modern shock absorbers, which made sleeping just about impossible. But dinner was black tie, very formal, and would be the highlight of the trip. After dressing with some difficulty in the confines of our small stateroom, we started walking through the carriages to the dining car when I noticed heads turning, people smiling, grinning at Donna and nodding approvingly. It seems her top had sprung loose, exposing her left breast to its full advantage. "Holy shit, how embarrassing!" she says, remembering the episode.

Donna's wardrobe malfunction aside, just getting from one place to the next could be an adventure in itself. "It was thrilling to watch the countryside spinning by on a bullet train in China," Donald says. "The Chinese spent $360 billion on high-speed rail from Beijing to Shanghai, and at 350 kilometers per hour, nothing comes close. Another but less dramatic ride took us 1,600 kilometers on the Blue Train from Cape Town to Pretoria overlooking South Africa's mountain ranges and vast savannahs. We had a very large, comfortable stateroom. I remember being horrified when they served their national symbol for dinner—grilled springbok."

By trains, boat, sports car, and sometimes elephant, they were early passengers as well on the supersonic Aerospatiale/ BAC Concorde turbojet, he says. "We flew New York–London and Nice–Washington, D.C., at over 1,300 miles per hour, or Mach 2.04. For three-and-a-half

hours across the Atlantic at 60,000 feet, you could make out the curvature of the Earth. I can't believe they took it out of service. Some years later friends invited us to a New Year's Eve party in Palm Springs with some high rollers including the president of Lockheed and the Saudi billionaire and arms dealer Adnan Khashoggi, who was showing us a brochure of his newly outfitted private DC-10. Lockheed was part of a group effort to sell Khashoggi a refurbished Concorde as a private jet. The next day we stopped by the Polo Lounge for lunch. The maître d' looked at us like, 'There is no way you're ever going to get a table,' when out of the blue Adnan spots Donna and waves her over. The maître d' sees this, snaps his fingers, and, like magic, a table appears."

One of their more extraordinary trips was with the tour group Backstage with the Arts, a joint venture with tour operator TCS, hotel operator Four Seasons, and La Fugue, an opera travel group based in Europe. Living up to its name, the tour took travelers behind the curtain for unique performances and art exhibits in Paris, Portugal, Milan, Istanbul, St Petersburg, and Prague.

"It's not just that it was super luxe, it was all the surprises that awaited us at every stop," Donna says. "In Lisbon, we arrived for cocktails and candlelight in the Jeronimos Monastery, a sixteenth century architectural masterpiece, which is magical enough in itself. After the cocktails and beautifully catered appetizers, we were asked to walk quietly down a long, ancient, arched candlelit corridor. It was enchanting, with soft music beckoning. We sat in chairs and were treated to the sounds of a lone oboe musician playing *Gabriel's Oboe* by Ennio Morricone, followed by a quartet, making the evening more magical.

"As we arrived in Milan, we stopped to pay a visit to Giuseppe Verdi's tomb. In his will, Verdi bequeathed that all his royalties would go into the retirement home for opera singers and musicians where his tomb is located. As we turned to walk back through the courtyard, a large chorus appeared, dressed in black, singing his most famous aria, 'Va Pensiero.' The inhabitants of the home were hanging out the window, banging on the walls in appreciation. Later in Milan, we met with the director of La Scala, the historic opera house. We were led on a backstage tour and watched a rehearsal."

The tourists never knew what to expect next. "In St. Petersburg, while touring St. Issac's Cathedral, we turned around to be met by a famed children's chorus," Donna continues, "and in Vladimir's Palace, while having cocktails, the Red Orchestra made its grand entrance. In Prague's Strahov Monastery, a full symphony orchestra played, hidden behind a metal screen on the proscenium. We ended the tour in Paris. We dined at the Jules Verne Restaurant in the Eiffel Tower and were treated to a post-dinner performance of three musicians hanging somehow from above us at unprecedented heights and playing amplified sounds on the tower's steel beams. It was a completely exhilarating and inspired trip."

They've traveled to the Mideast a few times: Israel, Jordan, Lebanon, the United Arab Emirates. They stayed in a desert camp outside of Dubai that was supposed to rival the safari camps of Africa. The animals, however, were imported from the forests and savannahs of Africa and died from the extreme heat of the desert.

"We've been to India twice," Donald says. "One time we went with a group of friends and did the grand tour of the Golden Triangle, traveling to the cities of Delhi, Jaipur, and Agra. We played elephant polo, stayed at hotels that are unmatched in splendor, and spent a night with the camels in a tented safari camp. We returned later on our own in search of tigers from the back of an elephant. I've got some great pictures of tigers. They were damn hard to get. You can go on a tiger safari and never

Trying on traditional Indian apparel.

A camel caravan through the "lost" city of Petra, Jordan, the site of scenes in the movie Indiana Jones and the Last Crusade.

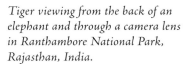

Tiger viewing from the back of an elephant and through a camera lens in Ranthambore National Park, Rajasthan, India.

see one. They're nocturnal and very shy. These are the Bengal tigers, the big ones, up to a thousand pounds, and even though you feel safe on the top of an elephant, it has happened where tigers have leapt up onto the elephant and taken out the *mahout*.

"We met friends in Bangkok and cruised the Irrawaddy River in Myanmar on the road to Mandalay. Pretty exotic, even for seasoned travelers. Donna and I recently chartered a 100-foot yacht and cruised from Phuket through the Straits of Malacca to Langkawi in Malaysia. We've been to China on the Yangzee, traveled in New Zealand by a helicopter, and taken river trips in Papua New Guinea with Kelly, where we danced with the Huli Wigmen, a tribe of indigenous people in the country's highlands. It's a culture barely known to the outside world."

A chance meeting with a stranger led to an impromptu trip to Sri Lanka in the late seventies. Donna recalls the details: "We met this character in a white suit at a gambling casino in Haiti who was having legal problems with all the massage parlors he owned in Mississippi. His legal issues were most likely sending him to jail and preventing him from going on a trip that he had previously booked. So he offered his Sri Lanka tickets to Donald, and Donald, not one to spurn such an offer, jumped at the opportunity. We spent Christmas of 1978 touring the country and rode elephants on the beach. It turned out to be a very timely trip. Civil war broke out in 1983, and the country was closed to tourism for the next thirty years."

If judged by the incessant incidents of conflict and violence in the post-9/11 no-travel-zone world, Donald and Donna's journeys have been surprisingly problem free. "People generally have been extremely nice to us," Donald says. "We've always been treated well, and I have the highest regard for the people we've met."

There have been a few near disasters. "I wouldn't recommend traveling to Paris on May 3," says Donald. "It's the annual reenactment of the student uprising of 1968. We were meeting friends for dinner on the Left Bank and got caught up in the confrontation between an angry mob of students and the gendarmes dressed in full riot gear. They lobbed tear gas canisters over our heads as we were exiting the taxi right in the crosshairs of all this excitement."

A cruise down the Nile turned out to be a bust. "Out of all the Middle Eastern countries we've been to, Egypt was the most unpredictable," Donna says. "Our guides were inexplicably misleading and deceitful. That was really the only bad trip we've ever had. Although in Rome with Kelly, walking around the Colosseum, we were pickpocketed. I looked down and my fanny pack was open and there were things missing. These little kids, gypsies, were distracting me by shoving newspapers in my face with stories of terrible calamities in the world. Meanwhile, they're pickpocketing me. So I grabbed a bunch of them by the shirt collar." Nearly stripping the young bandits naked, she found Kelly's passport in one boy's clothes. "Donald held two of them by their collars while I searched the other one, and Kelly was pretending she didn't know us—Parents? Not mine! They had incredible sleight of hand and were fearlessly passing money back and forth between them. Finally I screamed 'Polizia!' And they dropped everything and ran off. Although Kelly was happy to have her passport back, she wasn't so sure about her parents."

The Japanese understand hospitality probably better than any country in the world, says Donald. "They treat visitors as honored guests. Every hotel, every restaurant, department store, wherever you go, people are extremely polite. It's the gold standard. But you would not want to live there. As an indigenous society, they are not so welcoming of strangers who live among them."

Among the most captivating trips were the African safaris. "The first time we went to Central Africa," Donald says, "we went with our friends, Bonnie and Leon Joseph, and Joe and Ellen Checota, and we all took our children. They were in high school. There were eleven of us, and I planned it for the group—a Hemingway kind of safari where we walked a lot and also rode in Jeeps. We visited Mount Kilimanjaro in Tanzania and walked in the Ngorongoro Crater, the world's largest intact volcanic crater where, if you're lucky, you can get a glimpse of each of the so-called Big Five predators—lions, leopards, rhinos, African elephant, and African buffalo.

"We also went to the Masai Mara, a preserved savannah wilderness in southwestern Kenya," he says. "Along the way we met the Masai, who were herding their cattle. Ellen had brought a Polaroid camera along, and the Masai were very curious and excited to see pictures of themselves."

All © Donald Baumgartner

Top: Two rhino in Moremi Game Reserve, Botswana. Middle left: Cheetah at Mpumalanga, Kruger National Park in South Africa. Middle right: An elephant crossing the Chobe River, Botswana. Bottom: Leopard in Sabi Sands Game Reserve, Greater Kruger National Park.

"Of all the places we've traveled," Donna says, "the safaris in Africa are at the top of the list. They are the most rewarding. You become immediately enveloped in the surroundings, in the life of the villages, the clamor of everyday life, and the wonder of the animals. You become engaged in their survival. They are all under threat either from poachers or the laws of the jungle. On one safari, the camp brought in a small group of villagers to entertain us, and we ended up dancing with them and sharing in their celebration of life."

"We used a plane to go from one spot to the other," Donald says. "Down in the bush, we would see elephants on the move and herds of Cape buffalo. In the open jeeps, we were plenty close to different prides of lion. The guides are incredibly knowledgeable. They know the prides. They know the lives these lions have had. They can read the scars on their faces."

"There is nothing to compare to being out in the wild on the savannah watching the animals live their lives," adds Donna. "We saw a baby elephant

African lions in Etosha National Park, Namibia, on the plains and after a hunt, below.

Opposite: Nap time on the jungle floor of the Odzala Rainforest, Democratic Republic of Congo.

only minutes old taking its first steps, and not far away a male lion was munching on an young elephant surrounded by his lioness and offspring, who where showing remarkable restraint waiting for permission to dine. It's the whole cycle of life in an afternoon from a jeep."

Another safari took them deep into the jungle in the Democratic Republic of Congo in central Africa. "We went into the Congo looking for gorillas to photograph," says Donald. "There are highland and lowland gorillas. I wanted to find the lowland gorilla because I thought we would be able to do it on the Congo River and that would be easier for me on a boat than climbing a mountain. And the guides said, no, no, you have to walk. No boat. Well, walking through a jungle with a machete, cutting your way hour after hour through brush tangled with vines is no picnic. We are right on the equator, it's over 100 degrees and extremely humid. The sweat is pouring off of me. We finally find the gorilla family. There they are. I'm taking pictures of these wonderful creatures, and I decide I'm going to stay and live with the gorillas. I'm not walking back."

"He laid down right there on the jungle floor," says Donna. "He said he was done. So we all sat down. There was one other couple and their guide—we just sat and waited. And Donald took a nap."

© Donald Baumgartner

King of the jungle and a Western lowland gorilla, Odzala Rainforest, Democratic Republic of Congo.

"It was just totally exhausting," says Donald. "But I got some great shots of the gorillas." An entire wall in Donald's office is filled with photos of wildlife from their African travels—lions, elephants, zebras, and gorillas taken from elephant back, jeep, small boat, and on foot.

In 2014, Donald and Donna traveled to the Kingdom of Bhutan in the Himalayan Mountains. They had read that Bhutan had a reputation for being the "Happiest Place on Earth." Once one of the poorest countries in the world, the tiny country with a population of 800,000 people—the only remaining Buddhist kingdom in the world—now receives high scores for its quality of life.

"We wanted to see what the happiest place in the world looked like," Donald says. So they booked a flight and a room at a luxurious Aman Hotel with a view of snow-capped peaks 24,000 feet above sea level. "Knowing the quality of Aman Hotels and the quality of their food and service. I thought, what the hell, let's try Bhutan. We've never been there. Let's see what it's like.

"Bhutan is way up high, next to Nepal," he says, pointing to a pushpin halfway between India and China. "It's run as a monarchy by a king and queen. The queen was drop-dead gorgeous, and the king is a benevolent king. It's a small country with a lot of hydropower. They've got dams and they sell electricity to India. With such a small population, they all can live off the sales of their hydroelectric power. The quality of life is high because there's almost no poverty, and the hard labor is done by temporary laborers from Bangladesh. They are brought in for maximum of two years. Year after year the Bhutanese are voted the happiest people in the world. Denmark is second usually. They compete with Denmark for happy place."

Donald and Donna receive a ceremonial welcome to Bhutan, the "happiest country in the world."

Donna at the Tiger's Nest, a Himalayan Buddhist monastery in Bhutan.

The people of Bhutan were indeed happy folks, as illustrated by the display of phalluses that are painted on houses and buildings throughout the land. Apparently in Bhutan, the belief exists that the image of a penis is a symbol of good luck and drives away evil and malice. "People have pictures of penises on their buildings and penis door knockers, which I didn't quite understand," says Donald. "It's part of their happy culture, I guess, because the penises are always portrayed in a very happy state."

The trip to Bhutan was just one stop in an exceptional year of travel for the couple. All told, in 2013 they visited Bhutan, Cuba, Ecuador, the Galapagos Islands, Taiwan, Bangkok, Hong Kong, Venice, Verona, Tuscany, Pisa, Paris, South Africa, the Congo, Colorado, New York City (twice), and San Francisco Bay to watch the America's Cup boat races aboard a yacht.

Beginning in 1973, traveling became a yearly holiday tradition during the Christmas season for the extended Baumgartner family. It began in Florida, where JR lived with Thelma and their daughters, Carolyn and Roberta. Sometime after JR retired, he bought property in British Honduras, which was renamed Belize when it gained independence from Great Britain. "When Dad

Growing larger by the year, the extended Baumgartner family spends Christmas vacations at tropical sites such as Florida's Captiva Island.

moved down there, it was called British Honduras, and he liked that." Donald says. "And one day they changed the name to Belize, and it really infuriated him. 'How can you live in a country where you wake up one morning and the name is changed?' he complained. 'I liked British Honduras well enough.'"

"Belize City was so primitive when he first moved down there," says Roberta, who was a young child at the time. "The city was really nasty. It had open sewers and had been ravaged by hurricane after hurricane. The people couldn't rebuild fast enough. Over the years it did get better. They fixed the sewers and started from scratch with new buildings, new roads."

JR and his family lived downtown in Belize City in a big white house built on stilts. He purchased a property twelve miles into the forest along the Belize River to develop a "plantation," which he named Ridge Lagoon. "He imported large, earth-moving machines so he could build his empire on the river," Roberta says. "Eventually he sold or lent the machines out to the government so the country could build its road system. So he had a hand in helping Belize get on its feet."

The Christmas vacations began alternating between Florida and Belize. "Back then, it was not developed," says Sally, who spent an entire summer at

JR and his grandson, John, tow an airboat at JR's plantation, Ridge Lagoon, in Belize.

Three generations of Baumgartners—Donald, John, and JR.

the plantation with her brother, John. "Now it's eco-tourism, and so everybody wants to go and see the rainforest and the animals that exist there. My grandfather was huge with the Audubon Society. There are birds there that are very rare, and he would put Audubon people up at Ridge Lagoon and take them up the river in his airboat. In the middle of his plantation, he had a workshop with machines. That was his love of machinery. My grandmother was a wonderful sport living in Belize, leaving her Fort Lauderdale existence and her church and the Coral Ridge Yacht Club. All of a sudden, she's in the middle of this jungle. She put up with whatever he wanted. He was happy there. He would just tinker with stuff. He brought in swans and dredged out a pond and called it Thelma's Pond. Unfortunately, the crocodiles got into the pond and ate those beautiful white swans. We used to water ski on the Belize River, which had crocodiles in it too. We were young and didn't know." As part of his empire, JR started a chicken production company called Mayan Broilers. "He hatched the eggs, he raised the pullets, and then he sold the chickens to the grocery stores," Roberta says. "He wanted to feed the people. Meat was very expensive, and people would eat goat, mainly. My dad loved fried chicken, and chickens were cheaper to raise, so he thought that would be the best thing. It didn't work out, though. It was poorly managed."

Sally remembers the chicken plant. "One of my cousins, Sheryl, still can't eat chicken," she says. "She was a young child and took a tour of Mayan Broilers. She saw the chickens being placed on a conveyor and then their heads were chopped off. I didn't go on the tour, so I don't know exactly what happened to the chickens. But whatever it was, Sheryl to this day—and she's now in her fifties—will not eat chicken."

As the youngest kids grew older, the family began to spend Christmas holidays at resorts in Hawaii, Cabo San Lucas, Puerto Vallarta, Jamaica, and Costa Rica.

"It started when JR and Thelma and Grandpa's mom, Mae Lucille, and Elmer joined in," says Jessica Baumgartner, John's daughter and Donald's oldest grandchild. "They wanted to keep all their kids together at Christmas, so that meant Donald's four parents, his four kids, along with Jean, and then Carolyn and Roberta, their husbands, and more kids. Then the grandkids started popping up. So it just started expanding and expanding. It's kind of like a Christmas pyramid scam. We just all want to get in on all of these fun Christmas trips." As many as thirty-five family members have turned out in recent years for the annual vacations.

Added to the rotation was Donald and Donna's log home near Vail. "It's made for comfort," says Jessica. "You don't feel like you have to dress up. You know, you kick off your ski boots, and you walk around in in your socks and your leggings and your T-shirt. No fuss, no muss. Every morning, Grandpa makes the eggs, the best scrambled eggs you've ever had in your life. I've asked him what he does to the eggs. 'Do you add cream or something? Do you add sour cream?' And he says, 'Nope. I don't do anything.' I'm, like, sure. He would *not* share his secret recipe with me."

One year Jessica worked as a waitress in Aspen at a Japanese restaurant named Matsuhisa, run by the world-renowned chef Nobu Matsuhisa, who also owns restaurants in London, Los Angeles, and one in New York that's co-owned by Robert DeNiro. The Aspen location was a magnet for Hollywood stars. "I waited on Mariah Carey. I waited on Arnold Schwarzenegger. I waited on Jack Nicholson," says Jessica. "Because people in L.A. couldn't get into Beverly Hills

Matsuhisa, they'd fly to Aspen to eat there. So when it opened, my grandfather was really excited to try it. He and Donna, or Bubbi, came to visit with maybe ten friends. I sat with them at this big, round table in the middle of the restaurant, and he let me order for everybody, which was a really big deal to me. It was a little intimidating, I'm not going to lie, but I thought, *If I can do it for Jack Nicholson, I can do it for my grandpa.*

"So we ordered a bunch of food and everything was amazing," she says. "Then we ordered this high-end sake, Junmai and Daiginjo, that are served cold in these little bamboo cups. My grandfather started sending bottles of the Junmai and Daiginjo to the chefs at the sushi bar; it's kind of customary when you're happy with your food. And the chefs were getting a little wasted because he kept sending them more and more. Soon they were screaming across the restaurant. 'Kanpai! Grandpa-san, Kanpai!' It's a Japanese toast, 'Cheers!' We've got this big table right in the middle of this very fancy restaurant, and they're screaming it across the room, 'Kanpai, Grandpa-san.' It was so funny. There's now a Matsuhisa in Vail, and whenever I go to Vail, Grandpa and Bubbi take me to Matsuhisa. Every time, we do a Kanpai, Grandpa-san toast."

The family trips tend to be in warm and exotic locations, and the planned events are almost always active—jet skiing, snorkeling, tubing, fishing, swimming with dolphins, along with snowboarding and skiing when in the Rockies. "We were on a cruise ship for one Christmas, and the entire family decided to do a Karaoke Night," says Tammy Jarrar, the younger of Sally's two daughters and the mother of Donald and Donna's first great-grandchild, Bella. "My grandpa and Bubbi picked out 'I Got You Babe' and sang it together. It was a very cute couple moment."

Donald and Donna have attended all of her graduations and her wedding, says Tammy, who lives in California. "I graduated from Lebanese American University; my father is from Lebanon. Grandfather brought the family to my graduation in Beirut. And after my wedding to my husband, Talal, they toured Lebanon. Talal and I showed them around. Then we went to Jordan and stayed in Amman. From there, they went to Petra, where they swam in the Dead Sea and got all covered in mud. They were up for all of these things."

Donald receives a gift from his great-granddaughter, Bella.

Baumgartner vacations are not without a little drama. On a trip to the Bahamas in 1994, Donald suffered a gallbladder attack. "I was in Nassau at Christmas with the family," he says. "I came down for breakfast, and my daughter, Lisa, had this whole fish on her plate—head, eyes, tail, the whole damn thing. She was carving away at it, and all of a sudden I got extremely nauseous. I thought it was from watching Lisa eat this damn fish. But it wouldn't let up. So they rushed me to the hospital in Nassau and discovered that my gallbladder had happily welded itself to my liver. They had to remove it. They put me on a local anesthetic, and they've got some local doctor, who probably just made it out of the University of Grenada, trying to get at my gallbladder. I'm half awake while he's trying to fish it out through my naval. He kept saying, 'I got it, I got it, I haven't got it. I got it, I got it, I haven't got it.' It was a nightmare. Donna was in the OR standing behind a screen with a window and watched the whole thing. This was our anniversary, after all. Fifteen years to the day.

"After the surgery, I got peritonitis. I had a raging fever and was in agony forever and eternity. The pain was much worse than when I passed a kidney stone on the top of Vail Mountain and had to ski all the way down hunched over my skis. In Nassau, they kept me in the hospital for eight days. I thought I was going to die for sure. My first inclination was to get Medevac'd to a major hospital in Miami. But my temperature was up in the 104-105 range, at the top of the thermometer, and I just couldn't be moved. They couldn't even get me to an airplane. So I put up with the local doctors. And they soon discovered they had a tourist in the hospital with a credit card. Every doctor came by and swiped my card. I had a foot doctor come by. I had an eye doctor come by. A psychiatrist! I mean, I got examined by every doctor on staff. Swipe, swipe, swipe, swipe.

"That's about as close to death as I've ever been. I no longer have a gall bladder and I have not missed it at all. The appendix is totally useless, and the gallbladder is a close second. If you have to lose an organ, get rid of your gallbladder. It doesn't matter a hell of a lot, and you won't have people saying you've got a lot of gall."

Family events are ongoing year-round. Thanksgiving dinners are hosted by Donald and Donna. "Donald cooks the turkey," Donna says. "The kids bring the sides while I challenge myself every year to build an even more elaborate cornucopia of several varieties of squash, kale, herbs, and fruit than the year before. It could weigh as much as a couple hundred pounds. As the eighteen or twenty of us are seated around the table, Donald begins with his annual reading of stories 'And the Fair Land,' a tribute to America, and 'The Desolate Wilderness,' a chronicle of the Pilgrims' arrival at Plymouth, as they have appeared in *The Wall Street Journal* every year since 1961." Particularly relevant even today is the poetic "And the Fair Land," as demonstrated by this excerpt:

> We can remind ourselves that for all our social discord
> we yet remain the longest enduring society of free men
> governing themselves without benefit of kings or dictators.
> Being so, we are the marvel and the mystery of the world . . .

"Donald has never made it to the end with out choking up," Donna says. Donald was introduced to narrative poetry when he was a high school freshman. "I was swept away," he says. "I memorized any number of poems, including Longfellow's 'Wreck of the Hesperus' and Robert Browning's 'Herve Riel.' Another winner at that time was Shakespeare's Henry V 'Band of Brothers' speech before the Battle of Agincourt."

For the 4th of July, the family flocks to Sturgeon Bay, Wisconsin, the site of a house built on the ship canal connecting Green Bay with Lake Michigan. "This was a place my Dad loved dearly and visited often, a place where he would spend his final days," Donald says. In his will, JR made a donation to the nearby Door County Maritime Museum to establish the Baumgartner Gallery, which includes a lighthouse exhibit and a collection of ship models. His grandson, John Baumgartner, paid it forward in 2018 with a contribution to help construct an observation tower at the museum.

Right up to the last year of his life, the Skipper was on the water. In Florida in 2000, he took the helm of his sixty-six-foot motor yacht, *The Ranger*, and, with family and friends aboard, sailed from Fort Lauderdale to Key West. Months later, he battened down the hatches and sold his last yacht, *The Isabella*. On September 30, 2000, John Robert Baumgartner passed away in Sturgeon Bay at age ninety-three.

Father and son ply the waters of Lake Michigan, a familiar pastime throughout their lives.

Donald was seventy when his father died. At JR's memorial, he read Longfellow's poem "Burial of the Minnisink," then spoke movingly about the all-encompassing influence his father had on his life.

> He was my father.
> He was my mentor.
> He was my friend.
> Few sons could be so blessed as to have a father so full of life, so full of excitement, so full of adventure.
> He didn't just fill my life; he overwhelmed it with his presence.
> Where he went, I followed.
> He manufactured machinery, I manufacture machinery.
> He loved the sea, I love the sea.
> It would be hard, no, impossible to conceive of where my life would have gone without his powerful influence.

In ninety-three years, a lot of water had passed under this man's keel. Cruising with Dad was always an experience. I guess he loved a challenge because we never left the harbor in clear weather or calm water. Or, for that matter, with enough fuel. When the going got tough, Pop was at his best, even if he had to create a crisis.

Most of you here, and certainly everyone in the family, has a favorite story. I would like to remember Dad at the wheel in a Lake Superior gale. We were trout fishing on his eighty-three-foot motor yacht, *Trenora*, on the north shore of Lake Superior. It was either late September or early October. We left Michipicoten Island early in the morning for Sault Ste. Marie. The weather was overcast with winds from the north at twenty-five knots and waves ten to twelve feet. By the time we were abreast of Caribou Island, the wind had backed into the northwest, and the weather station there was reporting a steady fifty knots!

We were caught in a Force-Ten whole gale, and things were only getting worse as we entered the shallower water of Whitefish Bay. The waves breaking over the transom were running twenty feet or higher. The scene was right out of the movie *Perfect Storm*. The Skipper had been at the wheel for at least eight hours, but refused to let me relieve him. He was grinning from ear to ear and obviously enjoying himself *way too much*.

That was my father. And I will never think of him any other way. Nor would I want to.

CHAPTER 14

Conquest and Loss

Throughout his life, Donald has focused on staying healthy and fit. He played football and threw the shot put at Shorewood High School and played football at the University of Wisconsin.

He was in his late forties when he and Donna got together. She had been working as a pistol-packing, badge-wearing, mini-skirted Cook County sheriff in the Chicago courts. "I had married this hot, vital young lady sixteen years my junior. Dick Fritz, my physician and a friend, said to me, 'You know, we ought to take your testosterone count and make sure you're up for this young woman.' He took a blood sample, the results came back, and it was normal. So Dick said, 'You should think about supplements anyway.' He sent me to the hospital, and once a week I'd get a shot of testosterone. Well, my GOD! What a difference that shot in the ass made, and I'm not just talking about putting a smile on Donna's face. Racing cars, crossing oceans, expanding the business . . . I was *driven*.

"At the same time I was supplementing with testosterone, I started a weight training program. I read about this guy who just moved back to Milwaukee after living in Saudi Arabia where he weight trained the Royal Saudi Air Force. I thought that sounded about right and had Donna call him shortly after my fiftieth birthday. I worked with Mike Jellich from 1980 to 2000. One day I was in New York City and went to the hotel gym to work out. A young lady with a very thick Brooklyn accent came up to me. She looked me over, up and down, and said, 'What are you doing? Look in the mirror. You're *perfect* already! So look in the mirror!' I guess I had gotten pretty well buffed."

Donald was an avid skier most of his life. He didn't hold back. As he does behind the wheel of his sports cars, he put the pedal to the metal, flying down the slopes as fast as he could. When he was seventy-one, he took a bad fall on a run on Vail Mountain and tore the ACL (anterior cruciate ligament) in his right knee. He was carted off the mountain to the ER. Surgery was needed to repair the knee, and he was admitted to the renowned Steadman Hawkins Clinic, a sports medicine facility in Vail.

The surgery started on an unexpectedly bawdy note: "I was on a gurney on my way to surgery, pushed by two nurses, with an anxious Donna hanging on the side," Donald remembers. "One of the nurses saw I still had my shorts on under my hospital gown and asked me to remove them. Donna kissed me goodbye and wished me luck as we entered the OR, and one nurse turned to the other and said, 'Have you ever seen anything so big?' The other nurse replied, 'Oh my God, *no*. It's enormous!' I was taken aback, so I said to them, 'Will you please give me back my shorts.' The nurses laughed. 'No, no,' one of them said. 'We were talking about your wife's diamond.'"

Years later he had a casual conversation with another doctor, also his friend, and again got a bit of unsolicited advice. This time the advice turned urgent.

It was May 2000. Donald was at a Tina Turner concert with Donna at the Bradley Center in Milwaukee when he ran into his cardiologist, Dr. David Slosky. "I asked him what was new in the world of cardiology," says Donald. "And he told me about a new machine that scans the arteries for blockage, for calcification. He gave me his phone number and told me to make an appointment."

Donald wasn't too worried—he had recently passed a stress test with flying colors—but he made the appointment just the same. The results of the scan were alarming: There was serious blockage. Dr. Slosky followed up with an angiogram. Donald had 87 percent blockage of his coronary artery, the proverbial "widow maker." Donna was called into the doctor's office to hear the prognosis, and that afternoon Donald was wheeled into an operating room at St. Luke's Medical Center. The surgery lasted nine hours, a quadruple bypass. The anesthesia wore off and he regained consciousness, along with his sense of humor. "A quadruple bypass, one for each of my four kids," he quipped.

But his comment was more than a clever joke. His children could be stressful, taxing, all-consuming. Over the years, he spent a great deal of time, money, and heartache dealing with the results of some of their poor decisions.

Donald returned from the hospital on the first day of June. The sun was streaming down, the peonies were full flush. He felt resilient. He would repair his health and he would move on. Meanwhile, his daughter Kelly's marriage had just dissolved. And his daughter Lisa seemed destined for destruction.

Lisa had been an insurmountable challenge. Neglected as a young child by her alcoholic mother Nancy in Jamaica, and finally rescued by her older sister Sally and cared for by her family, she struggled to maintain equilibrium, using marijuana, alcohol, and other substances to mask her problems.

"Lisa was an unsolvable problem for Donna, for me, for Sally, for John," says Donald. "Nobody could do anything with her. While she was living with us, we had her at the University School, and she got into trouble there and got her butt kicked out of the school. Eventually she got her high school diploma, got into college, and it looked like she was on a pretty good track, with Donna pushing her along on that track. We got her enrolled in Loretto Heights College in Denver. We were excited and decided to get more serious about skiing in Colorado, hoping to visit Lisa often. But unfortunately she was expelled before Thanksgiving in her first semester. She moved home and went to the University of Wisconsin-Milwaukee. She took chemistry and physics in the same semester and got As in both. I thought that was plenty damned impressive. She graduated from UWM with a bachelor of science degree in nursing. She took pride in being a nurse and great pride

Lisa Baumgartner as a young nurse.

in being purposeful, but she had continuing trouble with drugs. She tested positive and lost her nursing license. She lost her career and lost her way."

"Her pride just totally tanked when she lost her license and couldn't go back to nursing," Donna says. "Lisa really wanted to be proud of herself. She really wanted her dad to be proud. Pot sort of mediated a lot of what was going on with her in her brain. But she couldn't keep it together, she was just so self-destructive."

Lisa's struggle with drug abuse led to the loss of her nursing license.

Donald and Donna sent her to a number of treatment programs. "We sent her off to the Betty Ford center in California," Donald says. "They called me from the center and said Lisa was wasting their time and my money—she didn't want to be cured. Not giving up, we sent her to Hazelden. We thought everything would be fine when she came back. We bought her a house, we furnished the house, and got everything all set up for her, even filled the freezer. She was in the house for a very short period of time before it burned to the ground. Somehow she must have started the fire, most likely from smoking in bed."

While she was in college at UWM, Lisa met Jorge Aguad, who was visiting Milwaukee to attend a friend's wedding. Jorge was a world-class surfer from a well-to-do Peruvian family. Lisa and Jorge eloped and moved to Peru, where they lived with his family. They soon had a child, a baby boy named Gabriel. The marriage was destined for failure, however, as the two strayed far from the beaten path, both of them falling into the clutches of serious drug problems. Their son, Gabe, a charmer as a child, was the unfortunate beneficiary of his parents' multiple disorders as he grew older.

The couple divorced and Lisa returned to the states, first living in Florida, then back to Milwaukee. There she married her second husband, Dean Gardner, a close childhood friend of sister Sally and brother John. The couple had a son, Jacob. But the marriage had little chance, as Lisa's bad habits grew worse. Arrested for possession of marijuana in 1996, she divorced her husband and moved to Daytona Beach, Florida, where her mother was living. Her son, Jacob, went to work for his father in his Milwaukee-area restaurant, Poco Loco, and now attends culinary school in Milwaukee.

One day Donald got a call from Florida. Lisa was on her deathbed. Her liver was giving out, and she wasn't expected to survive more than a few days. "We dropped everything, chartered a plane, and flew down there," Donald says. "She was bright orange when I saw her. She couldn't hold a piece of Kleenex to her nose, she was so weak. I scooped her up in my arms. I said, 'I forgive you for everything and I still love you, Lisa.' She got better, her liver regenerated, and she recovered. The doctors told her, 'If you have another drink, it'll kill you.' But she didn't listen—she made her way to the nearest bar and had that drink. That was Lisa."

She was gone. Described by her family as a once-effervescent, charming, charismatic young woman, Lisa died at age fifty-three from complications due to liver failure. Donald was numb. There was never enough he could do to make things right with his problem child or with his alcoholic wives. "I was helpless. I was totally helpless. I did what the hell I could. I tried very hard with Cam. I tried very hard with Lisa. And I had zero success. I had high expectations that were unrealistic. I thought I could change them, make them better. There was no question in my mind that I could keep Cam from drinking and keep Lisa off of drugs and on the straight and narrow, and I failed miserably in both situations."

His long-time friend, Molly Abrohams, had witnessed Lisa's downfall firsthand. She had tutored her as a young girl, and watched despairingly as Lisa burned out. "Lisa was a bright star in Donald's eyes for so many years, but there seemed to be no desire on her part to change," says Molly. "Donald loved her, and she disappointed him so many times it hurt. It hurt him so badly that he had to protect himself finally by pretty much giving up."

Donald is a citizen of the world, as evidenced by the pushpin-laden map in his basement. He had set foot on six continents by the time he was seventy-nine. With his eightieth birthday approaching, he began to plan a trip to Antarctica. He thought he should stand on his seventh continent "while he was still young," says Donna.

Donald and Donna would take an expedition ship *The Prince Albert* from Cape Horn's Tierra del Fuego, at the very tip of South America, across the Drake Passage to Antarctica's South Shetland Islands, a 500-mile voyage.

A world explorer, Donald had conquered his seventh continent, Antarctica, with Donna by the time he was eighty.

"One of the things I'd always wanted to do before I died was sail across the Drake Passage," he says. "This particular body of water is among the roughest water in the world." With thirty-foot waves on the surface, and trenches nearly 20,000-feet deep below, the infamous passage was named after the sixteenth-century explorer Sir Francis Drake, whose ship was blown toward

Antarctica in a storm coming though the Straits of Magellan off Cape Horn. Drake and his crew survived the storm and sailed from Atlantic waters to Pacific waters, the second excursion to circumnavigate the world.

Stormy, turbulent, and frigid—the passage was right in Donald's wheelhouse. "These were some of the roughest waters I've ever seen. The ships that make it down to the Antarctic are pretty sturdy, and, my God, they have to be. The waves look like mountains coming at you."

The overnight, fifteen-hour crossing was not for the faint of heart. "The boat rolled and pitched to such a severe degree that dishes were flying everywhere," says Donna. "I think we were the only ones in the dining room that night including the injured maître d." When they reached the frozen landmass the following morning, they hiked on an iceberg and plunged, very briefly, into the frigid waters, satisfying Donald's ambitious goal.

"When you cross the Drake Passage and go through the Magellan Straits, you think back all the way to Magellan," he says, "who crossed these waters in these wooden sailing ships. And you wonder how in the hell they ever did it. These were some plenty tough guys."

In the eighty years between 1930 and 2010, Donald had racked up a slew of accomplishments: He had stood on each of the seven continents of the world, sailed the Atlantic Ocean, built a local manufacturing company into multi-million-dollar global market leader, accepted a business award from the President of the United States, oversaw the construction of a world-class art museum, owned Rolls-Royces and Italian sports cars, helped design a log home in the mountains, hopped a freight train, swam with the sharks, cried at many an opera—*and* sur-
vived peritonitis and quadruple bypass surgery. With his family and friends gathered around—more than 200 of them—he would celebrate his eightieth year with a big birthday bash, Vegas style.

It was black tie, a lavish event at the Wynn Las Vegas hotel. Beauty and glamour dominated, making the evening a memory maker for all who attended. "People came in from Texas, California, Chicago, Florida, New York, and North Carolina," says Donna. "Three of Donald's children and six of his grandchildren attended. Molly's daughter, Alison, sang; she has an extraordinary voice. My mom was there; she was ninety-three and dressed to the nines. It was a complete, outrageous hoot."

Donald's eightieth birthday drew family and friends to Las Vegas for a lavish party.

Top: Donald and son John, center, with Donald's grandsons, left to right, Robert, Jacob, and Augie.

Middle: Grandchildren Augie and his sister Jessica. Donna and her mother, Geraldine.

Bottom: Granddaughters Tammy and Jennifer with their mother, Sally, center.

Women on stilts greeted guests at the door. One woman wore a champagne glass, offering drinks. Women in long, white dresses and white wigs stood on pedestals playing white violins. There were the James Bond Girls dressed in long, white coats with glittering *Goldfinger*-gold dresses beneath. Marilyn Monroe's lookalike was in the crowd, batting her eyelashes and swinging her red dress. A Dean Martin impersonator was there too, cocktail in hand and cigarette dangling from his lips, joking and crooning and dancing with the ladies.

Marilyn Monroe and Dean Martin impersonators flirted, crooned, and cracked jokes at the Vegas extravaganza.

It was a true Las Vegas show, one act after another, the happy hubbub pausing only when dinner was served and mouths were filled with delicacies. There were go-go dancers. There were women dressed only in lingerie, and a woman dressed only in balloons. "And there were people walking around with not too many clothes on," says Molly Abrohams, "sort of with bubbles all over them, and they were passing out hors d'oeuvres. There were Las Vegas showgirls, the dancers wearing the big headdresses and kicking up their *whatever*. And of course they were all over Donald. Donald is a big flirt, and Donna handles everything with aplomb." Donald's relationship

Vegas showgirls were no match for the happy couple.

with women has been central to his life. His mother's four sisters, the smart and independent Hayes Girls, were a huge influence. "Women love him, women of all generations," says Molly. "He really appreciates women for the things they've accomplished—his daughters, his friends. He respects them for it. Women have been important to him, and Donna is the best."

He's a ladies' man; he enjoys being in the company of women. In fact, he usually prefers their company. "There's something genuinely endearing about Donald," notes Donna, who, at the time of his eightieth birthday, had lived with him for nearly half of his life. "He's naturally a generous man and very open. He is both disarming and engaging, with a keen and timely sense of humor. Donald exudes good taste. He's a gifted conversationalist and an incredible icebreaker, with impeccable timing. People are drawn to him, they want to be around him, especially the ladies. He's easy on the eyes, smartly dressed, and is knowledgeable about everything. Sometimes guys just don't know what to make of him."

Years ago Donna and the wives of a small group of neighborhood friends decided to form a women-only club. They dubbed themselves the Double Bubble Girls and met regularly for champagne and gossip. One day the husbands planned on going to a basketball game on the night of a Double Bubble gathering. Donald was invited to the game, and his friends expected him to go along, but he passed. "Instead of going out with you guys, I'd rather hang out with the ladies tonight. I think I'll stay with the Double Bubble girls instead and get them into some better champagne." Recognizing a wise choice, the ladies welcomed Donald not only as a bearer of champagne but as a man of discerning taste, and from that night on made him an honorary member of the Double Bubble.

The Sheik and his harem: The Double Bubble Girls celebrate Donald's sixtieth birthday.

CHAPTER 15

"My Cup Runneth Over"

One summer morning Donald woke with a start, sat straight up in bed, and uttered a single word: ESOP. Donna had no idea what he meant, but as he would explain later, he had found the answer to his future.

It was the middle of 2015. Business was booming at Paper Machinery Corporation. The company had survived a 20 percent layoff following the terrorist attacks of 9/11 and weathered the 2008-2009 recession with only a minor downturn. The size of the company, with 240 employees, had doubled since 2001.

It was a pivotal time for Donald and his son, John. As president of the company, John's leadership provided a level of confidence to his father, as Donald and Donna traveled and spent more time involved with the arts. John, though, was thinking about getting out. With the economy on the upswing and PMC the dominant manufacturer in its field, he started to talk about retiring. He was pushing sixty-five and wanted to spend more time pursing his own pastimes—boating, horseback riding, fishing, hunting, hanging out at his second home in Sturgeon Bay.

"I always had an agreement with my father on how I would buy the company *from* the family to keep it *in* the family," says John. "That option would be exercised if something happened to Dad driving his Ferrari, flying

John and Donald reached a creative agreement in 2016 on the future of their family business.

around the world, going into the Congo. I always had a succession plan, a good buyout with a fair agreement, where I would take care of Donna and my sisters. There was one exception: Dad didn't want to sell to me while he was still alive."

John was the man behind the desk running the show. But for how long, he didn't know. "If my children ever were capable of running the business, it would be twenty years from now, and I'd be my dad's age. Dad was able to travel the world because I was able to run the family business. My father had me, but I didn't have me. And there is nobody you can hire that's going to look after the family business like family."

It's a dilemma many family-owned businesses face, and with limited options. "John was thinking of retiring," says Donald. "And I wasn't quite ready for that." Donald needed a plan, an exit strategy. A buyout didn't sit well with him. There was no way he would sell his company to an out-of-town competitor or conglomerate or private equity group.

The best solution, he decided, would be an Employee Stock Ownership Plan, an ESOP.

An Employee Stock Ownership Plan is basically an employee retirement plan, generated by the sale of company stock to an ESOP fund. Shares are allocated to the employees based on earnings and years of service, and when employees leave, they cash in their shares, which are bought back by the company at its fair market value.

To purchase the company's stock, which is typically held by majority owners, the ESOP could choose to borrow the money. "The Employee Stock Ownership Plan owns the shares, but it has all this debt," explains Scott Koehler, the company's chief financial officer. As the company earns a profit, it contributes cash to the ESOP so it can repay off the debt. "Basically the company buys itself."

Designing the ESOP was a long, arduous—and sometimes frustrating—process. "I consulted Ben Abrohams, my friend and a retired partner at the Foley & Lardner law firm," says Donald. "The immediate reaction I got was: Don't do an ESOP. They didn't like the idea at all. But I couldn't get it out of my mind."

He was dead-set against going down the same road his father taken. "When we talked about the ESOP," says Abrohams, "one of the points Donald made to the professionals we talked to was that his dad had formed three different companies over the years and sold every one of them. Then they all moved out of town. So that was a motivating factor for Donald to do the ESOP, to keep the employees with the company."

In September 2015, Abrohams introduced Donald to Steve Barth, a business lawyer and partner at Foley & Lardner who specializes in mergers and acquisitions. Given PMC's backstory, Barth knew the importance of the company to Donald and his family. Yet in a market that was booming for mature, well-managed companies, Barth felt obligated to recommend selling PMC outright instead of forming an ESOP.

"My strong advice to Donald, over several meetings and one-on-one conversations, was that he should go through a sale process," Barth says, "sell the company either to a strategic buyer or to a private equity firm. We had initially explored the ESOP. As we were getting some indications of PMC's value I was absolutely convinced—and I'm still convinced—that going to a sale process probably would have netted him another $100 million at least in cash up front."

Donald stood firm in his decision to preserve the future of PMC and its employees. "He said to me, 'I don't care, Steve.' In fact, he got mad at me. Since I do this for a living, and this would be the one time he would ever go through the process, I thought it was my duty to kind of insist: 'Donald, it's 100 million dollars. Are you kidding me?' And he got mad at me. He literally got mad at me and reiterated the importance of the employees and customers and the community and the culture.

"And, you know, that's why he's inspirational to me," says Barth. "There have been others who have done really good things for their employees in a sale process. But Donald sets the bar at a new level of height. I've been doing mergers and acquisitions for thirty-four years—buy side, sell side, big deals, small deals, and everything in between. Lots of founding sellers talk a great game when they say they really want to do what's in the best interests of the company and their employees. But Donald is one of the very few who not only walked the talk, but he invented the talk and the walk.

"I hate ESOPs. I've done quite a number of them. Under certain circumstances they still continue to be the right thing to do. But in this M & A market, where valuations are extremely high, I strongly advise clients not do them because they generally result in far less money, at least up front, to the seller. They are extremely complicated. They are very costly because of all of the parties involved. There's lots of risk to getting it done because of all the moving pieces. But to Donald's great credit, and my endless lifelong admiration, he was very direct and constant with me about what he wanted to do. He's one of my favorite people and clients of all time, somebody who continues to inspire me."

Donald spoke with advisors at Baird, a wealth management and private equity firm, then with his bankers at JP Morgan Chase, who introduced him to a Minneapolis financial company that specializes in ESOPs. "It all started to sound good," Donald recalls. "I was concerned that John would not be happy with the idea. He was a little skeptical at first, but he came on board quickly enough. He knew I wanted to do it, and he went along with it. He asked a lot of good questions but certainly didn't put any pressure on me not to do the ESOP."

On May 1, 2016, PMC's principal shareholders—Donald, John and the family trusts—sold their stock to the ESOP, which borrowed the money to pay the Baumgartners. In the sale, they received some cash upfront, Koehler says. "But the way it was negotiated, the Baumgartners took back some IOUs, seller notes. They are now being paid an amount of interest and then, over a period of time, as the company pays off the debt, the Baumgartner family will be paid off too."

Donald knew he could get more from a straight-up strategic sale versus an ESOP. "So I have to wait a little bit for the money. What the hell, what's the difference?" he shrugs. "By doing the ESOP, it allowed me the opportunity to stay on as chairman of the board of the company, to keep my office, to keep my staff and privileges.

Donald, Donna, John, and Ben Abrohams, Donald's friend and attorney, now control PMC's seven-member board of directors. Rounding it out are its longtime managers, President Luca Dellomodarme, Senior Vice President Mike Kazmierski, and CFO Scott Koehler. "These are the guys that do the day-to-day work. They're enormously competent and smart as hell," says Donald. "I've been traveling a lot and enjoying myself, and John's been running the place for a long time. And now, I'm still there. I'm overseeing the operation at a distance, to be sure, but I'm still watching everything because these guys owe me a lot of money, or they're going to owe my estate a lot of money. I knew it wasn't going to be a drastic change in my life, and I was damned thrilled to do what I did."

The plan satisfied John as well. "Dad likes all the goodwill that comes with it. It's been a habit for him. He's been coming into PMC all my life. Doing the ESOP was difficult. And I thank my father. In a large part, I think he did it for me. I envisioned myself dying at my desk."

As a high-tech entrepreneur, Donald's daughter, Kelly, has started and sold businesses of her own. When her father started talking about reorganizing PMC, she put him in touch with a philanthropic family foundation she knew in Chicago. "He was looking at options, including private equity funds," says Kelly. "It was clear very early on that he really wasn't interested in private equity, even though it was a seller's market and he could have done extraordinarily well. PMC is a very strategic company that has got a near monopoly and a great space. For the right private equity player, that could have been a gem in their portfolio. But my father was very clear from the beginning that he really saw this as an opportunity to do an ESOP."

Donald's decision was a personal move. "He felt not just a kinship with the people who helped build it, but a responsibility," Kelly adds. "Unlike a lot of leaders, particularly today, he doesn't believe in the false narrative of the leader as the most valuable part of the organization, that the CEO should be paid a thousand to one what the small, lowest player is paid. Over the years he poured the vast majority of the profits back into the company. And even though he lives very well and has always lived well, he never pulled out money that would harm the company."

The process of putting the ESOP plan into place was as secretive as a Navy SEALS operation. Not even Donald's oldest child, Sally, was told. Although she'd heard rumors, she didn't know the certainties of the plan until her father made the announcement to employees and other family members at company headquarters. "I had mixed feelings, in a way," she says. "I mean, it was wonderful that he was giving the whole business to the employees, and that's great. But still, I felt kind of choked up, to be honest. It was like the loss of a family member all of a sudden, and I didn't really know how to take it."

Indeed, four generations of Baumgartners have been employed at the company—from JR to Donald to Donald's children to his grandchildren. Some still are. Sally's oldest daughter, Jennifer, known by the nickname "Jaja," has worked at PMC for five years as a data entry tech. Sally's daughter Tammy was in the purchasing department. John's son, Robert, works with engineers writing software, and John's son, Augie, recently left his job as a lathe operator to go back to school. Lisa's son Gabe worked briefly on the production floor.

Sally remains somewhat skeptical about the arrangement, concerned that the family business environment will be lost. "One of the reasons people liked working there before is because of how nice Dad and John have been to them. Whenever it's somebody's birthday or retirement or the Packers win or any kind of excuse, Dad would bring in sandwiches. He would have parties, barbecues, picnics. It's a family business, and now it doesn't feel like it. So I don't know what will happen, we'll have to see. I think the employees will miss my father. They love him. He was the kind of company owner that would come out onto the shop floor, shake people's hands, talk to them, 'How are you doing?' Just a real tangible kind of person that you could feel comfortable talking to." As a gesture of appreciation and good cheer, on Donald's eightieth birthday he had individual pizzas delivered to each of PMC's 230 employees.

The ESOP generated a lot of chatter in the banking community, says Koehler. "ESOPs aren't unusual, but they are infrequent. I know this deal certainly got a lot of notice inside of JP Morgan. Among bankers this was a really, really good deal." A top executive of JP Morgan Chase called Donald after the deal was announced and invited Donald and Donna to New York where, according to Donna, "We were we treated to lunch and given a tour of the JPM art collection."

The ESOP story also got great press, with headlines touting Paper Machinery as "employee-owned" and proclaiming Donald "a hero for the entire country." Letters of congratulations flooded Donald's inbox and Donna's Facebook page, notes of awe and wonder from employees, business executives, community leaders, elected officials, close friends, distant relatives, Donald's personal trainer, his next-door neighbor, his banker, the director of the art museum, the president of the YMCA, and many more.

> Not only is this great news for your employees but also for the people of this city who have a desire to see Milwaukee flourish in the years ahead.... This will be your everlasting legacy.
> — Stacy Terris

> I am proud to know you and what you have created—a lasting legacy for Milwaukee. Workers of the world appreciate you!
> — Carl Mueller

> Donald and Donna,
> You are amazing role models for our community.
> — Andy Nunemaker

> Dear Donald and Donna,
> So rarely have we met owners who bothered to see their employees as the true building blocks of a company. . . . This act, with hearts of pure gold, has catapulted you into a stratosphere we can hardly express. You are super-stars!
> — Libby and Patrick Castro

I believe, as you do, that it is an exceptionally worthwhile endeavor to provide jobs for people with decent pay and benefits. You deserve the respect and admiration of our entire community.

— Bruce Eben Pindyck

Donald,

Last year, leaving the Oriental Theatre after a Film Festival screening, I accosted you on the sidewalk to express thanks for all you have done for the community. Hearing yesterday that you turned your company over to the employees was a welcome infusion of extraordinary news and, for me, like icing on the cake.

— Jake Fuller

Dear Donald & Family,

We know that you have always been invested in the betterment of our community, so doing this only increased our appreciation for all that you & Donna have done. We are lucky to have you in Milwaukee.

— Sincerely, Ed and Diane Zore

You two renew my faith in doing good, and the absolute goodness in the two of you is so life affirming.

— Geralyn Cannon

D&D,

Today's front-page story is just another reason why you two are my favorite couple in Milwaukee. And why you are a Donald I can love. . . .

— Pam Kassner

I have tears!!! The Baumgartners are precious people and I'm blessed to call them friends. . . . You are amazing!!!

— Julie Mills

Dear Donald and Donna,

It is so good to know that people with your generosity of character and heart are here in Milwaukee. There are few who would do what you just did. Congratulations on this change in your life, and changing so many of your employees lives as well. I always knew you were a class act.

— Julia Taylor

Months after the ESOP deal was announced, Foley lawyer Steve Barth hosted a small dinner party at Rare Steakhouse in Milwaukee. "It really was just an occasion to pay tribute to Donald and John and the management team for such a wonderful transaction," he says.

One of the treats of the night was a red wine that Barth ordered for the group. "I fancy myself as a California cabernet connoisseur," he says, "but I can't hold a candle to Donald's collection. I knew I was up against it. I knew I'd better come up with something good. So we had Plumpjack Reserve, one of my favorites, and I think it went over pretty well. We put a big dent in Rare's wine cellar that night, I can tell you that."

By coincidence, Bud and Sue Selig happened to be dining at the same restaurant that night. A friend of the Baumgartners and friend and long-time client of Ben Abrohams, Selig stopped by the celebration party to offer his congratulations. "He came over to give a toast to Donald and Donna and John. It was a great treat and a real surprise."

A few months later, Foley & Lardner presented PMC with its national Private Company Board of Directors of the Year Award. The ceremony was held at the Hyatt Hotel in Chicago on the day after Donald Trump was elected President. With protesters marching in the streets, Donald accepted the award for the board with grace, humor, and poignancy.

"Donald's an incredible speaker. He was the hit of the evening," Barth says. "The entire audience was in love with him for what he and the board had done. And by the way, we reprised the same wine, the Plumpjack Reserve, at that dinner. It was the icing on the cake."

In an event held each year by the Milwaukee Press Club, Donald was feted for his business, civic, and philanthropic contributions to the community. The ceremony was a light-hearted, comical ceremony in which selected individuals are inducted into a pseudo-fraternal organization, The Order of the Knights of Bohemia.

Family and friends, including former Baseball Commissioner Bud Selig, far left, celebrated Donald's induction into the Milwaukee Press Club's Order of the Knights of Bohemia.

In the backroom of the downtown Newsroom Pub, Donald was seated in a straight-back wooden chair in front of a cheerful crowd of family, friends, colleagues, and members of the press. His white mane of hair was thick and leonine. He wore a vicuña blazer over a white shirt opened at the collar, Zilli loafers, and no socks. More like a playful roast than starchy, formal investiture, members of the public were invited to speak on behalf of the newly inducted Knight of Bohemia. Kelly Fitzsimmons offered a waggish tribute to her good-natured father:

> Bohemian? You look at my father with his great haircut, his sharp suits, and the crazy cars that he drives, and there's something off here. But I have to tell you, I was there in the 1970s, and I have photographic evidence that this man is truly Bohemian. . . . I've spent a lot of time asking my dad what the secret of his success was, which finally, this summer, I was able

to get from his lips. Here's a man who had sixty-two years of success in business and most of those years were profitable. How did he do this? I took my dad aside on a mountain as we were walking down and asked, "Dad what is the secret of your success? Can you boil it down to one thing?" And he said, "Honey, I've been thinking about this a lot. And I think what it comes down to is, I'm impatient." Really, Dad? You're impatient? I wonder if anybody else would have guessed this. So we got down the mountain to the car, and I said to my mom, "Dad finally told me what the secret of his success is. He boiled it down to one word, one thing. Can you guess what it is?" And Mom looked at me and said, "His libido?" But there was a third person who weighed in on my father's success— my grandfather. Many years ago, when I was a small child, my dad bought one of his first majorly fancy cars. And Grandpa was in town. He was there, looking at the car, walking around, kicking the tires. Dad's all excited. "What do you think, Dad?" he said to Grandpa. Grandpa looked at the car, he looked at my dad, and said, "Donald, I finally understand why you're successful." And my grandfather looked him dead in the eye and said, "Because you're lucky." So the secret of my dad's success is impatience, libido, and luck.

Bonnie Bockl Joseph pitched in with her own tongue-in-cheek testimonial of her longtime pal, who frequently refers to her as "my communist friend."

It's so easy to support the nomination of Donald Baumgartner for King Bohemian award. A true Bohemian, one without a home, his father told him he was Swiss and later admitted that he did not like the French so that's why he said they were Swiss. But I'm sure that Donald is a Wandering Jew. He spent weeks with friends at Palm Beach, and at the end, they thought he was Jewish. We've been friends for thirty-five years. We agree on so much: How handsome he is, how well dressed he is, how well his red suede Zilli shoes go with his Brunello Cucinelli jeans. And how juicy his fabulous wife is . . . And his cars—Rolls, Bentleys, Ferraris, Lamborghinis, and now, the one and only orange McLaren P1. Donald and I agree on most everything. We sometimes even agree on politics. Okay. Never. But I have tried to get him to accept unions, to like Hillary, to love liberal causes, to vote for Democrats. I'm an uber-liberal, prochoice, pro-gun control, tree hugger. Donald is not, but he's always generous. Maybe he heard my pleas to listen, to care, to tend to the less fortunate. Maybe it worked too well. You're not a liberal? Not a Democrat? But Donald, your ESOP semi-giveaway to your employees has made you a communist! So, Comrade, love and welcome to the Bohemian world of the homeless.

Knighted as a Bohemian, a white silken sash draped across his chest, Donald signed his name to a small, framed chalkboard, which now hangs among the signatures of presidents and poets, athletes and artists, film stars and rock stars on the historic walls of the Milwaukee Press Club headquarters.

A year after the Employee Stock Ownership Plan went into effect, business was humming at Paper Machinery Corporation. For the company newsletter, Michael Hansen, a top sales rep at PMC—and one time son-in-law—composed a mind-boggling mathematical perspective of the world of paper cups:

Each year 356,000,000,000 paper cups are produced worldwide. That's 356 billion. Eight years ago the total number of cups was 210 billion. That is a healthy increase of 170 percent in less than a decade. North America accounts for 145 billion cups per year. And it's no surprise that Asia, specifically China, represents the fastest growing segment. During the last eight years, the world market has seen annual growth of 6.7 percent. If we assume a more modest future growth of 3 percent annually, that would

Donald's signature hangs on the wall of the Newsroom Pub amid the names of presidents, poets, and pop stars.

equate to over 10 billion more cups required each year. That is the equivalent to the yearly capacity of over 70 PMC-1003 machines. . . . Unfortunately, PMC is not blessed with 100 percent of the increased cup market every year. There are low-speed machines built in China, Korea, and India. And there are high-speed machines that compete directly with PMC built in Germany. But, thanks to everyone at PMC, we dominate the world paper cup market and plan to continue to do so indefinitely.

Donald's decision to form the ESOP was the right move, he was sure of it. To know that his company would succeed was gratifying, humbling. "I was born lucky," he says. "I was lucky to have hard-working, ambitious parents who knew how to make a living and how to have fun. I was lucky to be able to attend an excellent, small, private school. I was lucky with the expansion of fast food. And I sure as hell was lucky when my cousin Donna entered my life. My cup truly runneth over!

With the sale of his stock to the ESOP, Donald stepped up his philanthropic gift-giving almost immediately. Just two weeks after PMC ownership was transferred to its employees, he and Donna announced they would give $8 million to the Milwaukee Art Museum's endowment. It was the largest gift to the endowment in the museum's history.

"We are very proud of the Milwaukee Art Museum as an institution and as a vital part of the city in which we've lived and worked," Donald said at the time. "Our gift is a way to celebrate past accomplishments and support future directors as they lead Milwaukee's most acclaimed cultural institution."

The donation came shortly after Dan Keegan announced that he was retiring after serving as museum director for more than eight years. "We've been so inspired by Dan Keegan's leadership and vision for the future, in particular his passion for securing the viability of the museum for generations to come," said Donna. "We wanted to carry on his legacy and keep the momentum going." The next day, the museum announced it would hire Marcelle Polednik as Keegan's successor. With a curatorial and management background at art museums in Jacksonville, Florida; Monterey, California; and New York City, Polednik would become the first Donna and Donald Baumgartner Director of the Milwaukee Art Museum.

The Baumgartners' double shot of generosity was stunning, as two friends noted in a congratulatory message:

> Dear Donna and Donald,
> We read of your gift to the employees and thought it was rare and fabulous. Today, in the newspaper, we learned of your endowment gift to the MAM. Honestly, you are shining examples of people who make the world a better place by your presence.
>
> — Phil and Reva

Without a doubt, the Baumgartners had made a mark as a couple who cares deeply about the community and the betterment of its citizens. The ESOP was a personal example of that by Donald and his family. The endowment gift to the art museum further signalled that the arts were regarded as critically important.

"Everybody in the arts that I'm involved in know the Bamgartners," says friend Carmen Haberman, board member of the Herzfeld Foundation and cofounder of the Milwaukee Film Festival. "They're very recognizable names now." Donna and Donald are purposely not associated with a foundation. As individual givers, Haberman views them as relatively new up-and-comers in the philanthropic community. "I would say, as far as major individuals, they're on the climb."

That has now changed dramatically. In addition to the endowment donation, successive contributions made by Donald and Donna to the Grammy-winning Florentine Opera ($1.5 million to support the Studio Artists Program), Milwaukee Film ($1.5 million for the revitalization of the Oriental Theatre), Milwaukee Symphony Orchestra ($1.5 million toward the rehab of the Warner Grand Theatre), and Milwaukee Ballet ($10 million toward its new building) placed them among the pantheon of the city's giving community.

"They've come to the point of being recognized as being in the top tier of philanthropists in Milwaukee," says Russell Bowman, former Milwaukee Art Museum director who continues to do business in the city as an art advisor.

"They've made such a significant impact," says Michael Pink, artistic director of Milwaukee Ballet. "Certainly as part of the history of this ballet company, their names will be right up there at the top in terms of the people who have provided constant support." In recognition of the Baumgartners' unprecedented donation, the ballet named its new center after them.

Like other beneficiaries of the city's major donors, Pink wonders who will take their place. The top tier is occupied by old-guard givers whose contributions will not sustain the city's arts groups and nonprofits forever. Who will be the next generation of givers?

"Without sounding too morbid, there's no question that one of the major challenges for this city is that we look at our philanthropic greats and recognize that they're coming to the end of their lives," Pink says. "We just know that without Donald leading the Milwaukee Art Museum, that wonderful edifice would not be standing down on the lakefront. To continue to support this level of excellence, it's the legacy part that is crucial. Nothing would be more disappointing for the city, for everybody involved, if suddenly, a few of your major key donors are no longer here and there's nobody standing in the wings to pick up the mantle."

Beyond the provisional support of foundations and public funds, and the often arbitrary allocation of corporate sponsorships—which, in an era of mergers, buyouts and overseas moves, is lagging—the transfer of that responsibility falls to individual donors and their families.

"We need to get more people's skin in the game," says Pink, "especially at this juncture where the cultural make-up of the city has changed. The skyline, the buildings, things are happening. There's going to be movement within the city that in the next five or ten years will really redefine Milwaukee, and with that comes the fact we've had this extraordinary arts scene. People like Donald and Donna and many others have all been trying to make sure we protect it and preserve it."

Partly by example, and partly by gently twisting a few arms, Donald has persuaded his family to take up the cause. Along with his father, sister, Jean, and half-sisters, Carolyn and Roberta, the next generation of Baumgartners has made gifts to Milwaukee's art museum, opera, and ballet. In an agreement set up by Donald and Donna, each of Donald's three children donate 5 percent of their trust-fund payments to a not-for-profit or charitable organization.

From his very first donation of $3,000 to the fledgling Milwaukee Ballet in the 1970s, Donald has been an avid and active patron of the arts. "I've been giving money away ever since I had money to give away. And as long as I'm around, I'm not going to stop."

The Baumgartners show little inclination or interest in slowing down. "There's still plenty of planet to cover," as Donna says. In the course of one recent calendar year, they were perpetually on the move, visiting their home in Colorado for a family ski trip, flying to London for a play, New York City for a ballet, Cooperstown, New York, for the induction of their friend Bud Selig into the Baseball Hall of Fame, back to Colorado for a dance festival, Monte Carlo for the Grand Prix Road Race, British Columbia for wine tastings and a mountain driving tour in Donald's McLaren P1 dream machine, to the Venice Biennale and Verona for an opera festival, then off to the coast of Croatia for a ten-day family vacation on not one but two chartered yachts.

While reviewing their appointment book one morning, Donna noticed that the month of September was shaping up to be relatively uneventful.

"Well, I'll just have to do something about that," Donald said, without missing a beat.